Imagine No Religion

≫ an autobiography ≪

Blase Bonpane

From Central America to the Middle East, the life story
of a leader in the movement for social justice and peace.

Red Hen Press 🐔 *Pasadena, CA*

Imagine No Religion

Book layout by Leila Benoun
Book design by Mark E. Cull

ISBN 978-1-59709-180-0 (eBook)
ISBN 978-1-59709-435-1 (hardcover)
ISBN 978-1-59709-553-2 (tradepaper/alternate edition)

Library of Congress Cataloging-in-Publication Data

Bonpane, Blase.
  Imagine no religion : an autobiography : from Central America to the Middle East,
the life story of a leader in the movement for social justice and peace / Blase Bonpane.
— 1st ed.
    p. cm.
  Includes bibliographical references and index.
  ISBN 978-1-59709-670-6 (alk. paper)
  1. Bonpane, Blase. 2. Catholic ex-priests—Biography. 3. Social reformers—
Biography. 4. Office of the Americas. I. Title.
  BX4668.3.B67A3 2011
  282.092—dc23
  [B]
                          2011033907

The Los Angeles County Arts Commission, the National Endowment for the Arts, and
Department of Cultural Affairs City of Los Angeles partially support Red Hen Press.

First Edition

Published by
Red Hen Press
www.redhen.org

Imagine No Religion

This is for you Theresa,
the mother of two great children
and the grandmother of five future peacemakers.
You are the one who makes everything happen.
I love you.

Contents

Preface.. *xi*

Introduction.. *xiii*

1. The Escape..1

2. Odyssey to Maryknoll...10

3. Uninhibited Apostolate...16

4. Assignment to Central America............................22

5. Renegade Priest...29

6. Cuba..34

7. The Peace Movement..38

8. New Incarnation...43

9. Our Wedding..50

10. Surveillance...54

11. Campaign/Chicano
    Moratorium/Santa Paula......................................56

12. La Paz..63

13. Return to Academia/
    The Peace Movement...71

14. The Movement to Abolish Nuclear Weapons
    and the Struggle of the Sandinistas...................79

15. Nicaraguan Revolution...................82

16. Office of the Americas
    and Nicaraguan Delegations...................87

17. Media Requests...................92

18. Beginning of the International March
    for Peace in Central America...................94

19. The Long March
    through Central America...................103

20. The Celebration...................113

21. Reflections on the International
    March for Peace...................117

22. Returning Home...................126

23. El Salvador...................128

24. Demonstrations...................132

25. Liberation Theology...................146

26. Last Delegation to
    Nicaragua and Reflections...................154

27. Delegation to Iraq...................159

28. L.A. Uprisings & Campaign
    for House of Representatives...................168

29. Cuba Again...................182

30. Chiapas...................187

31. A Respite..192

32. Let's Not Talk About Jesus.............................198

33. A Moral Revolution......................................201

Personal Reflections..206

Postscript: A Conversation with God................207

Index..209

Preface

This is the personal story of the life of Blase Bonpane, a Maryknoll priest who, prior to any books on the subject, was in the vanguard of liberation theology.

In the wake of the Second Vatican Council 1962–1965 many religious people, especially those serving in Latin America, began to understand a spirituality that transcends sectarianism.

Having come from an upward mobile Italian American family marked by both love of the Church and a touch of Southern Italian anti-clericalism, Blase was accustomed to hearing his parents express real differences with their clerical institution.

He went into the seminary despite the avid protests of his parents. His father, a Judge of the Superior Court in Los Angeles said, "If I had five sons and one was an idiot, he could become a priest."

This odyssey of Blase Bonpane takes us from his high school and college days to his service in Guatemala during a violent revolution, his expulsion from that country for "subversion" and the years that followed.

After receiving gag order from the Church, which he could not accept in conscience, Blase met with the editorial board of the *Washington Post* and released all of the material he had regarding the US military presence in Guatemala. This action led to his separation from the Maryknoll Fathers.

Blase accepted a teaching post at the University of California Los Angeles (UCLA) and while serving in academia he met the former Maryknoll Sister, Theresa Killeen who had served in Southern Chile. They married in 1970. Their adventures included working daily and directly with César Chávez at his headquarters in La Paz, California, creating solidarity with the Central American Revolution, forming the Office of the Americas and working in the forefront of the international movement for justice and peace while raising two children.

Blase has worked on the ground for international peace in Mexico, Guatemala, El Salvador, Nicaragua, Costa Rica, Honduras, Panama, Columbia, Ecuador, Peru, Colombia, Cuba, Japan and Iraq. He led the

US contingent of the International March for Peace in Central America from Panama to Mexico in 1985–1986.

This book is dedicated to his wife, Theresa, to whom he attributes the wisdom to found the Office of the Americas and to organize and initiate a new dimension in peace making by way of direct solidarity with the victims of US military intervention.

Introduction

After my expulsion from Guatemala as a Maryknoll Father, I wrote, *Guerrillas of Peace: Liberation Theology and the Central American Revolution.* Our time was primarily devoted to the peace movement, and the holocaust of Vietnam. The great blessing of marriage made it possible to, "be the change we wanted to see happen." Theresa and I were able to do the work we had begun in religious life but without being bound to its strictures. In that period we had the experience of working daily with César Chávez in the administration of the United Farm Workers headquarters at La Paz, California. There was also academia and frequent demonstrations for peace and farm labor. When the US interventions began in Central America, we and our compañeros organized The Office of the Americas. From the day of its inception it appeared to be the right organization at the right time. Constant travel followed including a new concept in solidarity of visiting the wars and letting our delegates come home to write their op-eds, and speak in their schools and organizations to denounce the evils of "Our Latin Vietnam."

As the peace accords developed in Central America, we were stunned by a massive blitzkrieg in Iraq in 1991. That massacre is still underway. Much of our time has since been dedicated to ending the bloodshed in Iraq, Afghanistan, Pakistan, and now Libya.

My work was interrupted in 1999 by colon cancer and again in 2000 by kidney cancer. This led to a change in tempo for me. The "blessing close to the wound" was to be closer to home and to the wisdom of Theresa and my children. Also my restrictions on international travel made it possible to dedicate more of my time to media. I realized that the impact of our work could be magnified by radio, TV, print, as well as the speaking circuit. It also gave me the opportunity to write the trilogy: *Guerrillas of Peace on the Air, Common Sense for the Twenty-First Century* and *Civilization is Possible.*

The title of this book requires an explanation. Religion has been a key part of my life. For years, however, I have realized that the name of one's religion is meaningless. Just as Jesus said there are the weeds and the wheat, they grow up together. Within any religious structure we can find rapists, murderers and saints. And perhaps worst of all, we can find the liars that manufacture fear, create war, defend planet busting nuclear instruments of biocide and the trashy catastrophe creating nuclear power plants that fuel and sustain them. In this reflection on my life, I am speaking for myself. I do not pretend to speak with any form of totalism, absolutism or religiosity. This may be seen as "one man's opinion."

Let's take a look at the etymology of the word "religion." It comes from the Latin "religo" which means to bind and cast aside, to relegate. In selecting a title for this book I was concerned about how to unbind, how to liberate. After now living for decades without the binding nature of religion, I find liturgy meaningful, a form of spiritual play, but I am not bound to it. I find meaning in the gathering of the faithful in mass mobilizations to denounce the insanity of war. I welcome experiences of prayer and worship outside of the Roman Catholic tradition. And it is obvious that this sense of the faithful is now part of the lives of many people who have a Catholic upbringing. Their pastors keep telling them that the church is not a smorgasbord but their instincts are otherwise.

The binding force in religion is dogma. Dogma, however, is primarily something to argue about. As we look at the history of dogma we find that it has been used as a cover for political power for centuries. This cover tells the faithful that God is on our side and, even more, that the other side is demonic. "We know how to define God and you don't." Let's look at just one example. A meaningless argument about the Holy Spirit has separated the Orthodox and Roman Churches for over a thousand years. The question was: does the Holy Spirit proceed from the Father and the Son ("filioque" in Latin) or from the Father only? Neither side had any idea what they were talking about. What was the issue? The issue was whether Rome would be the ecclesiastical capital or would it be Constantinople? The Romans insisted that the Holy Spirit proceeded from the Father and the Son, the Greeks said the Holy Spirit proceeds from the Father only. And such was the cover for a political conflict.

I do not think that Jesus is sectarian. I don't think we should be sectarian either. I believe that authentic spirituality must be non-sectarian. Take a look at the nonsectarian Jesus, Luke 10:25:

> There was a lawyer who, to disconcert him, stood up and said to him, 'Master, what must I do to inherit eternal life?' He said to him, 'What is written in the law? What do you read there?' He replied, 'You must love the Lord your God with all your heart, with all your soul, with all your strength, and with all your mind, and your neighbor as yourself.' 'You have answered right,' said Jesus, 'do this and life is yours.'

But the man was anxious to justify himself and said to Jesus, 'And who is my neighbor?' Jesus replied, 'A man was once on his way down from Jerusalem to Jericho and fell into the hand of brigands; they took all he had, beat him and then made off, leaving him half dead. Now a priest happened to be traveling down the same road, but when he saw the man, he passed by on the other side. In the same way a Levite who came to the place saw him, and passed by on the other side. But a Samaritan traveller who came upon him was moved with compassion when he saw him. He went up and bandaged his wounds, pouring oil and wine on them. He then lifted him to his own mount, carried him to the inn and looked after him. Next day, he took out two denarii and handed them to the innkeeper. 'Look after him,' he said 'and on my way back I will make good any extra expense you have.' Which of these three, do you think, proved himself a neighbor to the man who fell into the brigands hands?' The one who took pity on him,' he replied. Jesus said to him, 'Go and do the same yourself.'

This is what I mean by non-sectarian. Compassion is a life-style not a dogma.

Did Jesus have a religion? Yes, it was Judaism. But he was unbound and constantly spoke of the Spirit acting outside of his sect. Imagine asking Jesus: Are you a Presbyterian? A Methodist? A Roman Catholic? Can you possibly imagine an affirmative answer? Jesus gave us a life-style to be imitated and remembered. He teaches us to be the change we want to see in society, and his admirer Mahatma Gandhi taught the same message. Gandhi was a Hindu. Yes, Jesus is a secular humanist (secular: in the world; humanist: of, for and incarnate with humanity). He is a living spokesperson for ongoing life, for prayer and meditation. Jesus tells us that our service to God is our service to each other. He sees humanity as interconnected with all creation. Together with Socrates he affirms, "You can kill me but you cannot hurt me." At death life is changed and not taken away. My understanding of Jesus is that he did not distinguish between natural and supernatural. Everything had a spiritual component. All creation is divine.

And how does religion become corrupted? The greatest occupational hazard is the infection of self-righteousness. Fundamentalism is created by the virus of self-righteousness. "Now I have my religion, my full approval by and from God. Now I have the truth, I can identify the other as evil. And when my self- righteousness reaches perfection, I will be ready to kill the devil; that is anyone who differs with my truth. And such has been the history of political religion.

What religion do I say no to? The religion of nation. This is an affirmation that what my country does is God's will. This is the God and country religion and I think it is the prime religion of citizens of the United States. If the United States is not our religion, why would we tolerate one genocidal massacre after another? As we proceed to consciousness, the nation state must no longer be a sacred cow to be worshiped.

A noncritical approach to nation is a religious approach. It is not a rational approach. But the religious approach to a patriotism, early defined as the last refuge of scoundrels, dominates our culture from Kindergarten through graduate school. It is called American exceptionalism.

The sect becomes cult when it becomes exclusive. If I bind myself to the cult leader rather than act on an informed conscience, I am in a cult. This is what I mean by imagine no religion; no cult, no sect. Historically religion has accommodated to the state in a sycophantic fashion. Our bishops have not been a strong voice for peace in a warfare state. On the contrary they have maintained the subservience that the bishops showed to Constantine at Nicaea in the fourth century.

Aside from nation, there is the religion of sectarian political dogma. This sect promotes a pre-conceived formula of how to change the world by ideology. But it does not work that way. The common good of humanity must be foremost. I would like to recommend the Universal Declaration of Human Rights, that great United Nations document of December 10, 1948. It is an unbound document. It is not sectarian.

Whatever happens politically must be humane and humanitarian. Humane Norwegian capitalism would certainly be better than Pol Pot socialism. The essence of a polity is not the ideology but the performance.

Dogmas are dictated by humans who often have a political agenda. Just reflect on the great Protestant/Catholic Wars in the wake of the Reformation. Need we mention Sunni and Shia? Martin Luther had a great message against the sale of indulgences and other abuses of Papal authority. The foundation of a religion in his name, however, was of doubtful value.

What is the "constitution" of a religion? Dogma. We will tell you all about God. And in order to be a member you must agree with us. If you fail to agree we will denounce you as an apostate, a heretic, and history tells us we have the right to kill you. Thanks very much to 600 years of inquisition in the name of God and dogma. We want to Christianize you, and we'll do it with the sword of the Conquistadores. We will fight as soldiers of God in Crusades because we have the truth. And by the way we will also take your treasures with us.

Would it not be much better to say to each other, "Let's share our sacred stories." What a revelation this would be. You say that in your tradition there was a virgin birth? That's what we say too. You say there were actually many virgin births recorded in religious traditions. Perhaps that was really a way of saying that something great was happening. You say your sacred messenger is divine. That is what we say. You speak of people going right up to heaven in the body. We say that too. How much we have in common once we see these figurative concepts in place of attempted literalism. And you indigenous folks tell me that the raven created the world. Well we have some tough stories to understand as well, something about a tree and fruit and a man and a woman. Sharing sacred stories is enlightening and inspiring in the absence of self-righteousness and absolutism.

Imagining no religion is not an argument for atheism. I am not at all impressed with the reasoning of the new pop atheists. Their arguments are cyclic, There is no God because there is no God because I said so. Thank you very much. At the same time, I respect anyone who cannot affirm the existence of God. Just think what they might have been taught about God? Hell fire here, hell fire there. Say a bad word and go to hell, miss Church on Sunday go to hell. Aye! Guilt is wholesaled, forgiveness is retailed. The understandable response of many people can easily be, "I don't believe in God." Such a comment might be translated, "I don't believe in that sect."

Then there is the theologian Mark Twain. Huckleberry Finn wrote a letter to Miss Watson telling her the location of Jim, the runaway slave because his religion told him he would be lost and go to hell if he did not give such information. Then Huck began to reflect and to meditate on the love that Jim had for him. He tore up the letter to Miss Watson and said, "All right, then, I'll go to hell." This was Huck's unbinding and liberation from sectarian nonsense.

And what of science? Science, the sacred pursuit of what is true. Science is reading of the book of nature. Every page of the Grand Canyon and it striations is another sacred message about the history of the planet. But on occasion science gets into a trap. "Matter can neither be created nor destroyed," is one of science's great laws. OK then, how did the universe begin? By a big bang? Please dear scientists try to do better than that. Here is where the word "meta" comes in. Metaphysics takes us beyond physics. If matter can neither be created nor destroyed then we must look to Metaphysics . . . not to a big bang.

The war between some religions and science generally only demonstrates the failed education of the religionist. The scientific method is rational and when scientists are into the theoretical realm they will say so. On the contrary, many religious proclamations are simply based on "authority." The science of Logic rejects arguments from authority as having no basis in the truth of the argument. This is called the ad baculum fallacy, the fallacy of the club, the stick, the threat. This is the fallacy of militarism. Do what you are told, follow orders, keep your mouth shut. As the authority I have the ability to flunk you, to jail you or to kill you. Do what I say. Such reasoning attempts to destroy critical thought. Sadly it is probably the most prominent method in our political, educational and religious institutions.

My perspective in the title of this book is a cry for reverence. And reverence is not to be found in dogma. Reverence leads us to confirm that we know little or nothing about God, it is anti-dogmatic. The more we claim to know about God, the more irreverent we can be. Listen to the TV evangelists! "God will do this." "God won't do that." "The tsunami came to Japan because of homosexuality." These faithless preachers are making God into their image and likeness. And such preaching has historic antecedents. As we look at the Old Testament we see tribal anthropology. We see the tribal chief saying who God should slay, and what the tribal chief is really saying is who he or she thinks should be slain. This perspective can help us to understand the "mean God" of the Old Law. Once again we have a smorgasbord of some wonderful stories, many of which are meaningful.

What I am trying to say is that we should respect and reverence the pursuit of the spiritual together with agnostics and atheists. I simply reject any fundamentalisms, political or religious. I am not asking you to leave your faith. I am asking you to leave your sectarianism.

And what is your faith? It certainly must not be a rote formula recited with unthinking repetition. Your faith must be how you live your life, what you are willing to hope and what you are willing to do. I don't see Jesus as an exclusivist and I don't want to get into the trap of rapping different verses of the Bible at each other in conflict. We are aware of the glosses, the additions and subtractions to the canon of the New Testament as established in 397 AD.

How many sorrowful mothers were told that their unbaptized baby could not go to heaven to the beatific vision? But it's OK Mom, your child will be naturally happy in Limbo as a second class citizen, you and the rest of your family might go to heaven after a few thousand years in Purgatory. The dogmatists are saying too much and they don't know what they are talking about. Oh yes, they recently said, "Limbo?. . . never mind."

The liturgy? Thomas Merton found a great spirituality in his Buddhist colleagues at prayer. I hazard to say that he understood the title of this book better than I do. Drop the sectarianism.

The Emperor Constantine wanted one church, one empire and one emperor and that is what he got at Nicaea. He paid the way of the bishops to attend this council, they all agreed on a creed followed by a political mandate. We will eliminate those who do not affirm this dogma. Kill those who differ. What was missing here? They forgot to focus on the singular Law of Jesus, that we love one another. Thus began the history of Christendom. We will kill you if you differ with one of our defined dogmas. And you are justified to kill in the name of God in our crusades, our conquest of the Americas, and in any imperial wars fought by Christian soldiers.

The history of religion is a history of separation. But the hope, "That all be one," demands that we accept our connectedness, not our separateness. We are each other. Service of God is service of each other.

In my years as a Maryknoll priest I did not urge people to become Catholic, I simply gave them the message from the life of Jesus. I talked about conversion in their life-style, not conversion to a religion. I spoke of the unconventional wisdom of the Sermon on the Mount in opposition to the boring conventional wisdom of the monetary world.

A historic and cosmic view of the study of asceticism gives us a variety of the signs of authentic spirituality. Spirituality becomes visible in the following qualities: Understanding, Knowledge, Reverence, Wisdom, Counsel, Awe, Fortitude, together with: Justice, Love, Joy, Endurance, Compassion, Faith, Temperance.

These are listed in a plethora of ways in various works on ethics and morality. But what we have here, contrary to dogma, is a global consensus on behavior. And this is how all can be one. These qualities can make up the fabric of our lives.

Individuals can make a global call in the name of these qualities. Note the challenge of Dr. Helen Caldicott. As founder of Physicians for Social Responsibility, She was asked: "What actions can we as responsible citizens take in the face of the nuclear danger?" Her response:

This is the ultimate spiritual and religious issue ever to face the human race. For what is our responsibility to God to preserve the creation and evolution? We are the curators of possibly, the only life in the universe and our responsibility is enormous. We must therefore dedicate every waking and sleeping moment to the preservation of creation. But first, action must be preceded by education. We are all physicians to a planet that is in the intensive care unit.

Dr. Helen Caldicott is speaking as an international authority on a moral issue. Please note, this is not the fallacy of the appeal to authority (the stick, the baculum), "Do what I say or else." This is the authority that derives from competence, and excellence in one's field.

To sum up I offer the following opinions, not dogmas.

Yes, to prayer, meditation, creative liturgies, base communities organized for observation, judgment and action on issues of justice. Respect for all with discernment, the ability to denounce injustice and to organize against it.

Yes, to the reverence that celebrates how little we can know about the deity, not any claim to say we know all about it. No, to all forms of self-righteousness. Yes, to our connectedness with all creation.

Respect for people who are bound to religion, yet unafraid to demonstrate how their "faith" may be used as a cloak for malice.

Respect for those who cannot affirm any deity. No, to the religiosity of the state and all sacred cows. No, to all fundamentalisms—political or religious.

No, to all sectarian cults, economic, political, or religious.

No, to totalism, absolutism.

No, to the official stories of church and state. Let them demonstrate their credibility by action rather than defending themselves with threats of war or eternal punishment.

Yes, to the primacy of conscience.

Yes, to the universally accepted spiritual qualities.

No, to being bound and cast aside in a sect.

May the unbinding of religiosity be the catalyst of a continuing moral revolution which was conceived in Latin America, which has morphed into the Middle East and Asia and which we pray will restructure the United States before our warfare state destroys itself and much of the planet.

I think that Percy Bysshe Shelly said it all so well in the Epilogue of his play *Prometheus Unbound* which was published in 1820.

To suffer woes which Hope thinks infinite;
To forgive wrongs darker than death or night;
To defy Power, which seems omnipotent;
To love, and bear; to hope till Hope creates
From its own wreck the thing it contemplates;
Neither to change, nor falter, nor repent;
This like thy glory, Titan, is to be
Good, great and joyous, beautiful and free;
This is alone Life, Joy, Empire and Victory.

After almost a half century of being unbound from religious ties, these are my reflections. My mentor in the pursuit of authenticity is my best friend, my beloved Theresa who led the way in this quest.

What follows in this book are some of my thankful and grateful recollections of a joyful journey.

Imagine No Religion

Chapter 1

The Escape

June 28, 1950. I had been waiting in my room (2307 Chislehurst Drive, Hollywood) for all to be asleep. This was "The Fort," our family home since 1939. It was gloriously set on a curve below the Griffith Observatory. The lot was shaped like an arrowhead with tiny frontage rising up to an acre of lawn, lantana, jacaranda, geraniums, lemons, oranges and decomposed granite. The house was California Spanish, on four levels. It was one-of-a-kind architecture shaped to the hillside which held it firm. The essential red tile roof covered rotund rooms with Romanesque ceilings of hand-painted angels, cupids, and buxom beauties.

At approximately 1:00 AM, I picked up my suitcase and descended the staircase past the hall which lead to my parent's room, down the wooden staircase to the garage, out the sheet-metal fire-door and departed down the steep driveway in my mother's car. I parked the car near a Pacific Electric stop, left the keys under the rug and clicked away down to the Greyhound Station. This was the most bizarre thing I had ever done.

My note was waiting for my parents when they awoke. My mother cried. My father was furious. "If I had five sons and one was an idiot, he could become a priest," he said. As the near empty Greyhound roared through the Mojave Desert, I began to put the puzzle of my life together.

My current escape from home had a precedent. My father, Blase Augustus Buonpane (he dropped the "u" in our last name after we moved to California) was born in Vitulazio, Provincia di Caserta, Regione Campania, Italy, near Naples, December 16, 1892. His last memory in Italy was of being awakened by his grandmother, Domenica Cecelia Buonpane, who said, "Wake up, young man, you are going to America." He arrived in the US in 1896, with his mother, at the age of four. His father, Elpidio, was not permitted to leave the stone quarry in Blooms Run, Pennsylvania when his wife, Mary Jane, and son landed at Ellis Island. Grandma and Dad took the train to the site of the quarry. The little family moved as much as thirteen times in one year, following the stone cutting jobs available to my grandfather.

My Dad, Judge Blase A. Bonpane, 1970.

In 1902 grandpa moved the family to Youngstown, to establish Ohio's first Italian language newspaper, *La Nuova Italia*. By the age of eight, Dad was setting the type, writing articles, and helping to deliver the paper. Elpidio, who was principally self-schooled, did not see any reason why Dad needed more schooling. This led to Dad's ultimate escape from Youngstown to pursue a high school education in Cleveland. In 1910, Cleveland's Central High School was a great intellectual and multicultural experience for Dad. His teachers were a symphony of intelligence, pedagogical skill, and compassion. They even recognized that he was hungry. They invited him to meals at their homes. He wrote to some of them as long as they lived.

Dad met my mother, Florence Marcogiuseppi while at Central High. He knew instantly that this was his wife to be. She was not so sure. She was distant to him and rich. Her father had arrived from Italy about the same time as Elpidio. Grandpa Michael Marcogiuseppi was a pillar of steel and love of life. Upon arrival in the US from Anzi, Provincia di

My Grandfather, Elpidio Buonpane, 1902.

Potenza, Italy, he saw men digging a ditch. He jumped into the ditch and dug for several days until he was placed on the payroll. He sold fruit, he established a market to sell dried fruits, dried beans and rice, and then he bought an apartment building and became a landlord. By 1910, he was driving his own Stanley Steamer.

"Grandpa, what did you do when the Black Hand came by and demanded 'protection money'?" was one of my teenage questions. "I tol' them to go to hell," he responded. His strength was contagious, and so was his piety. He and his wife Angela Rosa were at Mass and Communion daily. It was a wonderful piety that never interfered with the realities of life. When their son Vincent, a wildly successful businessman and lawyer, brought his fifth wife home, they received her warmly. Michael and Angela had a vibrant morality, but they did not moralize. So both grandfathers first came to the United States alone.

I don't think that Mom understood that one of my objectives was to subvert the kind of priesthood that was repulsive to her. My mother would cry when I spoke of my vocation. She did not realize that I did not intend to become one of those guys who babbled about at what part of the Mass your tardiness became a mortal sin, or whether you chewed the meat after you realized it was Friday. I recall writing a letter to "The Priest who celebrated the Noon Mass on Monday" and sending it to St. Joseph's Church in Los Angeles. I asked him why he insisted on mumbling through the Mass and then racing through the prayers after

Mass. "Would it not be better to say one Hail Mary slowly than to say three Hail Marys rapidly?"

Blase and sisters, 1929

My mother was an excellent theologian. "Take it with a grain of salt," was her frequent comment when referring to pontifications by the ecclesiastical institution. This theology was applied to the threats of slaughter (mortal sin) connected to eating meat on Friday, missing Mass on days of obligation, and the like. The fact is, we did not eat meat on Friday, we did generally go to Mass on Sunday, and we even went to Catholic schools some of the time. The liturgical celebrations that Mom witnessed as a child in "Little Italy" were disgusting to her. This included brass bands marching into Church, money pinned on statues and emotional expressions of "piety" and superstition. Long before Vatican Council II, she could distinguish between essentials and accidentals. For many high level bureaucrats in ecclesiastical life, religion was nothing but a mess

4

of accidentals and she knew it. She seemed to understand that there is a priority to Law in the Christian tradition. The Law is:

I give you a new commandment: Love one another. And you're to love one another the way I have loved you. This is how all will know that you're my disciples: that you truly love one another. John 13:34–35.

This was my mother's logic and theology. It was rock solid. Any other manifestation of law in Christianity must be subservient to this Law. The fact that priests and bishops so often made a religion out of inconsequential and lesser issues was self-condemning. She saw no merit in laws of clerical celibacy, heavy handed decisions about who could be married in the church, buried in "consecrated ground," no meat on Friday, no food or water before communion, Holy Days of Obligation. Mom's theology in the midst of a petty bourgeois culture was getting through to me; "You can't take it with you," she would say.

As the bus continued to roar through the desert, I recalled earlier solitary departures. I learned to love silence while biking hundreds of copies of the *Los Angeles Times* through the Hollywood hills at 4:00 AM seven days a week. The newspaper exploited us. "You are businessmen," said our manager, "you will collect from all of your subscribers each month, pay your monthly bill to the *Los Angeles Times* and you get to keep everything left over." A simple translation: "The paper-boy will absorb all bad debts." My predawn departure from home every day was a contemplative experience, a mini-escape that led the way for this Greyhound trip through the desert. I loved the brisk night air and the miraculous transition to dawn and daylight that I had the luxury of witnessing daily.

But I did not simply leave home for the solitude. A vision of eternity had struck me at the age of seven in my second grade religion class at St. Ann's School in Cleveland Heights, Ohio. I had an experience of forever and ever and ever and ever and ever that struck me one evening with what in Spanish is called "*susto*" (fright). Saint Ann's was our neighborhood Catholic School. This was the "Church Triumphant." Father John M. Powers was the powerful and stereotypical Irish American pastor. The Sisters were Ursulines and my gifted sister Betty played spirited marches on the piano as we filed in and out of class. First Communion, May 17, 1936, was a spiritual experience. We were told it was the happiest day of our lives . . . and it was momentous. My parents were there at Mass. Mr. Parisi was directing the choir and we were all singing, "Oh Lord, I Am Not Worthy." The saccharine hymns were moving to me. My mother attended the PTA meetings. The cake was as sweet as the hymns, "On This Day Oh Beautiful Mother." For much of the first, second and third grades I was a dreamer, drawing pictures of wars, not listening in class and not really interested in diagramming a sentence.

5

My mother, Florence I. Bonpane.

During second year at Loyola High School, we had an outdoor assembly. The guest speaker was Father Frank McKay of Maryknoll (The Catholic Foreign Mission Society of America). I was extremely impressed with his description of mission service to serve the poorest in Asia, Africa, and Latin America. There was a tone of light-hearted generosity and sense of "non-self" that reached me deeply. At the earliest opportunity, I made my way to his office in East Los Angeles and returned with the Maryknoll magazine, a book, *Men of Maryknoll*, and other descriptive literature. Mom was horrified when I told her of my interest in becoming a Maryknoll priest. Dad was still in the service, Judge Advocate General Department (military lawyers). It was 1944. Mom wept, "You have to finish high school, you have to finish college." And that is what I did.

  Little did Mom know that high school would only increase my desire for the Foreign Service as a Maryknoll Missioner. At Loyola High in Los Angeles, I became aware of the concept of life as a brief and joyful struggle on which eternity depends. This belief remains firmly in place today. The religious atmosphere I experienced at Loyola High led me to understand eternity as a perpetual now. Jesuits were surrogate fathers for me while Dad was in the service. The faculty was made up almost entirely of Jesuit priests and scholastics (seminarians). Expulsions were commonplace at Loyola High. There was a triumphant and near-arrogant atmosphere of being the best and brightest students as well as the toughest athletes.

There was a war on. The vast majority of us were in the ROTC. We practiced on a firing range with live ammunition, and we marched around the football field with alacrity. In these years of World War II, teenagers too young for the draft did not have an adolescence; they had to prepare for war. This was a time in the life of urban children when they were considered useless. But similar to rural children internationally, we were considered an asset and not a liability. Jobs were available to us that would have gone to the millions of adults now in military service were it not for the war. War or no war, I could not take the ROTC seriously. As a Lieutenant, I frequently broke into laughter while observing the performance of my platoon. It all seemed like comic opera to me.

My realization of physical strength came not from the ROTC, but from my hillside biking and frequent brawling with my next door buddy, Jack Goin. Jack and I were inseparable and fiercely competitive during our elementary and junior high school years. We would time our descent down the steep canyon behind my home and the ascent up the other side. The charge was through sage brush, cactus and ice plant which hung onto crumbling decomposed granite. It was a wild leaping down one side and a frantic scramble to the top of the other. It took from two and a half to three minutes. We frequently had serious rough-and-tumble fights of combined fist and wrestling. Our friendship was always renewed by the following morning. Jack went off to military school from 9th through 12th grade and went on to become one of the world's finest plastic surgeons.

Yet, I mistakenly associated sports with spiritual growth. Loyola was a confidence builder. Excellence in athletics was excellence in life. Boxing gave me a great deal of self confidence at Loyola High. I did not realize how tough my work schedule had made me. I became a good boxer and wondered why I did not try my best when fighting our school superstar Al Pollard. Al was a world-class football player and went on to play at West Point and for the Pittsburgh Steelers. He was not a great boxer. I could have won that day. But for some odd reason, perhaps in deference to his fame as a football player, I held back. It was a draw. Why did I not fight harder that day? The frustration of my football career was never to achieve a firm place on that first team. Tackle and guard were my positions on what became one of the best high school teams in the United States. We even played the great team from Boys Town, Nebraska, beating them of course.

I told my girlfriends about my plan to become a priest. They cried like my mother cried. I did not stop dating during high school or college. Normalcy was the idea. But it was a curious mix. Relationships with women developed through experiences at Loyola. Loyola was a boy's high school, but our social life was linked to the elite Marymount High School for girls. At little or no expense to the men of Loyola, our weekends were frequently at social events held at the Bel Air homes of these privileged young women. Prayer before a Marymount date: "OK, Jesus, I can get married to one of these beautiful Marymount women and carry out my Uncle Joe's famous saying, 'You can marry more in five minutes than you can make in a lifetime,' but I'll surrender that with the hope that you will let me be your instrument of peace. I thought that instead of having a few rich children, I would ask that for every sperm cell I possessed there to be one more child of God."

I graduated from High School in June of 1946. Dad was home from his service in his Second World War. I was anxious to go off to the seminary and serve on the mission fields afar. But my parents would not hear of it. Despite my protests, I would have to put aside my desire to enter the seminary for now.

When I began the University of Southern California in September of 1946, I frequently walked over to St. Vincent's Church at Figueroa and Adams to start the day with Mass. It was meaningful to pray for guidance and for the opportunity to finish college and depart for the seminary.

Externally, I must have appeared as most of the post-World War II freshmen. I played football, and was rushed by Kappa Sigma fraternity and became a pledge. I lived on the pledge porch of the house on 28th Street, fraternity row. We were dressed in gunny sacks for the week, more push-ups, no sleep, endless badgering by actives, and the drinking of a squid cocktail. There were no Jews, no African Americans, but somehow there was one Latin American, the son of a Guatemalan oligarch.

At the University of Southern California (USC), I was quickly shocked out of my high school belief that excellence in sports correlated with excellence in morals. Jeff Cravath was a football coach from central casting. He had his share of All Americans and a world class team. As soon as I signed up for spring practice in 1947, I was receiving a salary. There were some blackboards to be erased. Actually, no one seemed to care whether the slates were erased or not. This was simply one of many mechanisms used to pay for "amateur football." "It's time to prune off some of the dead wood," barked Cravath. I was carrying the ball in a scrimmage. Running as fullback, I plunged through center and was suddenly buried in a groaning bundle of guards and tackles averaging some 300 pounds each. By some powerful intuition, I determined that Jeff's comment was directed at me. This was the beginning of the end of my college football career.

But it was not too late for the Marines. The recruiters were in the locker-room. "Men, we think that some fine Marines will come from the best football teams in the United States. We are going to offer you an opportunity to receive a commission in the United States Marine Corps Reserve by training for six weeks every summer in Quantico, Virginia at the Marine Corps Platoon Leaders Class (PLC)." I accepted the offer. I felt like a trained ape. I was superman. Crawling under live ammunition, navigating the jungles of Virginia on night compass marches, firing every form of weapon, learning how to sneak up by stealth on "the enemy," and to do him in with a looped piano wire . . . sheer power! And our Catholic Chaplain sermonized, "Men, only 20% of the people of the US are Catholics. But 50% of the Marine Corps is Catholic!" Just think of it. I am so glad that they did not point me at any enemy at that age (nineteen). I think I would have eliminated any designated group of subversives, un-Americans, international communists, or anyone else for that matter.

Joining the Marine Corps reserves helped me get closer to entering the priesthood. After the summer Marine training at Quantico I went up to Maryknoll, New York to visit the "Marine Corps of the Catholic Church." And Maryknoll immediately became a spiritual Mecca for me. The seminarian who greeted me said that he had been a Marine in World War II. The spiritual power of the place was contagious. I was once again touched by the quality of light-hearted generosity and non-self which seemed to be present in everyone there. I vowed to return and to pursue my studies as a Maryknoll Father. And that is why, two years after this first visit, I was crossing the Mojave Desert by Greyhound.

"We are at the Texas border; Nigras will go to the back of the bus!" The driver's mandate snapped me out of my reverie. I had never heard a segregationist command before. I reflected on the privileged treatment I had received and how I had grown up with little awareness of social injustice. When my childhood friend and I broke into the house next door for the fun of it, someone called the police. When we were apprehended, the officers told us never to do that again. If I had not lived on Chislehurst Drive, it may have meant juvenile hall. That bus driver on the Texas border gave me an understanding of class and racial privilege that has endured.

Chapter 2

Odyssey to Maryknoll

The moon-like terrain of West Texas seemed to have shorter horizons than the rest of the world. I was on my way to San Antonio for a visit to the Seminary of the Oblates of Mary Immaculate. Why? This was the site of the seminary of the Oblates of Mary Immaculate and the headquarters for Father John P. Walsh, a high-ranking member of the Oblates of Mary Immaculate. My first seminary choice, Maryknoll, had informed me that I would not be accepted in spite of the fact that I was over twenty-one. They cited my parents' opposition. I was disturbed by their letter and was given the impression that the person responsible for admissions lacked courage.

When I arrived at the Oblate Seminary in San Antonio, I knew my stay would be brief. I had met Father Walsh a few years earlier while he was stationed at the Mission San Fernando in Southern California. He was one of the few priests who had the courage to come to our home and talk to my parents about my vocation. Even after finishing four years at USC, my parents still refused to accept my desire to enter the seminary. I had even applied to medical school so my parents would understand that seminary was not my second choice. I applied to Case Western Reserve Medical School in Cleveland. When the response to my application arrived in the mail, I brought the letter to St. Vincent's church before opening it. "Congratulations, you have been accepted. . ." I was aware that some of my letters of recommendation were due to my father's connections in Cleveland. Regardless, I wanted to show my parents that I had been accepted and could have gone to medical school if I wanted to; it was my second choice.

Father Walsh could not claim success in speaking to my parents, but after the session he suggested that I visit the Oblate Seminary in San Antonio. Upon meeting Father Walsh again in San Antonio, both he and I knew that this was not my final stop. He said, "Blase, I know that your first choice is Maryknoll, why don't you get on a plane to New York and talk to the superiors personally?" His words were wise and generous.

The DC-3 toddled off at a lazy speed as we flew out of San Antonio into a miraculous sunset, reversed course and pointed east. On to Houston, to New York and then to Maryknoll. What about miracles? St. Augustine's reflections were welcome. He asked why we pay so much attention to miracles that happen rarely, and why we are often unimpressed by the daily miracles of the sunset and the wheat growing. Are such miracles any less great because they happen often?

Maryknoll: a field stone structure constructed by Italian immigrants, just as I was. The green tile roof with an Asian upswing to the eaves. It was unique, strong, and marked by Latin graffiti in stone. *"Euntes docete omnes gentes"* (Go and teach all nations) screams at the visitor from the main entrance. This was known as Sunset Hill before the founders christened it Mary's Knoll (Maryknoll) in 1911.

"I wandered lonely as a cloud," as Wadsworth would say, and stood alone at the burial place of the founders, Bishop James Anthony Walsh and Father Fredrick Price. Theirs was the centerpiece of the Maryknoll cemetery. Dead priests, brothers, and sisters lay in this verdant graveyard terraced out of a hillside below the main building. Stones flat to the earth were inscribed with descriptive verses.

I was lost in prayer at the site of the founders' tomb. Looking up slightly, I saw red piping, a black cassock, a person. "You must be Bishop Walsh," said I. "No, Bishop Walsh is buried right here. I am Bishop Lane." I quickly realized that I was talking to the Superior General of Maryknoll.

There are times when the authoritarian, top down, nature of an ecclesiastical structure is welcome. After hearing my story, Bishop Raymond Lane assured me that I would be accepted by Maryknoll and that I should simply wait at my sister Betty's home in Albany until receiving my seminary assignment. And so it was. This Epiphany made the word "providential" part of my vocabulary.

I lived with my sister Betty and her family from June to September, 1950, until I received my specific assignment. I had resigned from the US Marine Corps Reserve and had received an honorable discharge on February 21, 1950. Providence again. I did not realize that it would have been impossible to resign at a later date due to the impending War with Korea. My colleagues in the Platoon Leaders Class went to Korea, and many died there. Marine second lieutenants were among the war's highest percentage of casualties. No wonder the Corps came to our locker room to recruit.

After daily anxiety at the mailbox of my sister's home on Crumitie Road in Loudonville, I received word that I had been accepted as a Maryknoll seminarian. I was instructed to report to Brookline, Massachusetts, for Special Studies on September 7, 1950.

I appeared at the entrance of the seminary with guitar and suitcase in hand. "I hope you can play it," commented Father John Rudin, the Rector, as he welcomed the newly arriving students. I could not. The Special Studies Program was designed for those who did not fit into any conventional category. It was for someone like me with four years of college and no degree, a place for war veterans and doubtful cases of all kinds. The one-year program was to be a period of sorting out these misfit cases.

In spite of the rigorous seminary schedule of prayer work and play, I felt a deep sense of liberation. I had followed my star and had landed in Bethlehem. I had broken with parental control.

My father's letters were brutal. "You are wasting your time." . . . "There is a real world out there and you are not part of it" . . . "You owe us some consideration" . . . "You are killing your mother." My letters back were dull and routine; the weather, the sports, and famous visitors to the seminary like the Bishop Thuc, brother of Diem, who was to become the Premiere of South Vietnam. I was determined to show love, honor, and respect for my parents, and equally determined to follow my vocation.

Visits home were a form of torture, but I determined to return home at every vacation opportunity. The pressure to leave the seminary was relentless. Dad was angry, Mom was crying. My old girlfriends were invited to family events. Mom hated the idea of celibacy. She loved family and all that it implied. Not to have a family was wrong. The very implication that celibacy is required for the Catholic priesthood is a myth. There is no reference to celibacy in the ordination liturgy. Some seventeen Byzantine Rites under the authority of the Pope have never stipulated any such law. There was a sense of liberation in the pursuit of a life of celibacy. I was convinced of a calling to be a spiritual father to many and that this would rightfully be achieved by abstinence from personal sexual relationships. I considered my graceless inclinations to be toward endless promiscuity. The goal of focusing my sexuality as a co-creator with God and passing on the gifts and fruits of the Spirit to many "children" was for me a concrete objective. The concept of channeling the base pursuit of promiscuity into energy for what needs to be done has never left me. I kept the Seminary rule which forbade dating while on vacations. In spite of the rigidity of the program, a sense of liberation stayed with me through eight years of life in the seminary.

During May of 1952 my mother contracted cancer. Dad implied that my conduct was responsible for her cancer. I left the Maryknoll College Seminary at Glen Ellyn, Illinois to visit her. She required a colostomy. I remained home during the summer of that year and took a job at the Pepsi bottling plant as a bottle washer. I washed and observed 70,000 clanging, ringing, and sometimes breaking bottles each day and belonged to the Bottlers Union. It was a good reintroduction to the working class. "Is it better to work here with this endless clatter or to spend some time in jail?" Seriously mused one of the tired employees.

"God knows what He is doing," wrote my seminary classmate, Vincent Capodanno, knowing that I was concerned about possibly being dropped from seminary ranks for my long absence. Some fifteen years later, as a Navy Chaplain, Vince was killed in Vietnam and received the Congressional Medal of Honor posthumously. He carried wounded Marines to safety until he was shot to death by the North Vietnamese. Just prior to his departure for Vietnam, I challenged Vince, "Don't you think that Chaplains simply give the message that God is on our side?" Vince responded, "I am not telling anyone God is on our side, I am going to serve the young people who are fighting there." And now Vince Capodanno is about to be canonized as a saint. He was truly a hero, but I dread thinking about how he might be "used" for military recruitment.

After a year at the Maryknoll Seminary in Brookline, Massachusetts and two years at the Maryknoll College at Glen Ellyn, Illinois, I received my Bachelor of Arts degree in philosophy.

That summer I was an assistant to Father John Coffield at Dolores Mission in East Los Angeles. He was an excellent example of what a pastor should be, frugal in his life style and generous to others. He also gave homilies that were relevant to people's lives and contemporary events. Inspired by Coffield, I was in sync with the youth in East Los Angeles. Such encounters furthered my commitment to social justice. In East Los Angeles, the gangs were there. The poverty was there. I set up a boxing ring in the parking lot of the parish and began boxing lessons for the youth of the area. They loved it. I went door to door to visit the families in the projects.

Postgraduate work began with the Maryknoll Novitiate at Bedford, Massachusetts. It was a monastic year. We studied Ascetic Theology, the art of spiritual pursuits.

After Novitiate, we were sent to Maryknoll, New York for our final four years of theology. "I have found the seminary to be very meaningful, Father General, the only place where I believe I am wasting time is in the classroom. I do not believe I am wasting time by teaching High School students. My students are from North Tarrytown, a working-class manufacturing center. They are tough and sometimes delinquent. We are communicating. I relish the art of teaching, the art of pedagogy. I do not think I am wasting time in sports, but if I am in the classroom and a very boring lecture is taking place, I cannot simply pick up a book and read. That would be insulting to the professor. If I were in the library, I could be studying, but in a boring lecture, I can only endure. You know we have some twenty-three hours of lecture each week, and I must say this is where I feel I am wasting time."

The new Superior General had a slight smile on his face. Bishop John Comber was a no-nonsense, practical man with a bush of white hair. He was short and stocky and was always ready to give directions about car care or how to get to various locations in Westchester County. "There is an obstacle-course component to the seminary," he responded. I was pleased that he did not attempt to defend sleep-inducing lectures.

During these final four years at Maryknoll, New York we had been ordained to Minor Orders; Porter, Lector, Acolyte and Exorcist. We had been ordained to Major Orders; Sub-Deacon and Deacon. All that remained was ordination to the Priesthood, which was scheduled for June 14, 1958.

Ordination picture, June 14, 1958, Maryknoll, New York.

My whole family arrived for that great day. I was so grateful to my parents for arriving and for leaving behind the years of criticism and opposition that had preceded my ordination. They had finally arrived at a certain tolerance of my calling. We sang the Veni Creator Spritus: "Creator Spirit, come and visit the souls that are Yours; fill with heavenly grace the hearts that You created." My three sisters were also present at the ordination. Margie had always been supportive of my calling. She had also disappointed our parents by entering religious life. She joined about three years after I did. She was now Sister Mary Anne and she was celebrated for her ability to rehabilitate disturbed children. She was to become the Director of Stanford Home, which under her guidance became known as one of the best facilities for disturbed children in California. My sister Fleurette had also supported me in spite of my parents' opposition, as did my sister Betty, who with her husband Ed gave me much needed hospitality while I awaited my first assignment to the Maryknoll Seminary at Brookline.

Our mission assignments were not a matter of choice. They were given in a quasi-military fashion. Congratulations you are assigned to "wherever."

Chapter 3

Uninhibited Apostolate

"This is your promotion sermon," said Father John Martin, my new superior. He gave me an eight-page pitch for Maryknoll that he expected me to use at each Mass. I had been assigned to the Maryknoll Development House in St. Louis, Missouri. Development was the "Siberia" of Maryknoll. As foreign missioners, we were prepared for assignments to Asia, Africa, or Latin America. But some were always assigned to this promotional work. We were to raise funds and to recruit vocational prospects for Maryknoll. I was horrified at the prospect of using the "sermon" assigned by Father John Martin.

The anecdotes and the theology were just not for me. As an ordained priest, I was aware of my new autonomy and immediately began to speak with my own material, hoping that my superior would not be disturbed. He said nothing about my failure to use his sermon. This was a welcome to a priestly fraternity that was internally quite tolerant. I covered some seven Midwest states from our headquarters in St. Louis. It was a contemplative assignment. Hours of silence, meditation and prayer while driving the great plains, followed by speaking at as many as eight masses on Sundays and in an endless number of classrooms on weekdays.

I began more innovations. Why speak only in Catholic institutions? I contacted Public High Schools and asked if I could give assembly talks on "World Problems." The answer was, "yes." Why not speak in colleges and universities rather than elementary and high schools? I contacted priests at the Newman Centers at state universities and found them receptive. Contrary to stereotypical images of religious life, I had a great sense of freedom and autonomy both in my seminary years and in this new priestly assignment.

One of the pressures I noted quickly was the distaste for innovation by my colleagues in the priesthood. Oddly enough, it was not my superiors. It was the rank and file who had become set in their ways. Actually, I had been expecting to receive criticism from my superiors. Reports had to go to headquarters in New York every week. How many schools did we visit? How many students heard us? How much literature did we give out? What churches had we scheduled for Sunday appeals? How much money was collected? How many sponsors? All of this was a challenge to me, and I honestly found it interesting. I practically lived in my car, covering the highways, schools and churches of the Great Plains. I was actually doing an unintended informal study of the Catholic clergy of the United States by visiting so many schools and churches each week. I will say that in general these clergymen were serious and dedicated professional people, as were the sisters. On a few rare occasions in my seven-year stint as a Maryknoll promoter, I was aware of being the guest of an alcoholic, psychotic, or pederast. But overall, I had a sense of effectiveness and success in my "sales work." I learned to pray behind the wheel of a car. Where could anyone be closer to death?

I saw death on the highways and gave sacraments to the dying. These were contemplative years of intense work, itinerant prayer and preaching. Looking back, this was a period of channeling my physical and psychic energy into a meaningful and uninhibited apostolate.

I was sent on to continue promotional work out of the Maryknoll House in Houston, Texas. I found even more space for innovation. It was that year, 1959, when a few Spaniards had come to the United States with a powerful program called the *Cursillos de Cristiandad*. This was a high-pressure theological-psychological crash course in Catholicism that was evangelical and charismatic (perhaps even cultish), and directed toward creating devout members of the church. It was a masterpiece of group dynamics. It had never been given in English. I worked with several priests throughout Texas who were interested in seeing the transition to the English cursillo.

Once again, I was surprised that I was not getting complaints from superiors in New York or locally. The Superior General, John Comber (the same Father General who I had told about the boring classes), came to visit Houston and to analyze our work. "Just keep doing what you are doing," he said. I told him about my use of radio and hope to utilize TV for the work of Maryknoll. He drank two beers with me that evening said, "That's fine, keep up the good work," and went to bed. After the Superior General went back to New York, I asked an infirm priest colleague for some counsel. "Father Farnan, why am I not hassled for all of the new things I am trying? I know about the Peter Principle and how hot air rises so that many people in high places get there by not making any waves. But I keep receiving approval from headquarters and now I am assigned as Superior in Denver!" The tough-talking and wise priest, who was almost doubled in half with arthritis, responded curtly, "Blase, no one fights Santa Claus." Now I understood. Both funds and recruits were coming from my work and those were the basics of my assignment. Had I simply done the innovative things and not produced funds and vocations, the story would have been very different.

From Houston, I covered Texas and Oklahoma. I was especially impressed with the Oklahoma Catholics and their progressive clergy. Speaking with the Principal of Catholic High School in Oklahoma City, Father Carlin, and the priests who worked with him was an intellectual experience. They were in touch with major issues that would be coming up at Vatican II. This high school faculty had a serious interest in our mission work and were ready to leave their diocese and serve in Guatemala. Father Carlin did this as did many of his brother priests. The best known of these Oklahoma priest missioners was Father Stanley Rother who could soon be canonized as a saint for his martyrdom at the hands of the barbaric Guatemalan military.

A large youth gathering was organized at the Benedictine Monastery outside of Oklahoma City. As a speaker, I expressed my objection to the scanty clothing worn by the young women at the conference. My Oklahoma priest friends quickly asked me if it was my problem or the young women's problem. It was my problem. This insight helped me to understand that often the moralizing of clergy is an expression of envy.

In 1962, I was appointed Regional Superior of the Rocky Mountain Area. Our Maryknoll headquarters was in Denver, Colorado. I frankly could not understand why I had been tolerated so long. There were so many innovations, including my participation in bringing the *Cursillos de Cristiandad* to Texas (in Spanish) and later to Wyoming and Colorado (in English). These "Christianity Courses" were an intensive immersion in Catholicism from Thursday evening to late Sunday. There was little sleep, and presentations of up to seven hours in length were given on the seven Sacraments. The courses stirred up the faith of many Catholics. Although it was a powerful experience, the long hours and shortage of sleep received some well-deserved criticism.

I was comfortable with my new responsibilities as Regional Superior. I continued outreach to the universities and to the Major Seminary in Denver. Just as in Oklahoma, there were diocesan priests who were ready and willing to go off to a mission assignment. This approach had the potential for conflict with some of the local bishops if they should consider me as "stealing" their clergy. But the conflict did not happen. I found particular inspiration in the leadership of Charles Buswell, Bishop of Pueblo, Colorado. Vatican II was now in session, and Charles absorbed the spirit of Pope John XXIII to the fullest. At a large gathering of people of all faiths, Bishop Buswell presided at Mass. Many Bishops would have explained courteously that only Catholics were welcome to receive Holy Communion at such a Mass. Contrary to my expectations,

Bishop Buswell addressed the ecumenical gathering and said, "Would anyone with love in their heart please come and receive communion." My years in Denver were the years of the Second Vatican Council, 1962–1965. An irreversible mutation took place in our concept of the church. The triumphalism, legalism, and ritualism were not appropriate. The Vatican was actually asking us to make judgments in the field rather than constantly referring back to headquarters. In place of the Roman imperial model which had served since the Emperor Constantine, we were given the autonomous model of guerrilla warfare (to be applied nonviolently). How rapidly we received the message.

I enjoyed being a superior, but it was time for a new assignment. It was June of 1965. The Maryknoll Fathers had worked with the poorest of the poor in Asia, Africa, and Latin America. In the post-Vatican II era, the Maryknoll council decided that some of our priests should work in the universities of the poor nations. Father Gerard McCrane and I were selected to begin a new apostolate for Maryknoll, an outreach to the university students in Latin America. My assignment was to Guatemala with the qualification that before beginning work in that Central American country, I was to proceed to Georgetown University in Washington, D. C., and get a Master's in Latin American studies.

Every afternoon I would celebrate a folk Mass in the basement of Dahlgren Chapel. Students came in large numbers. My homilies were directed at the holocaust taking place in Vietnam and our response to it. By the winter of 1965 we were demonstrating in front of the White House to protest that evil war.

I received a call from the university chaplain, Father Geary. Expecting the worst, I arrived at his office ready to hear objections to my manner of celebrating Mass, the folk hymns, the laughter, the demonstrations. To my wonderment, Father Geary asked me to take over the retreat program for the entire university. He explained that the traditional retreats were not drawing any students. I joyfully agreed to accept his request. I asked that all retreats be co-educational and that talking be permitted.

Our site for retreats was outside of Washington at a Virginia hideaway run by Sisters who were most cooperative with new directions in the church. The sessions were called Weekends of Christian Living. Capacity crowds developed quickly. We dialogued about the Bible, the church, the council, and the many admissions of guilt on the part of the institution. We talked about sex, but not in the context of being the world's only evil. We denounced militarism while celebrating social justice, human rights, and the understanding that our response to people's needs was our access to God. We sang many folk hymns. I plunked the ukulele.

Conducting "Weekends of Christian Living" as Retreat Master for students at Georgetown University, 1965.

After memorable farewells from students who attended my daily masses and Weekends of Christian Living at Georgetown, it was time to depart for Guatemala. A sad goodbye to my parents in Los Angeles. They seemed more accepting of my calling ever since ordination day. While in Denver the previous year, Mom and Dad came to visit. They had accepted my being a priest and were happy with my new role, as Superior. Ambition has its place. "We must be humble enough to have our name in the paper daily, if necessary," said one spiritual director. Dad wanted to be a Superior Court Judge. He was a Republican and the Governor of California was a Democrat. Dad had an excellent file in the Governor's Office. He had been President of the Los Angeles Public Utilities Commission; he had practiced law with integrity for almost half a century. He was in his late sixties. Was he too old?

I determined it was time to do something for my father. I placed a call to the Governor's office in Sacramento. An appointment was made with Governor Pat Brown. I flew to Sacramento and we talked about my father. Governor Brown's key question was, "Is your father a compassionate man?" I answered in the affirmative.

The governor talked to me about his son, Jerry, who had seriously considered becoming a priest.

Shortly after this brief meeting Dad received his appointment as a Judge of the Superior Court.

It was not simply a result of my recommendation. There was also a large file in the Governor's office documenting Dad's excellence in the field of law.

Chapter 4

Assignment to Central America

I flew in to Guatemala on September 15, 1966. Firecrackers were going off everywhere. I fantasized that the celebration was for my arrival. Actually it was Central American Independence Day. Guatemala may be independent of Spain, but there has been no liberation. The Spanish-born newly independent oligarchy simply became imitators of the former *conquistadores*. The conquest continues.

Huehuetenango was my new home. Individual instruction in Spanish took up about four hours of every day. The high country is bone-chilling. I was never warm in Huehuetenango. We had a welcoming songfest one evening. The Maryknoll compound was surrounded by walls. Entry to the facility was attained by a honk of the horn (generally a Toyota jeep). A servant would run and open the gate for arriving priests and brothers. The common room had a huge fireplace.

I began singing with my trusty ukulele. The community entered in. The volume increased, and the raucous spirit generated echoes through the Cuchumatanes Mountains. We marched around the compound triumphantly. As the enthusiasm expanded, one of the priestly participants (it had to be Art Melville) seized my ukulele and struck me over the head. It was a friendly attack but it cracked the instrument. Such was the vibrant spirit of Maryknoll priests in Huehuetenango.

I began to work with the students from University of San Carlos immediately. The student center was called *Centro de Capacitación Social*. The *Cursillos de Capacitación Social* was a program designed to introduce university students to social questions by way of Roman Catholic social doctrine. Designed by Father Manuel Aguirre, S. J. of Venezuela, it was a polemic response to Marxist analysis, and the materials were rigidly anti-Marxist. However, the students at the University of San Carlos were already practicing a socialized democracy within their organization. They would go over all the materials to be used in the cursillo and translate the material into a mode that was understandable and applicable in Guatemala. (It should be noted that these *Cursillos de*

Capacitación were not related to the doctrinaire Cursillos we had been giving in the United States).

I quickly learned that the Guatemalan University students' main desire was to reach the Indians in the mountains. Students suggested that we spend a full six weeks in the mountain areas of Huehuetenango and Quiche. I thought it was a great idea. To my surprise, over ninety students volunteered to serve in thirty villages. Many of the villages that were selected were so isolated that there was no easy access other than small footpaths. We were pleased to realize that after a few days in these villages, visitors from other villages would come to request our presence.

During the regular university year, we structured brief weekend programs. The cursillos would take place at indigenous parishes. Pastors would simply announce the event, and the response was substantial. Our talks covered such topics as the common good, responsibility, the right to organize, as well as gave introductions on the process of organizing. The first cursillos were given to Spanish-speaking Indians who were mostly migratory workers who had some contact with urban centers.

I was embarrassed by the reverence the Indians showed toward me when they discovered I was a priest. On some occasions, they insisted I ride a horse when everyone else was walking. Yet, the university students had clever ways to deal with my unsolicited elite status. On one occasion, I was organizing in the community of *La Libertad* in Huehuetenango. A messenger from Aguacate came down asking for a priest to give the last sacraments to a dying elder. They brought down a mule and two guides led my way. There was no road, and often the trail was too steep for a mule. When I arrived at the old gentleman's bedside, the entire community was engaged in making his confession for him: "He was faithful to his wife and good to his children," "He would get angry sometimes," "He drank too much," and so on from various relatives. Trying to maintain a somber expression, I gave absolution and bid the small community goodbye after some tortillas and fresh milk. But as I came to the church grounds, I was ambushed. Some five students attacked with firecrackers. The mule lost its patience and I fell to the ground. The ability of Central Americans to joke in the midst of life and death struggles is majestic. We may be in danger, but we will not reject laughter, song, and poetry.

It was in Huehuetenango that the Indians began calling the teams of the *Cursillos de Capacitación Social* "guerrillas of peace." They knew the university students were unarmed, but they also understood that the goals and objectives of the group were revolutionary. Unfortunately, for the death squads, there was no distinction between armed struggle and non-violent struggle. As our movement grew into Zacapa, we had our first encounter with La Mano Blanca. After a five-day cursillo in Gualan, the student chairman received a letter from La Mano Blanca stating that he had been selected to be killed by their organization.

I decided to make a return trip to Gualan to see if I would be able to meet the director of La Mano Blanca, Mariano Sanchez. With the help of the local church, I was granted such a meeting. I told Mariano that our work in the villages was to promote social progress. I asked him if he knew the student who had received the death threat. At first he denied, but later stated matter-of-factly, "He is a communist." I asked him why he would make that statement, and he said, "We know him. His brother went to Havana, Cuba. We know that type. We heard him say he was willing to give his life for the poor."

This meeting was a moment of clarity for me. I had a gut-level realization that the conflict in Guatemala was actually a war between the rich and the poor, and that the poor and those who sought to help them were unequivocally categorized as communists. When I left my meeting with Mariano Sanchez and crossed the Motagua River by canoe, I was convinced that I was alive only because I was a United States citizen and a priest.

The plight of the Guatemalan people began to have a great influence on my theological development. On October 18, 1966, from a remote mountain location, I wrote:

A revolution is taking place throughout the world, and it would be a pleasure to be part of it and to help give direction to church people who are wondering just what their role will be. And now, to be here in Guatemala it is a privilege and honor to serve the Lord 'to the ends of the earth.' I do not intend to become accustomed to the poverty and destitution of these poor people. I do not intend to become accustomed to their sickness, ignorance and to the constant injustices they endure. I intend to do whatever I can to change these evils. God help me to be wise as a serpent and simple as a dove.

The combination of forces acting on me and the spirit of the people's resistance was getting through to me.

My work and the work of the university students in the mountain villages led to our mobilization of student organizers across Central America. We planned a Central American meeting of all members of the *Cursillos de Capacitación Social*. The meeting place was at the university in San Jose, Costa Rica. Many of the students who went to that historic meeting have since lost their lives in the Central American revolution.

The plan was to travel by car from Guatemala to Costa Rica. Our Guatemalan delegation was made up of some ten students, Sister Miriam

Peter, Father Jalon and Father Charles Reiley in two vans. Crossing each Central American border was a huge headache; questions, forms, car ownership, visas, highway border gates closed for two hours after noon, typed forms retyped for lack of carbon paper. In Honduras, we had to report directly to the police station.

In *Sierra de las Cuchumatanes* Mountains, Department of Huehuetenango, Guatemala, 1967.

Father Reiley insisted on driving in El Salvador. I reluctantly turned the wheel over to him. Being a passenger makes me nervous, and I am more comfortable behind the wheel rather than wondering what the driver is doing. After driving for five minutes, Charlie and the van were pushed off the road by a burly bus. We smoothly floated down into a ditch, which gently curtailed our momentum. If the incident had occurred at a less favorable place, we could have suffered fatalities. The offending bus did not stop. We were able to proceed out of the ditch and onward under our own vehicle's power. I had been warned previously that if there was an accident in El Salvador, it was not uncommon for one or both of the drivers to come out of their vehicles shooting. Our superior in Guatemala had warned us, "Even if you hit someone on the highway, drive on to the next police station or hospital to ask for help. If you stop, you may be attacked by the pedestrians."

As we proceeded into Nicaragua on our way to Costa Rica, "Vote for Somoza" signs appeared. The trappings of election fever were everywhere. It was a classic demonstration election. Somoza would win. He had opposition, but the opposition would not win. There was no possibility of that. Young women in straw hats were campaigning US style for the corrupt and vile Anastasio Somoza DeBayle.

Little boxes were for sale everywhere in Nicaragua. These were coffins for the endless deaths of children. Funerals were in process in every village. It may surprise some students of current Nicaraguan history to know that the opposition to Somoza during the 1967 campaign was known as UNO (*Unión Nacional Opositora*) or the National Union of Opposition. UNO was supporting candidate Dr. Fernando Aguero. The Socialist Party joined this effort to form a coalition with anti-Somoza middle and upper-class people. Newspaper publisher Pedro Joaquin Chamorro, and husband of later President Violeta Chamorro, knew that Somoza was in complete control of the ballot boxes. Pedro organized a mass demonstration to march on the Presidential Palace. It was January 22, 1967. We were in transit to Costa Rica. 60,000 people were marching. In his mercy, Somoza used his tanks and machine guns to kill only 1% of them (600 people). This massacre was the occasion for many middle and upper class people to identify with the newly formed FSLN (*Frente Sandinista de Liberación Nacional*) or the Sandinista National Liberation Front.

As we crossed into Costa Rica, the first comment made by one of the university women on seeing San Jose was, "*Que gringa!*" (How gringo!) It may be a gringo city, but it takes great pride in the fact that its army was eliminated in 1948. This great achievement of Pepe Figueres, who was later elected president, should be imitated by every Central American country. Costa Rica has an educational system and a health system. It seems clear that most countries can have education and health systems, or an army, but they can't have both.

The meeting was focused on Central American solidarity. Armed revolutionary forces were active from Guatemala to Panama. We considered our movement, *Los Cursillos de Capacitación Social*, to be the last chance for nonviolent change in Central America. We did not want to fail.

The US press concurred with our assessment of the situation. Vern Richey and David Mangurian, writing for the *Copley News Service*, identified our movement as being one of the last effective nonviolent programs in Central America. The journalists also surmised that the students and their leaders would be inclined to enter the armed struggle if their nonviolent program was abolished. (The reader may wish to refer to my book, *Guerrillas of Peace; Liberation Theology and the Central American Revolution*, Third Edition, www.iUniverse.com which covers, my Guatemala tenure).

By December of 1967, events moved with stunning speed. The lack of toleration for our movement generated by misleading reports by infiltrators to the church, military, and US authorities about our potential merger with rebel forces led to a government crackdown. The leadership of *El Centro de Capacitación Social* was listed by the secret police of Guatemala (*judiciales*). This meant the students had to disappear on their own accord or they might be "disappeared" by the secret police themselves. I began to help shuttle leaders out of Guatemala. Some were brought to the border with Mexico. Some left by air. But all knew there was a place to meet in Mexico in order to regroup and reorganize.

I was not certain of what I would do. My thought was that I should go back to the US and shout out the facts to every media outlet possible. I thought that if I could garner support in the US against US intervention in Guatemala, I could help save many lives. I would soon discover that my exodus from Guatemala would be made for me.

My remaining days in Guatemala were spent getting rid of the files of our student center and helping at-risk student leaders to get out of the country. When the final, and predictable, police and military attack destroyed our headquarters in Guatemala City, we were just grateful that the building was empty.

It is difficult to reconstruct the pace of activities of December, 1967. Students were still scattered throughout the mountains of Huehuetenango. It was necessary to pull them together and to thank God that some ninety of them were able to regroup without the loss of anyone. The coming together was celebrated by a dance. Prior to the dance there was a collective celebration of the sacrament of Penance. During the dance, there was a constant and continuous exchange of information among the dancers.

The Assistant Superior of Maryknoll, Father Rudy Kneuer, arrived at the dance to speak to me. He had an airline ticket in his hand and told me that I was to board a flight leaving Guatemala on Christmas Eve, 1967. I was amazed at the fury expressed by the Maryknoll Superior a few days later in Guatemala City. He asked me to meet him at the Las Vegas Restaurant in Guatemala City. He told me that if I did not tell him all that was taking place with the movement, I would be spitting out my teeth like Chiclets. Fortunately, his Assistant Superior was there as a witness to this tirade. In response to his threat of physical violence, I responded that any attack on my person would be to his detriment. This was the first near physical conflict I had experienced in decades. The Superior and his Assistant appeared shocked by my response.

At the dance, the marimba music continued, and everyone there shared life-risking secrets about points and methods of departure. Some were going into the rebel movement, some were leaving the country, and some hoped to stay and continue a relatively normal life in Guatemala. After careful consultation with the leadership of the movement, and my own personal reflection that I was needed in the US to speak about the situation in Guatemala, I decided to accept the Superior's order to leave. My personal plan, after helping various students to border areas, was to return to the United States and proclaim the realities of social injustice taking place in Guatemala to the mass media.

Chapter 5

Renegade Priest

Still stunned by the rapid exodus from Guatemala, I discovered that my plight had found its way into the US press. I accepted a speaking engagement in St. Louis at a national gathering on the Latin American Church for January of 1968. However, I was somewhat hindered by a gag order from the Superior General of Maryknoll, Father John McCormack and a summary assignment "under pain of suspension" to report to Hawaii.

My meeting with the Superior General was one-sided. "Father General, I understand you want to talk to me," I said. "No, I don't want to talk to you. You have been making a damn fool of yourself," he replied. He then went into a rant threatening suspension of my priestly faculties, inviting me to leave the Maryknoll Society and assurance that there was no position for me in the community. I left that meeting realizing there had been no dialogue, no hearing, no defense, and no humanity. If there was no position for me in Maryknoll, I concluded that I would have to find my own way.

Professor Don Bray from California State University Los Angeles was a participant in the St. Louis conference. His question was exhilarating: "Will you consider teaching at our university?" Of course I would consider it. If the church cut off my support, I would need to be financially self-sufficient. St. Paul was proud of his self-support as a tentmaker. I had recently requested a five-hundred-dollar loan from the seminary credit union, which was denied.

The St. Louis conference made it clear to me that people in the United States were ready to hear about US intervention, not only in Vietnam but also in Latin America. I had to fly on to Hawaii immediately as I was under threat of ecclesiastical suspension if my arrival was not timely. Fellow priests waiting for me at the Honolulu airport assured me that I was not suspended because the plane touched down at 11:55 PM. Five minutes later and the suspension would have taken effect. So much for canon law.

The following morning I asked about the conditions of my assignment as stated by the Superior General. The Hawaii superior, Father Stankard, assured me that the conditions of my assignment represented a firm mandate rather than a passing moment of anger on the part of Father McCormack. For me, it would have been a lack of faith to comply with the tyrannical orders I had received; do not speak about Latin America, do not write about Latin America, do not organize any student groups, and forget everything that happened in Guatemala. Such rigidity seemed to represent a quasi-religious conformity to US military policy. I did not share that belief.

I had never been an unhappy priest. Had it not been for this intransigent treatment, I might have tried to negotiate a workable solution. Thank God for the harshness of Father John McCormack, the Superior General. What might have happened if some understanding superior had tried to negotiate? If that had been the case, I might not now have my beautiful family. My decision was to take the next plane out of Hawaii. I was only on the island for fifteen hours before departing for Washington, D.C., and I had an editorial meeting with the *Washington Post*. Journalist Bill McKaye had extended the invitation.

My friend, attorney Jack Dowdy and his family took me in as I tried to find my compass as a renegade priest. I had no feeling of leaving anything. What I was doing was because of my faith, not in spite of it. I had to follow where the Spirit led.

I found an apartment about a block from the White House. I was not inclined to live in one of the numerous communes of the sixties. I don't think community is created by jamming a bunch of unlikely people into the same house and then fighting over who is going to do the dishes. Community is like-minded people in solidarity, some of whom might choose to live together.

My view of community is global, and I have always felt connected, even having a sense of community while driving on a freeway. Being disconnected, uprooted, is a painful form of death.

The uprooted feeling of being disconnected from Maryknoll was not lasting. I quickly recovered from my wounds and continued to follow the same Spirit and same prayer that had led me through years of missionary life. What prayer?

Veni, Sancte Spiritus,	Come Holy Spirit,
Et Emitte coelitus	Send forth the ray of
Lucis tuae radium.	Your heavenly light.
Veni, pater pauperum,	Come, Father of the poor,
Veni, dator munerum,	Come, giver of gifts,
Veni lumen cordium.	Come, light of the heart.
Consolator optime,	Highest consoler,
Dulcis hospes animae,	Sweet guest of the soul,

Dulce refrigerium.	Sweet refreshment.
In labore requies,	In labor, rest,
In aestu temperies,	In heat, coolness,
In fletu solatium.	In grief, solace.
O lux beatissima,	Oh, blessed light,
Reple cordis intima	Fill the inmost hearts
Tuorum fidelium.	Of your faithful.
Sine tuo numine,	Without your grace,
Nihil est in homine,	We are nothing,
Nihil est innoxium.	Nothing is right.
Lava quod est sordidum,	Wash that which is dirty,
Riga quod est aridum,	Water that which is dry,
Sana quod est saucium.	Make sound the sick.
Flecte quod est rigidum,	Bend the rigid,
Fove quod est frigidum,	Melt the frigid,
Rege quod est devium.	Straighten out the crooked.
Da tuis fidelibus,	Give to your faithful,
In te confidentibus,	Those who have hope in you,
Sacrum septenarium.	Your seven-fold gifts.
Da virtutis meritum,	Give us strength to finish
Da salutis exitum.	Our journey with courage.
Da perene gaudium.	Give eternal joy.
Amen. Alleluia.	Amen. Alleluia.

This is my mantra. This prayer recites itself in my soul as I speed down the highways and contemplate. It is a nonsectarian prayer because God is nonsectarian. Can you imagine a sectarian God? This recalls the story of the Catholic who went in search of God. After traveling the world, there was a long-awaited call home with the following report: "The good news is I have found God. The bad news is, I am calling from Salt Lake City."

We pray for a meaningful existence. Jean-Paul Sartre could find no meaning in life, could accept no God. But he came to a sublime conclusion: "There is as much meaning in life as I create. I have an obligation to create meaning, it is a moral imperative." What a superb and spiritual morality for a confirmed atheist.

I approached the great Eric Fromm in Cuernavaca, Mexico and expressed my concern about his "atheism." He groaned and explained, "My approach is that of the ancient rabbinical teachers. This is the name we do not take in vain. I am not referring to what is called swearing and cursing; I am referring to the arrogance of thinking that we can comprehend God. We do not say the name. So you may call me a non-theist if you wish." Fromm went on to explain the lack of reverence of those who "know all about God." God will do this, won't do that. It is the hubris of the TV evangelists. This is the essence of irreverence. The pursuit of the spirit requires reverence for the atheist and non-theist.

I put a phone in at my bachelor apartment. It began to ring. Speaking engagements flowed in constantly. Harvard, Yale, Cornell. Before long, there were one hundred venues. I was surprised to find out there were honoraria for these talks. I was actually able to support myself. Something began to happen at that time, which has led to my constant thanksgiving and has marked my "business" ever since. It is what I call the zero-cash-flow experience. I was spending money for travel, printing, and room and board. At month's end, I usually was at about zero. No debts, no deficit, and no ballast. It has been an experience of faith which I call the monthly miracle.

Another discovery of the moment: I was under constant personal surveillance by agencies of the US government. One of the operatives was David Skedule. He was everywhere. I boarded a plane, he was there. I gave a talk, he was there. I talked to him with a great deal of reserve. He offered me a sweater during a freezing visit to Cornell, and I accepted it and wore it for many months. At this time I developed a simple theory. I had no secrets; what I say to David Skedule, I will say on TV, radio or in the print media. When someone comes up to me who has a "secret" and must speak in whispers, I tell that person to speak up or go away, that my words are public, my position is public. I do not deal in secrets.

I received a letter from the dean at California State University, Los Angeles, offering me a full-time teaching position in Latin American Studies beginning in January of 1969. I accepted.

How could anyone teach about Latin America without experiencing Cuba? I decided to go there to see what all the fuss was about. I wrote to the State Department requesting permission. The State Department wrote me back denying permission. I left the day after receiving the negative letter from State. I presented myself to the Cuban Embassy in Mexico City and received a visa on a separate sheet of paper, not on my passport. Mexico City was in turmoil.

On August 27th, 1968 I saw 400,000 people marching in the streets, an amazing conglomeration of students, professors, peasants and common people. The demonstration continued on the following day in the main square, the *Zócalo*. *Granaderos* opened fire on the students after an action by police provocateurs. Police dressed as students took down the Mexican flag and put up the flag of anarchy to reign over the *Zócalo*. Police dressed as students began "sacrilegiously" ringing the bells of the Cathedral of Mexico, which reigns over the *Zócalo*. Students began to drop. They were dead from police and *granadero* bullets. This was the beginning of a blood bath that would continue into the fall as Mexico prepared to host the world in the Olympics of 1968. The Mexican newspapers "forgot" to cover this August massacre and headlined articles about the revolutionaries of 1910 supporting the government of President Díaz Ordaz. One of marchers carried a placard, "Porfirio Díaz Ordaz," identifying the incumbent with the dictator who preceded the revolution of 1910. Eduardo Galeano writes of the 1968 massacres:

> The students invade the streets. Such demonstrations have never been seen before in Mexico, so huge, so joyous, everyone linked arm in arm, singing and laughing. The students cry out against President Díaz Ordaz and his ministerial mummies, and all the others who have taken over Zapata's and Pancho Villa's revolution.
>
> In Tlatelolco, a plaza where Indians and *conquistadores* once fought to the death, a trap is sprung. The army blocks every exit with strategically placed tanks and machine guns. Inside the corral, readied for the sacrifice, the students are hopelessly jammed together. A continuous wall of rifles with fixed bayonets advances to seal the trap.
>
> Flares, one green, one red, give the signal. Hours later, a woman searches for her child, her shoes leaving bloody tracks on the ground.
>
> —Eduardo Galeano, *Memory of Fire, Century of the Wind*

In August of 1968, a police riot took place at the Democratic Convention in Chicago. Hundreds of casualties ensued. I was not at the convention but was present at the April 1968 peace march in Chicago. Mayor Daly's troops violently attacked our march in flying wedge formations, beating people indiscriminately, jamming protesters into paddy wagons with vicious and hateful alacrity. I stayed in a Chicago commune that night. Many people had wounds which needed treatment. Such was the atmosphere created by the war in Vietnam. Those who understood the evil nature of the conflict and tried to stop it were labeled as subversives and communists. We had just experienced Mayor Daly's dress rehearsal for the Democratic Convention in August.

The FBI was present in Mexico City to take pictures of me and the other US citizens boarding the Cuban plane bound for Havana. I reflected on the Spanish proverb, "politics is like playing the violin, you pick it up with your left hand but you play it with your right." Mexico's foreign policy may give the impression of progressive government by its long-standing recognition of Cuba. But Mexican domestic policy is sheer top-down authority.

Mario Vargas Llosa called it, "The perfect dictatorship."

Chapter 6

Cuba

A driver and a 1959 Cadillac were at my disposal. We covered the entire island in this gas-guzzler. I am not at ease with Cuban driving; it is analogous to the bullfight. Excellence is marked by the near miss. Crowds divide as the Red Sea while the smoking ancient luxury car plies the road. I was obviously shaken by the performance. Armando the driver, a revolutionary African Cuban, says, "*No temas, Blase, no temas!*" (Don't be afraid . . . don't be afraid.) The words had a deeper meaning to me. I applied his counsel to my outlaw status with church and state. Don't be afraid. Fear not . . . how biblical. "Don't let your hearts be distressed; don't be fearful," John 14:27.

I was a guest of the government in Cuba. The Cubans were interested in Liberation Theology. I spoke to a large gathering of university students at Jibacoa Beach. I talked about the role of religious people in the Latin American revolution. If you were a member of the religious community in Cuba, however, you could not be a member of the communist party. I spoke about the stereotypical "trinity" of military, oligarchy, and church in Latin America and the current contradictions to that stereotype. The young people were interested in the example of Dom Helder Camara, Bishop of Recife, Brazil, a progressive Bishop who was not in sync with that trinity of Brazil. Dom Helder said, "When I fed the poor, they called me a saint; when I asked why they were poor, they called me a Communist." The students were also impressed with Father Camilo Torres of Colombia. Camilo had run for president of Colombia and later became a commander in the guerrilla movement where he died in battle.

It was good to be with people who were in a process of experimentation, who celebrated life and who did not claim to have all the answers. Academic talk and revolutionary history took up about one hour of the evening. Then it was party time. The band started playing at about 8:00 PM and the music continued until 4:00 AM. This was a fine example for me. The US left was marked by grim fundamentalists who "knew the answers."

Yet, in the shadows of this and other meetings was an alleged member of the Students for a Democratic Society (SDS), Thomas Edward Mosher.

He was a paid informant of the FBI. Mosher later reported on my visit to the Committee on the Judiciary of the United States Senate before the Subcommittee to Investigate the Administration of the Internal Security Act and Other Internal Security Laws. Mosher explained how he had followed me in Cuba in 1968. As is often the case with such informants, he had a criminal record and was cooperating in order to have various charges dropped. There was nothing so exceptional about my visit. Perhaps he expected to get more points as an informant by creating an aura of mystery about my presence in Cuba.

In his testimony, Mosher described me as someone who approved violence and used my power as an American clergyman to legitimize revolution and violence: "The tenor of the conversation with Father Bonpane was more or less that priests and clergyman had to begin engaging in violence against property as distinguished from violence against persons, because as a propaganda technique that would legitimate violence." Of course, Mosher was working on a misinformed understanding of my involvement on the Berrigan Defense Committee. Mosher described my position in Cuba as one of mysterious political power and influence, "I cannot overemphasize enough the significance of the power of this individual, whom we were talking about, in being able to provide a private car, just like that, and take me out of the group" and "for me it was a measure of his political power when later that evening, he showed up, took me out of the entire group privately without anyone knowing it . . . and an armed guard . . . took us to a very luxurious home where Father Bonpane was being kept, some place behind Jibacao." Ultimately, to further malign and discredit what were only my peaceful activities in Cuba, Mosher explained, "Bonpane continually emphasized the necessity of SDS (Students for Democratic Society) and the Panthers working in the same direction. And he emphasized the availability of Cuba for secret discussions."[1]

Mosher's statements were quite ridiculous. First, given all of my activism in the US, why would I have to go to Cuba to have "secret" discussions? In fact, I went to Cuba because I was going to teach a course on Cuba in the US and I felt it was crucial that I experience Cuba first hand. As far as the luxurious home I stayed at, it was a modest place near the beach. And, the driver? It was Armando, the revolutionary African Cuban. Mosher's statements and testimony reflected the lack of discernment that we witness frequently in contemporary journalism.

1 Testimony of Thomas Edward Mosher. Hearings before the Subcommittee to Investigate the Administration of the Internal Security Act and other Internal Security Laws of the Committtee on the Judiciary United States Senate. 92nd Congress. First Session. Part 1. March 19; February 11, 12, 1971.

For example, mainstream journalists will typically make a comparison between the contemporary US militia movement to the peace and justice movement of the past four decades. Yet, in reality only the most negligible of fringe groups within the peace movement advocated armed resistance. If we exclude the numerous agent provocateurs and some marginal ideologues, we can correctly call the peace movement non-violent. On the contrary, 100% of the current militia movement favors violent change. And journalists compare the two movements as if they had something in common.

After living with the bloated bellies of Guatemala, the garbage dump people, the *barranca* people with cardboard houses, the street children, I was taken by the Cuban achievements. Frankly, the ideology was not important to me. The fruits of the revolution, however, are concrete and meaningful: by far the healthiest children in the Americas, no neglected children, no hungry children, no homeless, excellent schools, and excellent medical care. Jesus said, "By their fruits you shall know them." I was taken by these fruits of Cuba. On the streets of Cuba, I would frequently hear the phrase, "The revolution is for the children." Even though Cubans have fewer civil liberties than US citizens, they have a deeper commitment toward social justice. But our politicians have a harlot's forehead; they refuse to be ashamed. Yes, Cuba is heavy-handed. But if that is what it takes to give children a chance, it is worth it. There were no demonstrations permitted in Cuba, but what had I just seen in Chicago? State terrorism.

I also had several conversations with people who opposed the revolution. These were the traditional right-wing Catholics who were afraid that communism would undermine moral values. For these Catholics, the legalization of abortion was a big issue. The conservative clergy also knew that communism would diminish their status. Progressive clergy, on the other hand, opposed the Communist Party of Cuba because its ideological structure did not allow people who were active church members. This exclusion did not make sense to me. I had seen so many people in Guatemala who were in the revolution because of their faith and not in spite of it. From my perch at the Habana Libre Hotel (the former Havana Hilton) I wrote an article for *Pensamiento Crítico*, the magazine of critical thought in Cuba. I was pleased to be in Cuba some twenty-three years later at the time of the Party Congress of 1991, when the Cuban government offered a belated apology for its exclusion of believers from their midst. They said they had failed to understand that one could be faithful to their religion and to the objectives of the revolution.

For the African Cuban communities I spoke with, the revolution was a huge liberation. This community had previously been denied education, healthcare, and access to public spaces. The women I spoke to also perceived the revolution as an important path toward their liberation. Even though sexism still persists today, the revolution brought greater equality between men and women in the rearing of families and in employment. During my time in Cuba, I came to realize that we could learn so much from them. We could learn about Cuban medical care that has sent more doctors overseas than the entire World Health Organization. To our detriment, the US media remain almost incapable of saying a decent word about Cuba's achievements.

At the end of my stay, there was no way to get back to the US. I could not return to Mexico because of US pressure on that country. I opted for a seventeen-hour flight to Madrid by way of the Azores and Lisbon. Once in Madrid, I bought a ticket on TWA to New York. A flight of some 6,000 miles was required to return home from an island ninety miles off the Florida coast. So much for the travel ban!

Chapter 7

The Peace Movement

On my return from Cuba, I ran directly into the wrath of the exile community. I was speaking in Connecticut about Guatemala. A line of Cuban exiles came up to spit in my face by turns. I just continued my presentation and they did not bother me after that.

I spoke at Kent State in Ohio shortly before the murder of the students in 1970. The Associated Students at Kent State invited me to speak about the Vietnam War. My speech was filled with anger and outrage. I commented to the audience, "Oh, I see that the ROTC building is still standing," which in hindsight I regretted. My speaking and organizing during this period was unrelenting. One speaking engagement led to another. In Voluntown, Connecticut, we formed AVILA (Avoid Vietnam in Latin America), a loosely organized solidarity group that identified the similarity of US policy in Guatemala and Indochina.

I was invited to the home of two very generous and dedicated peace activists, Herb and Shirley Magidson on one of my trips to California. Saul Alinsky was there. He seemed to be disgusted by the peace movement. I don't think he understood that there were two movements in the United States. One was the counter-cultural movement represented by hippies, druggies, and flower children, which revolted Saul. The other peace movement was represented by leaders who often wore suits and ties in an effort to communicate with middle-class America. Occasionally these two movements converged. Theresa Killeen was at that meeting.

The Magidsons were gracious and generous in trying to get a handle on the movements of the '60s. The Black Panthers and many other movement people were welcome at their home. In 1967, Herb had been beaten and brutalized during a police riot of the LAPD at the Century City demonstration to stop the war in Vietnam. Herb used his personal funds to defend the demonstrators and to sue the LAPD. I followed the example of David Dellinger, the suit and tie component of the peace movement. Some of the counter-cultural-movement people would deride us for dressing so "middle class." But I wanted to respect the customs of the people we were trying to reach. I really did not think that naked kids on LSD were going to turn this society around. Sadly, some of those young people fried their brains out as they confronted the materialist war culture of the United States. I think of them when I see the sixty-year-old jewelry salespeople on Telegraph Avenue in Berkeley today.

With all of their warts, these movements for peace and counter culture created a positive mutation in the US culture. Our country will never be the same. The nation-state is as outdated as the city-states of old. The laws of the US can do little or nothing about the pollution of the oceans, the air, or issues of international conflict resolution. This must become the era of international law and order. The UN has a greater grasp on world problems and a greater potential for unity than the thirteen colonies did prior to the formation of the United States.

After World War I, the League of Nations was formed. Its greatest enemy was the Congress of the United States. World War II might not have followed if the League had not been destroyed. After World War II, the United Nations was formed. Its greatest enemy is the Congress of the United States. The twenty-first century must be the century of world government. Yes, this requires each nation state to give up some sovereignty. In the case of superpowers like the United States, the main problem has been intrusion by raw power into the sovereignty of smaller states. In over a half century of existence, the UN has made some very good decisions on behalf of the planet. Yes, it needs to be restructured. The best recommendations I have seen are those made by our Jeffersonian former Attorney General, Ramsey Clark in his book, *The Fire This Time*, Thunder's Mouth Press, 1992.

Larry and Renee Haun introduced me to Theresa because they thought we had so much in common. When directing the Denver Maryknoll House, I had signed Larry up as a member of our missionary community. He had previously served as a priest in the Diocese of Grand Island, Nebraska. Renee was a Maryknoll Sister serving in Chile where Larry was also assigned. Renee and Larry were married in 1967. I approached Theresa at the Magidson meeting as a pastor to parishioner. I was still quite uptight. But Larry and Renee persisted and arranged for me to visit the Alhambra House. They were certain that the right person for me was Theresa Killeen. They were so right. Theresa embodied the values I tried to live by; she was a liberated spirit who did not live in fear. Raised in a rigid Irish Catholic family, Theresa broke away from strict moral authority to define her own path. While serving in southern Chile, she decided to leave Maryknoll and to pursue family life. I knew this had taken much courage for someone who was such a model Maryknoll Sister. Prior to her departure from Maryknoll, Theresa was selected to be the

Mistress of Newly Professed Sisters. In Chile, she was Principal of the *Instituto Comercial*, a coeducational high school in Talcahuano. Mother General announced to Theresa (Sister Maura Killeen) that she had a surprise for her; she was to be the sister responsible for the formation of aspirants to Maryknoll. But Theresa had a surprise for the Mother General. She was leaving the community. On Theresa's departure from Chile she reflected on Soren Kierkegaard's leap of faith over the abyss and wrote:

Un salto es como pasar	A leap is to pass
de la luz a la obscuridad.	From light to darkness.
Es como pasar	It is to pass
por un abismo.	Over an abyss.
Es como pasar	It is to pass
desde el conocido	From the known
hacia el desconocido.	To the unknown.
Es como pasar	It is to pass
desde el miedo	From fear
hacia la esperanza.	To hope.
Y el timor	And fear
Porque es tan potente?	Why is it so strong?
El salto es la cruz	The leap is the cross
es morir um poco.	It is to die a little.
Llegare a la resurreccion.	And resurrection.
A la luz brillante.	Light follows.
A el conocimiento real.	Knowledge follows.
A la experiencia total.	Experience follows.
A la vida plena.	A full life follows
Y siguire saltando.	The leap continues
Y siguire muriendo	Dying yields
Para seguir viviendo.	To living.
Si, vale la pena vivir.	Living is worth it!
Vale la pena saltar.	Leaping is worth it!
Vivir es saltar!	Living is leaping!

This poem represents what I love and admire about Theresa. Theresa took such a leap of faith when she left the convent to pursue activist work. When I met Theresa, I could sense our mutual understanding of the need to break with tradition in order to make change.

Theresa, a skilled organizer, created the Alhambra House, a large residence which she leased as a transitional home for the many people pouring out of religious life in the late '60s. She was employed by Los

Angeles County as a social worker in East Los Angeles. It took years for us to realize that she was the same Maryknoll Sister who waited on my family at my ordination breakfast in June of 1958.

But now, 1968, it was time to dance. For once I did not have the collar on. Actually, I wore the collar long after Maryknoll had announced to the *Washington Post* that I had unilaterally separated myself from the community. Theresa and I danced. A vigil light ignited in my heart. I knew that something beautiful was happening here. Whoever wrote the song "May I Have This Dance for the Rest of My Life" knew how I felt toward Theresa in that moment.

I admired Theresa's courage and fearlessness. Theresa had channeled countless refugees from the vows of poverty, chastity, and obedience into the public school system. I don't think there was a dud in the lot. All the administration of the Los Angeles Unified School District needed was a call from Theresa and another job was filled. The Regional Superior of the Maryknoll Fathers in Los Angeles left his post and came to the Alhambra House to find Phyllis Huttenhoff as his future wife. Bob Menard, master teacher, with six years on a mule as founder of Alcoholics Anonymous in Yucatan, whose boundless energy and enthusiasm led him to be called "The Bounder," became the exemplar of teachers of English as a Second Language at the largest ESL institution in the world, Evans Adult School. He remains on the cover of their brochure.

Phyllis Huttenhoff, a good example of the type of person that came to the Alhambra House, had just left the Sisters of Charity in Leavenworth, Kansas. An experienced registered nurse and hospital administrator, Phyllis had been telling indigenous women of Peru about methods of family planning. She was bounced out of her order and returned to the states. Her rich aunt welcomed Phyllis into her home and later discovered, to her horror, that this former nun was not going to Mass on Sunday. Auntie ordered her out of the house in a Christian fashion, and Phyllis took refuge in the Alhambra House. Former priests, brothers, sisters, and even some displaced laypeople gathered at this Mecca to have a place to stay, to socialize, to learn how to write a résumé and look for jobs. The Los Angeles Unified School District became the great employer of these uprooted religious people. Once Theresa left social work and took a teaching position, administrators of the massive school district realized they had a treasure.

God, what joy to realize that one of our great school systems was so infested with Liberation Theology! And what a shame for J. Edgar Hoover that he never did a thorough inquisition on the matter. Right here in River City, students were receiving excellence in education together with the way of peace and justice. This was not union of Church and

State. This was union of spirituality and life. These were probably the best teachers the Los Angeles Unified School District ever had.

I went to see the musical *Hair* in Hollywood with Theresa, Phyllis, and Bob. This was the antithesis of religious life. It was a sermon on sexual liberation, and we got the message. Jesus said little or nothing about sex. But the ecclesiastical bureaucracy has had a compulsive, erotic, morbid, maudlin, controlling focus on the prurient. A great deal of harm has resulted.

Theresa and I would date on occasion, but I was still on the road much of the time, and she was surrounded by many friends and peace activities. Balancing our public and private lives was not always easy. While we dated, I was going from one event to another. I thought it was what I should be doing. Theresa was not always happy with it. I was too caught up in events.

I did no public relations. I simply responded to requests. Newsman Vern Richie had told me just after my expulsion from Guatemala that I had three months to make my point and then the matter would be dead. I think he was wrong. Many decades later, the issues have only intensified. Some of my speaking engagements can be restructured by simply reading the Freedom of Information files which the government kindly sent to me. I knew of the constant surveillance and even developed a custom of welcoming all in attendance: the group requesting my presence, the Boy Scouts, the CIA, FBI, DIA, and all others who might be there. It generally got a laugh but it really was not funny.

There was more stability, both psychological and financial, in my life now. I felt more at home with what I was doing. For composure, I learned how to walk slowly after the rushed pace of my speaking engagements. My teaching assignment began in January of 1969 at California State University, Los Angeles. I had lived on honoraria all during 1968, doing whatever I had to do, crisscrossing this country and Canada constantly, and actually finishing the year with no indebtedness. And that has been the story ever since. It has led me to believe the dubious axiom: Do what you love, the money will follow.

Chapter 8

New Incarnation

The values that led me to the priesthood were the same values that required me to leave the religious community. I have never left the priesthood. I have chosen to follow the most traditional theology on this one. You are a priest forever. The priesthood is a sacrament that leaves an indelible mark on the soul. You cannot become an "un-priest," even if you want to. I have never wanted to. It really was not a new life. It was a new incarnation.

There are no ex-priests. Poor seminary training and opportunism have led many bishops and church leaders to use the word ex-priest. Bad. Oh, yes, we can be in bad standing, we can be suspended (*suspensus*), interdicted (*interdictus*), shunned (*vitandus*) and excommunicated (*excommunicatus*). In the period between the thirteenth and nineteenth centuries we could have been burned at the stake. How the Roman Curia must long for those good old days! But none of the above punishments are relevant. Socrates understood it well: "You can kill me but you can't hurt me." If I baptize anyone, it is a baptism. If I give absolution to the sick and dying, it is as valid as the Pope's absolution. I have enjoyed this ecclesiastical reality not because I think the priesthood as we have known it has a future, but because my good standing is up to God, and my condition as a priest is unquestionable canonically. What tens of thousands of us renegades are doing is moving forward and identifying a ministry for the twenty-first century. New ideas generally are received with condemnation. History is clear on this. We do not want the priesthood to be an appendage on society in the future. It is a pity that the apostolic sharing as reported in the Acts of the Apostles became limited to clerics and members of religious communities. John the Baptist identified sharing as the key to preparing the way for the Messianic Era. The Mother of Jesus rejoiced in the rich going away empty, the poor being filled with good things, the mighty being put down from their seats, and the lowly exalted. Luke, 1. But goods that were meant for all became the property of the clergy. This was bad for the clergy and bad for the community. The sacraments became a diversion from praxis or reflective action. It makes sense to celebrate what we are going to do or to celebrate what we have done. It is a mistake to think that the celebration (sacrament) will do what has to be done. Have a party before you build the house or after you build the house, but never imply that the party is going to build the house.

My parents were happy that I had a regular job. They wanted me to live at our spacious family home on Chislehurst, but I opted for an apartment. I knew they would not like some of my movement or counter-cultural friends, and I needed space to find my way in this new life.

Speaking as a faculty member at UCLA Anti-Vietnam Rally, 1969.

My very first day on the faculty at California State University, Los Angeles was marked by a demonstration against the war in Vietnam. It was a relatively small peaceful demonstration of approximately one hundred students chanting "get out now!" I could see the shock and regret in the glare of administrators as they raised their eyebrows at my participation with those "radical students." Dean Dewey, who developed an antipathy for my presence at CSULA, was one of them.

44

The Latin American Studies Department faculty was a joy, a mix of scholarship and humanity. The doctors included Louis De Armond, Chair, together with Donald Bray, Timothy Harding and Joel Edelstein. The administration, however, was a drag. I have always considered the bell curve as a monstrosity designed in hell to declare to the vast majority of students, "Congratulations, you are mediocre." I prefer the pedagogy of Pablo Casals and his, "You are beautiful, you will never happen again." Dean Dewey did not like my grading practices. I graded some of the classes as a group. At least one class had either A's or incompletes. They studied together, they wrote together, and the entire experience was one of excellence, so the participants got A's. Incompletes were given to those who did not contribute their share of the work. After a confrontation in Dewey's office with Don Bray recommending that I return to CSULA, it was clear to me that the remainder of Dean Dewey's life would be dedicated to keeping me off of the CSULA campus. My contract was not renewed.

I do not socialize with students. Some of the worst professors are great socializers. I just teach. If they ask for counsel, I give it. I am not looking for playmates. The art of teaching is the art of leaving people alone. Let them see the light of truth in your own integrity, let them accept or reject your most carefully thought-out positions.

I would ask the first year students about their high school experience, how many thought that it was necessary to agree with their teachers' opinions in order to get a good grade. Sadly, most of the hands would go up. Such indoctrination is not teaching. Teachers who demand conformity of opinion, who grade on memorization, who exploit students, are not practicing constructive pedagogy. Consider the reverend that made up the lie about George Washington not telling a lie. Must we lie to the students so they will not tell lies?

A knock at the door. Several students arrived at my apartment from University of California Los Angeles (UCLA.) "We are here to hire you," they said. "You can't hire me," I responded. "Yes, we can. This is a new program called the Humanistic and Educational Needs of the Academic Community, or HENAC. It is funded by the Ford Foundation, a fifteen-unit course of student-directed learning. The students are allowed to select faculty. We are asking you to come to UCLA as a full-time professor." They were correct. I was hired by a department known as The Council for Educational Development.

Campus radicals of all varieties came to this "for credit" program. Classes were held all over campus and off campus. The majority were middle-class students on a quest for values. There were also the hippies, the Marxist-Leninists, the Maoists, and the anarchists. One common bond was absolute opposition to the Indochina War and the draft. I began on the HENAC faculty in the fall of 1969. As many of my life adventures, this one was intense, rapid and meaningful.

During one peace demonstration, the students were surrounding a recruiting station on campus. I saw security officers inside the building breaking the windows with their clubs. An all-news station began reporting that the students were breaking the windows. I immediately called the station using all of my professorial clout on the air to verify that the police were doing the breaking. It was just one more clear, provocateur action similar to the police "hippies" who were always on hand to burn flags.

Speaking as a faculty member at UCLA Anti-Vietnam Rally, 1969.

I was living at 1945 Corinth in West Los Angeles. The house was owned by a lawyer, Ron Hughes, who lived in the garage. I did not know that Ron was the lawyer for Charles Manson. Ron was a doper. In hindsight it is clear that some of the strange types who came to his garage home were Manson Family members. The Manson Family was suspect in Ron's subsequent disappearance.

The phone rang at 4:00 AM on December 8, 1969. "The police are attacking the Panther Headquarters." I knew some key Panthers; Elaine Browne, Geronimo Pratt and David Hilliard. They had invited me to be Minister of Religion for the Black Panther Party. I had been to the headquarters and had observed the sandbags and rifles. It did make me nervous to think that armed resistance would be used against the armies of the LAPD and the National Guard. As I had often done in Guatemala when things got tense, I put on my Roman collar.

Frightened and nervous, I drove to the site of the confrontation, parked and walked to the police command post. The police were obviously very nervous as well. I saw pistol-holding hands shaking. Various officers were approaching the chief and asking if they could go ahead with "the plan." I could not verify what the plan was, but I think they intended to bomb the Panther house in a manner similar to the attack on the MOVE headquarters in Philadelphia, which would take place some ten years later. I said, "They don't think they can come out of that building alive. They think they will be shot. May I speak with the people inside the building?" "They gave us their answer at 2:00 AM this morning," was the Chief's answer. He was referring to alleged shots that came from the Panther headquarters at that time.

I sensed something of an Irish brogue in the Captain's voice and a certain respect for the collar. We continued our dialogue and I was not hustled away. With elation I saw the press arrive. How many "subversives" have been saved by the press! Once the TV cameras were on the Panther Headquarters the occupants determined they could leave holding white flags. They knew they would not get shot while the cameras were rolling. (See *Los Angeles Times* article on Panther shoot-out, December 8, 1969.) The television coverage flashed my presence as a UCLA professor and a priest. When I returned to UCLA for the final weeks of the semester, I had a feeling that the administration did not like my participation as a frequent speaker at peace rallies, my presence at the shoot-out, nor the HENAC program itself.

The university administration had reservations about the program. A Ford Foundation representative came to campus to discuss the future of the program. One of the students asked him if the HENAC program was designed to concentrate all the student radicals in one place. He answered in the affirmative. Ford wanted to continue funding the program.

I, along with Angela Davis, Michael Tiger, Richard Flacks, and William Allen, was on a list of dangerous radical professors put out by the University of California Regents. Ronald Reagan was Governor of California at that time. He began a systematic destruction of the University of California. He could not attend Regents' meetings held on any UC campus because instant demonstrations resulted whenever he appeared. He did, however, attend an off-campus meeting of the Regents naming the five of us faculty members and asking that our positions at the university be re-examined. I read about it in the *Los Angeles Times*. Reagan accepted the real possibility of a bloodbath on the campuses of the UC system just as nonchalantly as he would later condone on-going bloodbaths in Nicaragua, El Salvador Guatemala, Grenada and Honduras. Jesus must have been thinking of Ronald when he said, "Father forgive them for they do not know what they are doing!" God, what a performance! Eight years onstage as governor and eight years as president. Never has the United States deteriorated so much and so fast.

On Christmas Eve of 1969, I celebrated Mass in the street in front of St. Basil's to protest the expenditure of funds for the new church. Theresa was also there. The street Mass was well-attended by *Católicos por la Raza* and its supporters. *Católicos por la Raza* was formed as the Chicano community became more aware of itself. The construction of St. Basil's Church became a point of conflict. In our judgment, the millions used to build this affluent structure would have been better spent on human needs. We asked Cardinal McIntyre to consider establishing a bail fund for the indigent. Most of the people being held in our jails were there for lack of bail. It seemed logical for the church to establish such a fund. The affluent faithful began to arrive for the scheduled Mass inside the new St. Basil's. Unexpectedly and unknown to me, some members of my street congregation began to filter into the church.

Doors were slammed to our kind. The excluded began to chant, "Let the poor people in, let the poor people in." A few of the street congregation were well-dressed enough to be accepted into the church with the Anglo community. They too began to chant loudly, "Why don't you let the poor people in?" The Cardinal was prepared for the attack. He had invited hoards of off-duty police to serve as "ushers," who were waiting for any such invasion.

I had not anticipated that the street congregation would disrupt the Mass within St. Basil's. But they did. Some were jailed, some were beaten. The spontaneity was an error. We determined not to tolerate such surprises in future demonstrations. Generally, things work out well when everyone agrees on the agenda. What happened at St. Basil's led to my belief that order and discipline is required to avoid counter-productive spontaneous acts. Those who are going to do civil disobedience must segregate themselves from those who want to demonstrate within the law. It is unfair to trap the legal demonstrators into an unexpected illegal posture.

In the gospel, that memorable Christmas Eve was about a couple expecting a baby and finding no room at the inn. Theresa and I were literally run off the street by charging "ushers" (police).

I was a friendly witness for the accused. Trials followed and Oscar Acosta, the "Brown Buffalo," was the defense attorney. The prosecutor asked about the ring on my finger in view of the fact that I was wearing a Roman collar in the courtroom. I explained that there has never been a moment in the Catholic Church when there was not a married clergy. I told the judge: "There are some seventeen Rites under the Pope of Rome that have no law of celibacy. Actually, the law of celibacy goes back to the Second Lateran Council of 1139. It has been a miserable law with a miserable history. It was designed to assure that no legitimate children of priests would inherit church property. The way to do this was to affirm that priests could not have legitimate children." The judge was interested, the courtroom was interested, but the judge finally made it clear that celibacy was not on trial in his courtroom. The law of celibacy, however, has hindered the spiritual life of the Catholic clergy for centuries. Celibacy is OK if it is freely chosen, but making it into a law is destructive.

Theresa and I went for a walk on Olvera Street, the ancient marketplace of an outstation of the Mission San Gabriel. Over 200 years ago the community was called Our Lady Queen of the Angels (*Nuestra Señora Reina de Los Angeles.*) We purchased some "friendship rings" and crossed the street to the Placita Church, which is actually the mother church of Los Angeles from which sprang the megalopolis we know today. I considered La Placita as my spiritual Mecca. As a youngster of fourteen, I was introduced to its chapel of perpetual adoration. Twenty-four hours a day, pilgrims come to this chapel to worship the Blessed Sacrament. I prayed there countless times regarding the key decisions of life; whether to defy my parents and join Maryknoll, whether to leave Maryknoll, and now in 1969, when Theresa and I were dating. We entered the venerable chapel, saw two kneelers set up for a wedding that would take place on the following day. We knelt down at the places prepared for the bride and groom and decided to get married.

Chapter 9

Our Wedding

Our wedding was planned for January 1, 1970. We did not print any invitations. Word of mouth at demonstrations and elsewhere spread the news of our coming nuptials. The wedding took place at my family home at 2307 Chislehurst Drive in Hollywood, the house I had escaped from some twenty years earlier.

We sang and celebrated. Some five priests and a minister presided. The gathered friends and relatives participated in the ceremony by offering their thoughts and words of wisdom. Our good friend Joel Edelstein wrote a poem that captured Theresa's and my commitment toward one another. This commitment, as Joel wrote, was also a commitment toward social justice:

There are many similarities
between the qualities
of a good marriage partner
and a revolutionary.
Both must have the capacity
to love universally
and, also, to love in particular.
Universal love is meaningless
if it remains an abstraction.
It must be particularized
in expression to another human being,
but also, marriage must not be a monastery.
It is home
but it is also a headquarters
in the struggle
that is an expression
of the love of humanity.
    —Joel Edelstein, "Poem for Blase and Theresa on the Day of their Mutual Commitment to each other and to Social Justice," January 1, 1970

The revolution was a recurring theme in the comments of the wedding guests. My poor cousin, Vincent Buonpane, Jr., was shocked at the references to the revolution and to the Black Panthers. He and my father had an adversarial exchange of letters after the wedding. Vince had been a bombardier during World War II and simply could not stomach the peace movement. Dad had become both supportive and defensive of my position.

My Dad's words at the wedding truly touched me. His acceptance of me and my new life, despite some of his previous doubts about my decisions, was invaluable. He expressed the following on that day:

I might say a few words. There are a lot of thoughts that come across our minds now as parents, but you probably understand that they're not very easy to articulate because they're clouded by sort of a consciousness that this is not real, that it's a dream. We hardly thought that this day would ever come to pass and let's see . . . that takes me back to review in my own mind a great many episodes and the agony of parents . . . how they feel when there is a divergence of judgment in life and disappointments on the part of parents. I had already prepared a nice room in my suite for my son, the lawyer. Then he did something which the higher courts have never done with my decisions, and that is, he reversed me. And so there wasn't anything we could do except to hope and pray that things would work out properly, and I think they have . . . eventually. It's taken Blase eighteen years to look around and to find someone that he would choose. I think the eighteen year period has been rewarding. We think the sum of it all makes a just man happy, choosing a good wife, and a better gift there can never be. A good wife is a crown to her husband. There are lots of things that I would like to say now but that would take a long time. But you can be assured that mother and I are not sitting here with blank minds. There are a lot of things going on in the brain that you can't see and many times it's a blessing that you can't see. Well, my gift is our blessing to Blase and Theresa. We love them both. We think that Theresa was a great choice for our son and we wish them both our blessing, our love, and our prayers for their everlasting happiness and good health and the hope that their love for their fellow man will become increasingly intense as the years go by.
    —Judge Blase Bonpane

During the ceremony, Theresa and I made a commitment toward one another that went beyond the traditional "for richer or poorer, in sickness and in health, 'til death do us part." We knew of the tension that would be present in trying to balance our public and private lives. We made that consideration part of our wedding vows.

This was my promise to her:

> Theresa, I can't help but think today of the traditional; for richer or for poorer, in sickness and in health, 'til death do us part. But I think of much more than that. I think not only of the traditional things, I think of a mission that I have always felt, all of my life. And I felt it marching to the particular drum that I have always marched to and that there was only one way to march to that music and that was alone. And then I realized that by going together we were marching better and the same drum did not stop. In fact, it's beating a little stronger. You have done as Jesus said and made it possible that we might have life and have it more abundantly. You've already done that by making it possible for me to fulfill my vocation more perfectly. The things I want to promise you are all of the traditional things and the consideration that I should always show you. I am eternally grateful to you and you are just an essential part of my mission on this earth. You are helping me to be more than I ever could have been.

Theresa returned my promise with words of love and generosity:

> Because I love you, I promise to try to help you always to grow and, I promise, to try to find the balance in generosity, between our need to be alone together as well as our brothers' and sisters' needs, to be involved with them. And, I promise to try to help us to always search for truth in our lives in big things and in small. And, I promise to try to help you to be everything that Blase was born to be.

How could I have ever found Theresa? It was not simply her brilliance and her beauty. She was often asked to show her identification when we ordered wine at restaurants. She was thirty-six years old and sometimes reminded me of a teenager. She was afraid of spiders and snakes, yet fearless of the consequences of living the truth. She never hesitated to bring delegates to witness the US war in Nicaragua. She became my most severe critic, and I needed that. Theresa recognized a hostility that came through in some of my speaking engagements. Indeed, it was rage at my government's behavior. She cautioned me not to direct that rage at the audience. Thank you, Theresa.

Theresa is an organizer. I frequently feel that I am being organized. In fact, I remind her that she was once appointed Mistress of the Newly Professed and now I am her only Newly Professed! She is sassy. I love her more every day and wonder what life would have been like without her. Perhaps I would be a cynical misanthrope by now had it not been for Theresa. We are very different and very complementary. I thank God for Theresa. She does not like the pomp and hypocrisy of organized religion. She cannot stand the preaching of disengaged clergy. She follows a defined spiritual path in communion with people and things that she grows, such as flowers.

After the wedding, we went to Palm Springs on our three-day honeymoon. We rode bikes and hiked and spoke of our future.

Chapter 10

Surveillance

After returning from our honeymoon, I went off to begin a new semester at UCLA. I eagerly maneuvered my mother's 1965 Ford into my cherished parking space. The prime purpose of such a university is to maintain a massive and hierarchical parking lot. I was proud of my parking spot as a UCLA faculty member and was quite unaccustomed to such acceptance and position of status.

A grim-faced attendant approached to inform me that the turf was no longer mine. I expected and discovered the worst. I had not been rehired. Please don't say that I was fired—I was not rehired. Thou hast conquered, oh Reagan! Aside from my activities on and off campus, my ever-present CIA files had been presented to the administration. J. Edgar had signed several chits explaining just how bad I was. That perverted, convoluted, toxic, bitter, paranoid, organized crime-saturated, racist, gatekeeper of Washington ruined as many people as possible in and out of academia. And his ghost still hovers over the J. Edgar Hoover Building. Just think of how fortunate we are to have FBI checks on all potential government servants. Anyone who has not served on the board of the National Rifle Association certainly should be suspect.

When Theresa came home from work that day she found me there and quickly surmised my plight. She was not terribly surprised. Theresa had witnessed my being recruited for some six other academic positions from the University of Southern California to California State University, Fresno. An incredible sameness was identifiable. After recruitment, studying my credentials, faculty and administration interviews, a position was offered. I was told to order books and submit my syllabus for the courses. In each case, I was later informed, "Something has come up," "We have cancelled the course," "We have closed the department," or "We don't have the students." Security checks had arrived in force on all of the campuses. We simply must not have professors who believe the draft is a form of slavery and who are not anxious to see the best of our youth die in places where they are not wanted. So much for earning a living.

This was the summer of 1970. Fortunately, Johnson's War on Poverty was still in motion. Instead of working in academia, I was now enlisted as Field Representative to work with the young people on the streets and parks of East Los Angeles. My job was to supervise students after school with constructive activities, such as sports. Theresa had made many friends in East Los Angeles while working with the Mexican American Opportunity Foundation. One of those friends was Tony Rios of the Community Service Organization. Tony, a patriarch of social action in East Los Angeles, had served as mentor to many of the Mexican American leaders in California, including a young organizer by the name of César Chávez. Tony Rios asked Theresa to assist with the administration of a summer program on behalf of the youth of East Los Angeles. The funds were granted through CSO and the program was called the Young Adult Leadership Project or YALP.

I was happy to have this position and entered the program with enthusiasm. I looked forward to helping students who had been overlooked and left out of the social and educational systems. Shortly after the program began, men in suits and ties came to the office. They asked Theresa, not knowing she was my wife, if I worked there. Everyone knew they represented some police agency, what with their plainclothes and all. They were FBI. She said I was in the field, which on that day was playing sports with the youth in Hollenbeck Park. I was called from my street work to come to the office immediately. On arrival, the FBI people said they had some questions for me. I said I would be happy to talk to them in my lawyer's office. They agreed. I quickly found a cooperative lawyer who would supervise the interview pro bono.

It turned out they were looking for Angela Davis. Their question: "Where is Angela Davis?" My response, "I have no idea." "We have her address book and your name is listed," they continued. "We taught on the same campus at the same time. I do not know where she is now," my final comment.

Chapter 11

Campaign/Chicano Moratorium/Santa Paula

Seeing the halls of academia fade into the sunset, I decided to apply for unemployment insurance. After realizing that mass mobilizations were not enough, I decided to apply as a candidate for the House of Representatives. I was beginning to feel unemployable. A government position, I thought, would be meaningful work. After discussions with my friends in the peace movement, we decided it would be wise to challenge any liberal in the House who had not yet come out against the war in Vietnam. We were now five years plus into that genocidal holocaust, and regardless of how good a representative might be on other issues, we determined that together with our mass mobilizations, electoral action had to be taken to stop the slaughter.

I filed in the Democratic Party primary as the sole opponent to incumbent congressman Edward Roybal. Bob Menard managed the campaign with constant help from Theresa and Bob's wife Phyllis. At one of the first campaign gatherings, Theresa became sick and nauseous. At first I thought it was her revulsion for the circus nature of electoral politics. We quickly realized that she was pregnant. Our daughter Colleen was on the way.

Theresa left her position at the Mexican American Opportunity Foundation in order to dedicate her full time to the campaign. As always, her strategy and tactics, office organization and coordination of volunteers were indispensable to the campaign. We talked peace from East Los Angeles to Hollywood, we talked about it in Spanish and in English, day in and day out. Loud speakers blared, leaflets for my campaign were left at every door. Theresa and I explained that the large percentage of African American and Latin American troops killed in battle was much higher than their representation in the population. In effect, they were cannon fodder.

The tension between the lack of economic and social resources in the Chicano community in the US and the high number of Chicanos in the military contributed to the Chicano Moratorium that took place months after my campaign in August of the same year, 1970—the largest demonstration of Mexican Americans in US history. Theresa and I were witness to the police brutality that took place at the Moratorium. We parked Theresa's VW bug on Lorena Street and marched through East Los Angeles together with our dear friend Shirley Cocker, who had served with Theresa in Chile as a Maryknoll Sister. The rally after the march was at Laguna Park, later renamed Salazar park. Sheriffs were poised at the entrance to the park and ready for action. Because we knew the police were ready for any excuse to pounce on the protestors, Theresa and I were very disturbed to see some Chicano youngsters who seemed completely unaware of the goals of the march, picking up rocks and bottles. They were not part of the political Chicanos who had planned the march. This was not intended to be a violent march. An irrational barrage of rocks and bottles were thrown by the apparently unconscious youth. The sheriffs exploded as a galloping herd, clubbing and tear-gassing everyone in sight. Theresa and I were directly in the sheriffs' path, and at the time, she was seven months pregnant. We crouched behind a Porta-Potty while the herd galloped on either side of us.

That same night, Theresa and I were fortunate to be able to stay overnight with Bob and Phyllis Menard, who lived in East Los Angeles. Due to the violence, we could not reach our car until the following day. By the end of the day, *Los Angeles Times* reporter Ruben Salazar was killed by a tear gas projectile fired by one of the sheriffs. There were lesser-known fatalities as well. The violence inflicted at the Chicano Moratorium was clearly a police riot.

As I reflected on my campaign months earlier, I knew that the fight for social justice among the Chicano community had made my campaign worthwhile. I was campaigning against the war, and a high percentage of Chicanos were serving in Vietnam. Even though incumbent congressman Roybal was Chicano and a liberal, he did not oppose the Vietnam War.

Going door to door during my campaign, I found segregated communities in our allegedly integrated Los Angeles. "Mommy, there is a white man at the door," was a reception I would frequently receive in the African American community. A white man meant trouble: a bill collector, police, God knows what—but trouble. I was just there to ask them to vote for me. One of my students from California State University, Los Angeles, an African American man named Pierce Austin, began walking with me in these areas. His presence helped a great deal. As soon as the families saw Pierce, they become more at ease with my presence. They began to realize that I was not just another white bill collector, but a person who spoke about issues they cared about.

The press gave an account of the dramatic upswing in my campaign. I was surprised that I had gotten that far. My Republican father was most helpful. Dad drove me to the bumper sticker makers and ordered thousands of the sticky things, and he paid the bill. He had lost his own campaign in 1936, buried in a Roosevelt landslide as he promoted Alf Landon for President and himself for the US House of Representatives. He knew what it was to lose. He lost our house in Cleveland as a combined result of that campaign and the Depression. Just like my father, I was following my dream.

US Congressional Candidate in Democratic Primary, 1970.

The media can work for or against a campaign, but beggars can't be choosers. I was invited as a guest on former congressperson and presidential candidate Robert Dornan's television program. Bob was "very Catholic." I was given full treatment on his program because he heard that a priest was running for Congress. The entire program was filled with "Father this and Father that." I had hoped to simply talk about peace and social justice in the US and the world. But when Bob was informed by eager sources that his esteemed Father Bonpane was married, he came in with a vengeance on his next program shouting, "Liar, Father Bonpane, liar. . ." raging and steaming in my absence about my status. I was not offended as I had become accustomed to such barrages. My Dad, however, was extremely offended and reminded me that we have the same name. I hoped that my public life was not going to affect my father's work as a judge.

Judge Blase Bonpane called Dornan and told him and his producer to come to our home. They came. Dad played a tape of the program and asked, "Why did you attack my son so viciously in his absence?" Bob explained it was because he is a good Catholic and thought I was a priest in good standing. Dad made it clear that ultimate "status" is a matter for the judgment of God, not Bob Dornan. My father's theology was far superior to Dornan's. As to the facts, his son came on the program as a priest, and that could not be disputed. Even though my Dad expressed some strong criticism of Dornan, he still conducted himself in a genteel manner, a trait that I and many others have admired about him. Dad's genteelness was a defining aspect of his personality in the courtroom. I was proud that Dad invited Dornan to our home to hold him accountable for his statements about my character.

I have seen Dornan several times over the past decades. Often he would be heckling in the audience, either ready to attack or paranoid that people were ready to attack him. Jane Fonda and I were speaking at Reseda High School demanding an end to the Indochina War. Dornan was in the audience raging against us. Years later, his producer called asking me to join Bob Dornan on a national radio talk show. I accepted with the qualification, "If Dornan starts red-baiting, I will walk out." Bob was surprisingly sedate that day. I think he was trying to create a new image of stability for himself. I consider him to be a classic victim of the war culture; he appeared to identify the foreign policy of the US as the foreign policy of Jesus.

As my campaign continued, a world-class artist came into our campaign headquarters and offered to make some signs. It was the great John August Swanson. Our midnight poster people did not realize that every poster they put up was a masterwork of silkscreen art. Professional graphic artists volunteered to produce superb brochures. Volunteers walked the precincts. We even had a victory party. Friends and supporters crowded into my shabby headquarters on West Pico and stayed until it was clear that I had been soundly defeated by incumbent Edward Roybal. I had expected the defeat. Even though I lost, I knew that we had accomplished a lot. It was an instructive experience for many people who worked on the campaign.

My supporters walked quietly away. Theresa and I were left with a personal debt of five thousand dollars, no jobs, and a child on the way. So, why enter into these impossible situations? Why not? During the campaign, I came to realize that we do not have to be successful, we have to be faithful. Faithful to what? To what we believe in. My campaign led me to believe that politics is an important route to making a difference. Even though we might not see immediate results, we must have faith that change is possible. I never accepted the idea of a symbolic campaign. People would ask if I was just doing this for educational purposes. I would always answer in the negative, saying I was running to win. Someone is going to win one of these "impossible" races someday. Of course we need proportional representation. It is a shame that the winner-take-all system is still part of our political landscape. But an educational process does take place. Our campaign made people aware of the connection between the war in Vietnam and the many social issues plaguing our country. Theresa did not think it was worth the effort.

A few months later, someone gave me an ad from the *Los Angeles Times*. The Santa Paula School District was looking for a bilingual, bicultural coordinator. I decided to apply. But where was Santa Paula? Just over an hour northwest of Los Angeles. There were some fifty-two candidates for this position. I went through the usual battery of interviews and hit it off very well with the interviewers. It was obvious, however, they were extremely far to the right. One of them asked, "If César Chávez comes to town, do you promise not to invite him to speak in Santa Paula?" After all, this was the lemon capital of the world. I said, "No, I don't promise any such thing." Despite my views, they hired me. This was curious given my perspective, but perhaps they felt obliged not to obstruct civil liberties.

Santa Paula was sharply divided between Mexican Americans and Anglos. One Mexican American, Arthur Gomez, had been elected to the school board. He was intelligent, caring, supportive, and courageous. He is now a Claretian priest.

Theresa and I were in the process of moving to 139 Mupu Street, in Santa Paula. During this time, Roberto Flores of the United Farm Workers called me from Oxnard to ask if I would celebrate a Mass for union members. I have often been so empowered by the faithful in various parts of the world. If *campesinos* asked for a Mass in Central America, I accepted their request. I had celebrated such Masses in Cuba, and many other places in the Americas. My desire to celebrate the Mass in Santa Paula was just another extension of my previous commitments toward the faithful in Latin America.

60

The newspapers covered the open-air farm worker Mass. The coverage was negative. The press did not focus on the large gathering of faithful farm workers at the Mass, but expressed shock that a married priest conducted the service. The local Catholic pastor heard about the Mass and was horrified to learn that I was coming to town as a school official. In response, local Congressman Teague distributed files on me throughout his Ventura County district. These files were taken from several Freedom of Information Act Hearings, such as Mosher's, that were used against me years earlier. Teague and his buddies came up with a leaflet listing my involvement in several "subversive" activities to build the case that I was a "radical." One of these radical activities was my role as Chairperson of the Berrigan Defense Committee. My peaceful activities in Guatemala were also labeled subversive. This was the heart of the Cold War. I was a "communist" who threatened the values of Santa Paula children.

Two days after Theresa and I moved to Santa Paula, *The Santa Paula Chronicle* came up with its stunning scoop, "Radical Background of Title VII Leader Bared." Day after day the paper screamed about my "radical past." I was an instant pariah in Santa Paula. I reported for work. The superintendent of Schools obviously wanted me to be on hold. They had no grounds to fire me, yet they were afraid to unleash me into the community. I was given some silly office work to do while the matter was pending for nine months.

The lemon capital was one ongoing bitter experience. I thought about quitting. I was frustrated. But there was a reason to be here. The Chicano community welcomed us, and addressing their plight was crucial to larger social change. I spoke in Spanish and English at community meetings. My bilingual presentations infuriated many of the "good Americans" that were present. Despite this, I brought Mexican folk music and dance to the schools and attempted to put parents and teachers in touch with the war that had taken this very location from Mexico in 1846. I tried to explain the racist history of the region where one could still hear remarks like, "Why, them meskins are happy singing in the trees, they don't need more education."

School board meetings became emotional gatherings. Board meeting attendance rose to the five-hundred-person level. Prior to my arrival they had had three or four people in the audience. Now that there was a danger of subverting the youth of the community, this was something "good white people" would not tolerate.

Santa Paula found three reasons I should be dismissed immediately: First, for not supporting the sacred Nixon Administration. Second, for bringing in a "foreign" language and "foreign" ways to my English-speaking country. And, third for supporting the United Farm Workers of America.

My demeanor was not always genteel. While I did try to be humorous, in hindsight I think my responses to allegations of the board and the public were often sarcastic, confrontational, and adversarial. Yes, I was angry. "We should show some concern for the Bonpane family, they are expecting a child," said a concerned citizen. "We have thrown pregnant women out of this town before," was the reply. "We don't want a communist baby born in Santa Paula." All of this created enormous stress for Theresa. She was isolated by the community except for a few Chicano friends, Molly King of the Baha'i Faith, and Dennis Renault, cartoonist for the *Ventura Star* and later for the *Sacramento Bee*.

In spite of the experience in Santa Paula as a "lemon," a whole new dimension was added to our lives while living in that atmosphere of siege. On the Feast of Our Lady of Guadalupe, December 12, 1970, our daughter Colleen Marie was born. Colleen seemed to take command of her life on the day of her birth. She is a teacher to her parents and gifted by God in plethora of ways. She and her husband John are both physicians and parents to three of our grandchildren, Blase Jairo, Chiara and Gianna. Colleen Marie is a healer to the multitudes as an obstetric gynecological surgeon and a perpetual joy to our hearts.

Needless to say, when César Chávez asked us to join him at La Paz, the headquarters of the United Farm Workers located near Tehachapi, Theresa and I did not hesitate. We packed our bags and left the isolated lemon-grove community of Santa Paula to serve in the administration of his movement.

Chapter 12

La Paz

Lonely mountain lions roamed the countryside, the Southern Pacific tracks cut through the rugged, dry hills of La Paz. A red shack on a knoll stood in humble splendor apart from the rest of the United Farm Workers community. It contained a single wood stove with segments of a metal chimney that would pop off with a certain regularity. It resembled a chicken house. Each room looked as if it had been built separately and possibly from crates that might have toppled from a roving freight train. Yes, there were rodents and birds and snakes. The shack was not airtight. Tehachapi mountain winds would create a musical effect day and night. The smell of the elderly and muddy pigs that lived next door would often waft in. Yet, this was our new home. Compared to how the farm workers lived, who were we to complain? Chicano friends from Santa Paula helped us move our few belongings. I put my desk into a garage near the UFW administration building and set up my office.

Theresa and I worked with César on a personal and daily basis. César wanted me to revive the newspaper *El Malcriado* (*The Brat*) and asked me to serve as editor. My job was to turn the newspaper into something of national importance, a respected paper that would be treated reverently. César discontinued the original version because he believed the paper did not represent the seriousness of the movement. My job was to write the editorials and coordinate the efforts of the others working on the staff. It took time before the union was ready to publish the first new issue under my direction; Theresa and I arrived in La Paz in September, and the first issue was published in March of 1972. César and I experimented with many incarnations of the paper. We asked: Was it for farm workers? Was it for our urban supporters? Was it for both? Was it to be in English or in Spanish? We tried to put all of these components into one bilingual production. When we finally published the first issue, it was very well received, and we produced 100,000 copies. Yet, we did not publish with regularity.

Since I had written several articles about the conflict between the UFW and the Teamsters, César called me aside to explain the current state of siege in the UFW. The benediction hymn *Tantum Ergo*, *"bella premuunt hostilium"*—enemies are on every side—captured the state of the union. Our concern regarding constant enemies of the UFW was not paranoia but reality. Law enforcement, the legislature, the courts, the growers, the Teamsters Union and almighty Governor Ronald Reagan considered our union to be brats needing to know their place.

Initially, César wanted Theresa and me to establish a Farm Workers University. But such a venture was simply not possible with so many immediate crises. Each day César would mention another critical issue requiring action. I did not consider his requests as interference with the university project; on the contrary, they were of necessity for the survival of the union.

As I worked on *El Malcriado*, Theresa took over El Taller Gráfico, the graphics shop. She quickly organized the disheveled files and resurrected un-cashed checks. She dug out ancient requests for bumper stickers, posters, and buttons, as well as contributions to the union. Theresa also formed a children's cooperative. All of the parents on the property were to share in child care. This project would conserve time for mothers and fathers to do their union work while knowing their children were in good hands.

César asked Dolores Huerta and me to go to Livingston and find out what happened with the killing of farm worker Romulo Avalos. Avalos was shot and killed by an INS agent in Livingston. The agent had shot Romulo through the hand and, some sixty seconds later, had shot him through the heart. He was referred to as an undocumented alien, even though he was born in Texas. This was the day I was scheduled to be in Los Angeles at the University of Southern California for my oral comprehensives as a doctoral candidate. I quickly called Dean Paul Hadley and told him I could not make it. Years later the Dean told me that the committee members were so angry at my flippant cancellation that they would never have approved my candidacy. After my impertinence, the doctorate was to remain on hold for over ten years. No regrets. I felt that the activist work I was doing with the UFW was more important than taking a test that would grant me access to the Ph.D.

Dolores, César, and I did our best to make the case of Romulo Avalos known to the national media. We wanted to make it clear to the public that undocumented aliens are not simply people who slip through cracks along the border. Growers recruit the undocumented to work their fields. They prefer undocumented workers because such people are considered to have no rights. They are expected to run rather than walk in the fields. They are expected to work twelve hours instead of eight hours. And when the crops are in, the growers will suddenly get religion and report to

64

the INS that they have discovered some "illegals" in their fields. This scheme often leads to non-payment of their meager salaries.

César and I drove to San Francisco to consider purchasing Chapman Press, a printing plant that was about to go out of business. The union was printing an endless number of leaflets, bumper stickers, newspapers, and posters at an outside press. Here was an opportunity for farm workers to learn a new trade and for the union to become independent of commercial printers. I called the Maryknoll house in San Francisco and asked if we could stay there. Father Bob Carlton was most gracious and accepted my proposal. Then I told him about the dogs. We had César's police dogs with us and his personal security man, former cop Andy Anzaldua. Carlton quickly declined his original offer. Actually, this was a good decision. The dogs were not friendly. We stayed elsewhere, bought out the entire Chapman Press and returned to La Paz.

People have often asked: What do you talk about with César Chávez on such occasions? We would often talk about the Bible. César was a very spiritual man. I found César to be analogous to a bishop or pastor of the flock or Father Superior. He was like Gandhi, driven toward peace and nonviolent action, yet always amidst a whirlwind of activity. I begged him not to go with the AFL-CIO, telling him of their awful work in Latin America with the American Institute for Free Labor Development (AIFLD), a CIA front known for breaking indigenous unions. I also mentioned to him AIFLD's history of rabid anti-communism. Leaders of the AFL-CIO had to first prove they were not communists and to further demonstrate their anti-communist track record. For this reason, Irish Catholics were frequently selected. Despite my position on the matter, César said he simply had to go with the AFL-CIO. "We don't have any money; we are a bread-and-butter union. If we don't go with the AFL-CIO, we can't continue." I understood César's position, but I simply did not trust the leadership of the AFL-CIO. Unfortunately, in the months and years ahead there were purges of "leftists" in the UFW leadership.

Often, I had to be armed at the La Paz headquarters of the UFW. Even in Central America, where there was a war in progress, I had never been armed. And, despite my training in arms at the Platoon Leaders Class in the Marine Corps Reserve at Quantico, Virginia, I was never in combat. One day, men from the US Department of Treasury came (T-men) to talk about a problem. They had uncovered a thirty-thousand-dollar plot to kill César. César played the tapes of the conversation between the T-men and some criminal elements. The tape revealed how the contract had been paid. The thugs offered to pay an additional five thousand dollars for destroying the UFW files. César said, "The files? We can never find anything anyway!" There was a roar of laughter from the staff. César's magnificent wife Helen chided all of us, "Go ahead and laugh; it's not your ass." The T-men brought the conversation back to a more serious note. They told us to take special security measures. Andy Anzaldua trained all of us as police.

I practiced with pistols and shotguns at a remote shooting range. I took turns on all-night vigils of the property. I was on sentry duty, which meant driving a jeep on the dirt roads of La Paz from 2:00 AM to 6:00 AM. This was an experience in starlight majesty. Fortunately, there were no surprises, and all weapons went unfired except on the range.

Theresa and I were feeling the crunch of life at the UFW headquarters. It reminded us both of religious life. Our emotional confinement was physically felt. Luckily, after many months in the red shack thrown between the Southern Pacific rail lines and the highway, Theresa and I were assigned to a fifty-foot mobile home unit, which was one of many the union had purchased. The wheels were removed and it was placed on concrete blocks. In comparison to the red shack, this was an experience of unbridled luxury. The plumbing worked and everything was new. Our new home no longer shook when the trains rattled by. Our daughter loved it, and so did we.

César came to our new mobile home and asked me to be available as his aide on Sundays. I told him that I needed at least one day a week free to be with my family. This new responsibility would add a day to the six days already taken up with the newspaper and troubleshooting for the UFW. César was not happy about my refusal to accept a routine seven-day work week.

Theresa was pregnant with our second child. When Theresa's labor pains began, we sped down to Bakersfield Memorial Hospital. At a railroad crossing, an endless freight train held us up for what seemed to be hours. I could hear the PA system blaring as we entered the hospital, "a Césarean emergency, a woman in labor." They were talking about Theresa. Our son Blase Martin was born on June 26, 1972. We had expected it would be June 29th. Within a few days we brought our new son, Blase Martin, home to La Paz in 105-degree heat. He seemed quite comfortable. The following morning at daybreak, César and the staff were at our door singing "Las Mañanitas." We will never forget that heartfelt greeting and our deep joy at now having two beautiful children. To us, the children were messengers from God to bring good news to the world.

Blase Martin arrived on June 26th, 1972. He was born with a creative and musical soul and an ability to lead. While a student at Santa Monica High School he was voted Youth Speaker of the California State Assembly in Sacramento. He teaches both high school and college in a remote rural setting. Blase and his wife Jen, a psychotherapist, are parents to our grandchildren Ossian and Nola. And now we count eleven members in our immediate family.

Prior to Blase Martin's birth we had been sent to Los Angeles to campaign against anti-farm-worker legislation. There were frequent changes in assignments due to constant emergencies. Knowing that I would not accept an assignment with months away from Theresa and the children, César asked us about the possibility of traveling together as a family to negotiate with growers. Theresa and I accepted this proposal, and we even looked at various mobile homes that might serve the proposed migratory living.

We arrived in Bell Gardens at night, while Colleen slept in the back seat. César had requested that we hold up on the negotiating plan and go to the San Fernando Valley to organize another street campaign in opposition to a ballot proposition designed by the growers. From a public phone, I called Reverend Hare, a Presbyterian minister who had been recommended as a friend of the UFW. He took us in. He and his gracious family made it possible for us to campaign all day and to reside at their modest home. Theresa and I, along with other union members, organized human billboards and mass leafleting to stop anti-farm-worker California Senate Bill 40, petitioning throughout that great suburban bathtub of smog.

At César's request, Theresa and I moved out of La Paz and established a UFW headquarters for the San Fernando Valley in a rented house on Canby Street in Northridge. Our house became a political headquarters and conveyed the sentiment Joel Edelstein had expressed in that poem he wrote for our wedding.

The house was filthy. The owner was Christine Jorgensen, of the famous sex change. Our friend Pauline Saxon helped us to clean it up and make it suitable for both our family and as a headquarters. One of the problems with this setting was its attraction for freeloaders and floaters. Theresa had plenty of assignments for people who were ready to work. I can recall one fellow who really wanted to talk. He told us exactly how the world should be changed. After listening intently, Theresa asked him to do some volunteer work. He seemed offended by her suggestion and explained that he was "a strategist for the far left." She showed him the door with a finality that must still ring in his ears: "We aren't looking for strategists for the far left. We are looking for people who can leaflet and who can work as human billboards."

Our work expanded rapidly, and we found a better rental on San Fernando Mission Road. With the help of excellent volunteer carpenters, the garage was converted into an office, and a Maryknoll-style sponsor program was developed. In our new office, Theresa and I held meetings to raise money for the union. By June of 1973, Theresa and I were raising a substantial sum of money, mostly through individual sponsors and occasional large donations. It got to the point that the teller at the local bank in Mission Hills would laugh when I asked her to add up the checks for me.

Blase and family: Blase-Martin, Colleen and Theresa, 1973.

Theresa and I were distraught when César wrote that the union could no longer pay for our medical bills or for the rent. Battles with the Teamsters and the courts had devastated the union's treasury. Two providential solutions to our financial problems arrived almost immediately. Tori Hill, who is now a librarian at the Library of Congress, moved in and helped substantially with our rent and superbly assisted us with childcare. And, in an unbelievable development, two men arrived at our front door saying they represented a special federal program for health care as a result of the Sylmar earthquake. We could receive full medical insurance on a sliding scale with our income. It was a miracle! Our income was nil, so the payments were zero. All medical expenses, glasses, and rides to and from the doctor were free.

I also applied for food stamps. What a humiliation. When I appeared at the local supermarket as a healthy-looking person and paid in food stamps, eyebrows were raised. I remember the ten-page application. The application was full of threats and more threats. At any time, the department of agriculture could come to our home and inspect our refrigerator. The fine print of the application stated that people who were not on food stamps were not allowed to eat any of the food. Such were the humble beginnings of my new role as "Development Director" of the United Farm Workers union.

While leafleting at California State University, Northridge, I met Professor Lawrence Littwin. He knew of me through the peace movement and asked why I was not teaching there. I explained my academic fate. Within a few days I received an offer from Professor Anthony Alcocer in the Department of Health Science. He asked me to teach a course on "The Chicano and Health." This was a required course for the Chicano studies program. Comprised of mostly Chicano students, the course focus was aimed at helping young Chicanos develop positive attitudes toward health and culture. We talked about food pesticides and the importance of purchasing healthy foods. This part-time teaching job brought in a few dollars, which helped Theresa and I continue the work of the UFW to fight against pesticide poisoning in the San Fernando Valley.

By March of 1974, I had the political bug again. It seemed to me, I could help the union most by running for the Assembly seat that was vacated by Assemblyman Robert Moretti. I could fight for the legislation we had been seeking from inside the government institutions rather than campaigning on the streets. Theresa and I drove up to La Paz to discuss the idea with César. He was supportive. He said we could use the printing presses for leaflets and bumper stickers. He said the union would offer campaign workers. Theresa accepted the management of the campaign. She expected to have a great deal of help from the union.

Theresa organized some two-hundred volunteers. The campaign for my election was outstanding. Even my mother had campaigned for me, standing at Reseda Boulevard and Sherman Way holding a "Bonpane for Assembly" sign. But there was a certain vacuum—the UFW came through with nothing. We have never understood the reason behind this turn of events. Perhaps the reasons were economic. Either way, I truly felt betrayed. Tom Bane ultimately won the primary and the general election.

The last time I saw César Chávez was at the funeral of Father Luis Olivares in 1993. He did not look well. His speech was halting and he used notes for his comments. A few weeks later, in a sweltering courtroom in Yuma, Arizona, he would withstand hours of grueling questions from attorneys hired by the growers who were fighting and winning a $2.9-million judgment against the UFW. César went home to rest that evening and died.

How can we criticize a man of such greatness? The truth that so many biographers miss is that people of greatness are still great despite their faults. Perfectionism is always a lie and a trap. If we try to develop a perfectionist approach to Mahatma Gandhi, Nelson Mandela, or César Chávez we are making a huge error. People do not become perfect and then do something for the world. They do something for the world and evolve into something better because of it. César Chávez was a great person. Our faults and his faults do not take that fact away; on the contrary, they make it more real. His spirit and dedication will stay with me and millions of others who continue to struggle for a better world.

Chapter 13

Return to Academia/
The Peace Movement

After I lost the campaign for Assembly of the State of California, Theresa and I were once again in debt. We had bills to pay, children to raise, and a war to end. I took on more teaching assignments at California State University, Northridge. Theresa went immediately to Kennedy Adult School and landed teaching positions for both of us. She soon became chair of the English as a Second Language Department and the union representative for the department. We were back on salary.

I did not make a sharp break with the UFW. I continued to be of service. But Theresa and I were no longer full-time UFW staff members. It was good to be away from the self-righteousness of an intentional community. This form of quasi-religious commune life might suit some. But Theresa and I preferred something more independent. There were few outside volunteers, accountants, technicians, artists, lawyers, ministers, or other professionals who could remain on the UFW staff for more than two or three years. It was too confining. It was during this time that the UFW used the Synanon Game to organize its members; Synanon was a therapy cult founded and led by Charles Dietrich in the 1970s. Chávez turned to Synanon because he was looking for better ways to organize people. It's ultimate premise, however, was to use mind games to create confrontational encounters intended to enact productive dialogues. While many individual workers were against it, the leaders of the UFW were not, and it became a very detrimental aspect of the organization. In fact, the UFW seemed to reach its low point when it used various adaptations of the Synanon Game. Our hope is that the United Farm Workers of America will continue its long, hard road representing farm labor throughout the United States.

With our new jobs, we decided to buy a house. We were so surprised to have a home of our own. Mom had given us $3,000 as half of the down payment on our new home in Reseda. We paid $29,000 for it. Dad said, "You are a capitalist now." And there is something to that statement. The line between renters and owners is an awful one. Renters pay and pay and get no equity. We capitalist owners in California generally sell our houses for much more than we paid for them. We literally get a free ride. Talk about "welfare."

The battle to end the war in Vietnam was still raging on our campuses. One day while I was teaching at Cal State Northridge, the Marines landed on the campus. They came in by helicopter, descending in front of the Oviatt Library and exiting their aircraft in camouflage. Cannons were pulled onto the campus by jeeps, and the recruiters set up their tables and displayed their super-slick promotional brochures. A spontaneous peaceful demonstration broke out among the students and faculty. I was one of them. With them, I shouted, "Troops off campus! Troops off campus! Troops off campus!" The troops finally left.

The Vietnam War ranks with that of the Third Reich. Three million people massacred, three hundred thousand Vietnamese MIAs. One of the great post-war myths was that the service people were upset because they did not have victory parades. What an insult to the fine young people who fought and died in Vietnam. They were not upset for lack of parades. They were upset because the United States government lied to them, used them and manipulated them into a slaughter that never should have happened. Nor were they poorly received by the peace movement. Peace people worked with them and showed them respect by forming GI coffeehouses where they could talk and read about reality. At some risk we spoke on their bases.

During ten years of opposition to the Vietnam War, I never saw a member of our movement burn a flag. That was the tactic of police provocateurs. Far more veterans died in post-war suicides than died in battle. While teaching, I heard constant and unsolicited stories from veterans of out and out mutiny during the conflict. "We fragged 'em," "We told 'em to go to hell," they reported.

The end of the Vietnam War left us in a state of emotional exhaustion. For ten years, Theresa and I had been trying to stop our country from killing people. By the time the Vietnam War ended in 1975, I had lost my faith in the integrity of most government agencies. In spite of this feeling, and with the intention of bringing the issue of nuclear war into the classrooms, I ran for the Los Angeles Board of Education. I lost my campaign, but the issue of education on the holocaust of nuclear war was not lost. Educators and board members continued to bring the topic of nuclear disaster into the curriculum.

At Cal State Northridge, my classes were jammed. I was now a member of the Political Science department. I taught introductory courses on US government, Latin American politics, and Cuba. I was hired on a basis of one semester only, no more. This hiring arrangement continued for fourteen semesters. I was seven years at Northridge with no tenure and limited benefits. I had hoped at some point to earn as much as the grounds keepers. That never happened. But every minute in the classroom was a joy.

I was a popular professor. One of the hardest things was to find a room big enough for the students trying to enroll. I was known to be tolerant of diverse opinions. I did not force my students to agree with me in the classroom. Students also liked my unconventional grading system. In fact, I did not believe in the grading system. I have never pictured myself as the students' judge. I want to teach them and not to judge them. I have always hated grades and grading. I have never given a test in the classroom. I have never given an "objective," machine-graded test. Students must speak and write. Once again, I would ask the question, as I did while teaching at California State University Los Angeles, "When you studied the social sciences in high school, did your grade depend on your willingness to agree with your teacher?" Most students would answer in the affirmative. Other faculty members were complaining about my large classes, my dialogical teaching, my grading, my politics, and my participation in demonstrations. Popularity is the kiss of death in academia. I did not try to be popular. I loved the students. My commitment to the students got through to them.

I wanted to challenge them to altruistic and idealistic ambitions. They loved it. I never asked them to regurgitate by rote what I taught them. By dialogue I wanted them to come up with new ideas. An "A" student is one who enters into the experience fully. This means he or she accepts or rejects the premises of the texts and the professor, uses critical thinking to explain his or her opinion, gives subjective verbal and written reports. All my tests were to be done at home. I have never understood why students are supposed to play the game of no dictionary, no books, and a lot of cheating. I wanted the students to take the questions home. I emphasized that instead of spending an hour on the exam, they should spend many hours, if necessary, and bring it back to me with no mistakes in spelling or grammar. I do not think the students came simply seeking an easy grade. I think they came because they were learning something.

Despite my popularity, I rarely socialized with my students. I tried to concentrate on pedagogy. Students are not looking for drinking buddies; they are looking for leadership, direction, information, analysis, critical thinking, synthesis, sincerity, and sometimes urgent counsel. Over the years, I have taught some thirty-five different courses. To academia, I was cheap labor, but I was doing what I loved.

"We want Bonpane! We want Bonpane," echoed down the halls. Students were demonstrating in the halls, demanding that I be retained. I found it embarrassing, but it was their doing. I was constantly on the stump for the peace movement on and off campus. There were ongoing pressures to fire me. The ideology of anticommunism was still the official story within the United States. I am not now nor have I ever been a communist, but I don't think a day went by without being called a communist. The mainstream conservative view of what to do with communists during those years was, "OK to kill." While the administration tried to fire me, the daily student paper, *The Sundial*, reported regularly on my plight. Larry Littwin was also my friend and protector. He ran interference for me against the administration. I don't think I would have been rehired fourteen times without his intercession and the student's support.

Even though I was rehired each academic term, my class assignments were given with the greatest lack of consideration possible. I might be informed a few days before the semester started or a few days after the semester started. If Professor X died of tenure or related diseases, I would be called in to replace him. Tenure certainly is the beginning of the death process for many. Complaints were coming in because of my grading practices, my course content, my politics, and the size of my classes. A dyspeptic tenured ash of a professor was sent in to observe my class. The very sight of him had a glacial effect. He gave me the worst possible evaluation. This was somewhat at variance with the overwhelming positive evaluations by students who also had their own written evaluation system.

The last courses I taught at California State University, Northridge (CSUN) were in the departments of sociology and mechanical engineering. For a year I had a full-time position as the lone philosophy professor at the newly founded Mission College in San Fernando. This was simultaneous with teaching at CSUN. During this time, I also had a friend at the *Los Angeles Times* who helped me publish various and sundry opinion and op-ed pieces. I wrote a popular article, "Money Myths of the 'Middle Class'," in which I argued that establishing a real economic democracy in this country depended on our ability to expose our economic mythology.

That same year, my mother died. She lived twenty-two years after her cancer required a colostomy operation. She continued her energetic, love-filled life until her last day. My sister and I witnessed an unforgettable transformation in her as she passed away. She was radiant in death and looked about fifty years younger than eighty-two. We stood at her bedside until hospital personnel dismissed us.

My Dad had a difficult time with her death. He simply could not accept the fact that my mother died before he did. He expected to be like most of us men: we die first. He was almost helpless without my

Mom, and he was vulnerable to a sweet young thing, some twenty years his junior, who took him for almost all he was worth. As a judge, Dad had publicly scolded people who took advantage of the aged in order to enrich themselves. And now he was the victim. It was a shock to our family to see him remarry after he had lost his ability to reason.

My mother's theology continually comes back to me. She was Catholic; that was our background. But she was truly non-sectarian. She could not think of giving preference to a person because of their Catholic faith. She evaluated people by the fruits of their lives and not by their sectarian preferences. I think the time has come for Catholic theologians to deal with this matter more profoundly. The Lutheran Dietrich Bonhoffer longed for a "religion-less" Christianity. What an insight! It is the religion part that is clearly divisive. It is the religion part that makes people arrogantly try to define the things of God. It is the religion part that inspired crusaders to slaughter Jews and Muslims in the Holy Land, to murder in the name of God during the Inquisition, and to conquer the New World for the Crown and the Cross. Bosnian Serb fascists of the 1990s called their slaughter, "a battle by Christendom against the inroads of Islamic fundamentalism."

We must get beyond the *ex opere operato* (the sacrament acting of itself) theology of what the sacraments do. Such rituals should celebrate what we are willing to do in following the Spirit.

Is a wife-beater with the sacrament of matrimony better than a couple deeply in love living together in mutual harmony and respect without the sacrament? Come off it! Is a baptized dictator better than a pacifist Buddhist monk? Is a pedophile priest better than an atheist humanist? An ordained millionaire is better than a hamburger flipper? A Mafiosi receiving the sacrament of the sick is better than an AIDS patient dying without it? A recidivist penitent is better than a reverent agnostic? A corrupt politician receiving the Eucharist is better than a Bedouin shepherd living without it?

How tragic that Church membership has been marked by sacraments received rather than services rendered to the poor. It is the focus on religion that ruins spirituality. I love to participate in the Eucharist. It is my spiritual path and the culture of my spirituality. I love it more now that I give no militaristic line authority to the ecclesiastical bureaucracy. I find that those who are still held by the imperial chains are precisely the ones who become the most bitter. They are the ones blabbering about how the institution should collapse of its own weight when they are still living off it as a babe at mother's breast.

Let us revere the seven sacraments. But let us stop telling people what the sacraments will do for them and start asking people what they will do for each other. By all means, we should celebrate what we are doing or what we are going to do or what we have done. I don't expect to see any religious states in the future. Such polities have failed miserably. Jefferson was confronted with this nonsense by fundamentalist colonies interested in burning witches and sending their enemies to hell. The First Amendment was essential to the establishment of the United States of America. It is even more essential now for our country and for the globe. Ethnic cleansing? Please! There is but one race on this planet. People must study enough philosophy to know that color, size, nationality, language, religion, and culture are accidents not essences.

Esquire Magazine visits our first home for its 1970 article on "Troublemakers."

With César Chávez and his aide, 1972.

Office of the Americas delegation to visit the Contra War, 1982.

With Ramsey Clark at the Citizens Tribunal on Iraq, 1991.

Chapter 14

The Movement to Abolish Nuclear Weapons and the Struggle of the Sandinistas

Dr. Richard Saxon invited me to go to Japan in the summer of 1976. His organization, Physicians for Social Responsibility (PSR), grew into an international movement with the founding of International Physicians for the Prevention of Nuclear War (IPPNW) in 1980. And by 1985 PSR shared the Nobel Peace Prize awarded to IPPNW "for spreading authoritative information and by creating an awareness of the catastrophic consequences of atomic warfare."

People from all over Japan marched to Tokyo for this international gathering to abolish nuclear weapons in 1976. The Japanese police did not harass the marchers and were mostly receptive to the thousands upon thousands of demonstrators.

I was privileged to speak to the gathering regarding the urgency of global abolition and how the US had the prime responsibility to lead because of its unforgivable annihilation of Hiroshima and Nagasaki. We met the Buddhists in the Sanga of Reverend Fuji who was approaching his 100th year. Reverend Sato, a former kamikaze pilot, told us of his experiences in war and now in peace making. I asked him if all Buddhists supported his position. "No, some Buddhists consider us devils because we march internationally," he explained. The spectrum of differing views on war and peace that was obvious in the Catholic Church was also visible in the Buddhist experience.

I went to Hiroshima on a bullet train going over 100 miles per hour. The Japanese were far ahead of the US in terms of public transit. I met survivors of the atomic bombing of 1945 at the Hiroshima hospital. These people's lives had been destroyed. As I spoke to some of them, I could not stop thinking about how the Pentagon myth, "Those bombs saved so many lives," was still alive in US folklore. International research has reached a consensus: the bombs were unnecessary. Surrender was in process. The bombs were used as a message to the Soviet Union that they would get no credit for entering the war against Japan. Further, these bombs were the beginning of the Cold War, an equally unnecessary experience (1945–1989). Every Soviet schoolchild knew that the US uses atom bombs against civilians. This terror led the Soviets to put their resources into arms, arms research, and nuclear weapons. These efforts to compete found the Soviet Union about fifteen years behind the US at all times. And the arms race, more than anything else, bankrupted the USSR. The military-industrial complex, more than anything else, is destroying the United States.

In Hiroshima, I was struck by the silence about the US barbarous attacks by the Japanese politicians. The only place I heard people talking about the atrocity was at the Hiroshima Peace Memorial Museum in the middle of the city. At that sacred memorial I saw the shadow of a vaporized person together with remnants of that city destroyed by the first A-bomb.

This Apocalyptic devastation was done by bombers safely distanced from the massacre. The A-bomb seemed to be considered such a "clean" action. And three days later the nuclear holocaust would be repeated in Nagasaki. These were civilians. These crimes will be remembered as the most repulsive acts of international terrorism. Perpetual war has been the legacy of the United States in the wake of this infamy.

By the time I returned from Japan, the Sandinista struggle in Nicaragua had become an international issue. Theresa and I marched in Los Angeles on behalf of the Sandinistas and against the Somoza dictatorship from 1976–1979. From that time until 1990, our lives would be very much aligned with the Nicaraguan struggle.

We marched on Broadway and sometimes in McArthur Park. The marchers were comprised mostly of Nicaraguans together with other Central Americans and Mexicans. I arranged for Father Ernesto Cardenal to speak to my classes at CSUN. Ernesto was a colleague of Father Thomas Merton at the Gethsemane Trappist Abbey in Kentucky. He had returned to Nicaragua to form a Liberation Theology Christian community on the Island of Solentiname. Ernesto spoke about the revolution taking place in Nicaragua in response to the Somoza dictatorship. He explained how the true God liberates and false gods enslave.

Father Miguel d'Escoto, a seminary colleague, also visited the campus and explained his role as foreign minister to the Sandinistas in Nicaragua. The students responded positively. The Vietnam Vets in the class were particularly struck by the situation in Nicaragua. They were the same students who had been vocal against the Vietnam War, declaring that it ended in a mutiny.

The Nicaraguan peace movement arrived at the CSUN campus and joined the students daring to protest what seemed like my imminent expulsion from the campus. Since I was hired as an adjunct, I was already hanging on by a thread each semester. This was 1978 and the

80

administration did not like my politics, grading policies, and the fact that my classes were so popular.

There were several editorial cartoons published in the student newspaper *Daily Sundial* from November to December that depicted my precarious position with the faculty. One cartoon showed my head in a chopping block with the Dean hovering over me wielding an axe. I continued on the faculty until 1979. It seems that my politics and teaching methods just did not fit the agenda of the administration. I was not rehired in 1980.

Without my teaching obligations at CSUN, my life became even more immersed in the Nicaraguan revolution. By 1979, the Sandinistas had won. The Sandinistas marched into Managua on July 19th of this memorable year. To celebrate, the local Nicaraguan community assembled at St. Joseph's Church at 12th Street and Los Angeles Street. In the absence of any other priest, and a church full of happy Nicaraguans, I put on the vestments and celebrated the Nicaraguan Peasant Mass, *Misa Campesina Nicaraguense*. After the Mass I came back into the sacristy, and a Franciscan priest who I had never met was waiting there. I introduced myself. He said in a rather somber voice, "I know who you are." It seems that my infamous reputation had reached him. My expulsion from Guatemala, support of the Nicaraguan revolution, and marriage status did not leave me in good standing with the Church. Yet, I was still a priest. One can never be an un-priest. Tu es sacerdos in aeternum (you are a priest forever).

Chapter 15

Nicaraguan Revolution

Like many historical realities, the events resulting in the takeover of the Nicaraguan Consulate in Los Angeles were so unbelievable that if they were encapsulated in a film, no one would believe them. It would seem too contrived.

Immediately after our Los Angeles demonstration celebrating the Sandinista victory on July 19, 1979, Manuel Valle, the march leader, stomped to the Consulate where the staff representing the Somoza government was still present. He said, "You know we Sandinistas have won. I am here on behalf of the new government of Nicaragua. It is time for you to leave." Unbelievably, the consul gave him the keys to the office and walked out together with his staff. The Sandinista banner went up instantly, together with the flag of Nicaragua. One problem, however, was that Manuel had not yet spoken to Managua about his self-appointment.

Manuel asked me to join him and to depart immediately for Managua requesting authorization papers for him to be the new consul of Nicaragua in Los Angeles. Our delegation included Manuel, myself, and Antonio Gonzalez, a reporter for a Spanish-language radio station in Los Angeles. US airlines had immediately stopped service to Managua. We flew to Guatemala City and were able to connect with a Panamanian Airline, COPA, to make the final leg into the César Sandino Airport.

Uniformed youngsters were everywhere at the airport. Two lovers long separated by revolutionary conflict spotted each other; they ran to embrace, their weapons intertwined, and an AK-47 burst blasted the ceiling of the air terminal. Everything was functioning: bags were inspected, papers were checked, everyone was effervescent, and everyone seemed to be fourteen years old. I was amazed that for a country that was undergoing a revolution and shift in government power, everything was running so smoothly.

We were met by the new minister of protocol. My God, it was Herty Lewites. I had known Herty through the Committee of Latin American Solidarity (COLAS) in Los Angeles. Herty greeted us with a machine pistol in his hand. It had no strap and no holster, so he could not put it down. "Yes, I am the same guy who was in COLAS in 1968. Yes, I was charged with shipping arms to Nicaragua and sent to the Federal prison at Terminal Island. All we want now is peace. Welcome."

I was present at the meeting of the new junta with Manuel. This was August, 1979, and an important moment in history. A five-person junta had been appointed by the Sandinista Directorate. They were chosen as a "Provisional Government of National Unity in which there will be real and effective struggle against dictatorship." They included Commander Daniel Ortega, who was later to be elected President; Moises Hassan; Sergio Ramirez, who was later to be elected Vice President; Alfonso Robelo, who later went to the Contras; and Violeta Barrios de Chamorro, widow of the murdered editor of *La Prensa*, who became President of Nicaragua in 1990.

Respite in Condega, Nicaragua during the International March for Peace in Central America, 1986.

Manuel Valle quickly received his official papers as Council of Nicaragua in Los Angeles. We talked with the new administration regarding legal problems relating to Nicaraguan planes, and ships that were located in US and other ports in the Caribbean. Members of the Nicaraguan bourgeoisie who had become revolutionaries entered into the planning for retrieval of Nicaraguan property abroad. Someone said, "Let's continue this discussion on Monday." An affluent looking Nicaraguan lawyer responded, "This is a revolution, we have to meet tomorrow" (Sunday). This junta became the executive instrument of the *Frente Sandinista de Liberación Nacional* (The Sandinista Front of National Liberation), or FSLN.

I met briefly with Father Ernesto Cardenal at the Intercontinental Hotel in Managua regarding his new role as Minister of Culture. This was the first time I had seen him since he spoke in my class at CSUN. We desperately wanted this revolution to succeed. This was not the Cuban revolution, nor any other revolution. The incorporation of the progressive clergy brought with it humane and non-dogmatic positions. Ivory-tower Marxists the world over were critical of the structures of Sandinismo. Ernesto and I talked about the profound humanity and changes in revolutionary Nicaragua. It was no longer a police state. I could walk the streets at Managua at midnight and feel safe. The prisons were no longer places of torture. There was humane treatment and prison reform. Former Somosista torturers were undergoing rehab.

While at the Nicaraguan airport I saw Mr. Pezzullo, the newly appointed US ambassador to Nicaragua. I extended my hand and introduced myself. Pezzullo patted my hand and said, "We threw you out of Guatemala some years ago, what are you doing here?" It was all very good-natured. Yet, any humanity that Lawrence Pezzullo might have shown to Nicaragua was cut short by the coming of the Reagan Administration. Pezzullo was an appointee of the Carter administration. With the Reagan Administration, a policy of hysterical propaganda and mass murder began immediately.

I returned to the States with Manuel on a mission to assist the newly-forming government of Nicaragua. *The New York Times* published my op-ed piece, "Normalcy in Nicaragua." In contrast to popular opinion of the Sandinistas as "bandits," I described Nicaraguans as not posing a threat to the US. Everything was running smoothly and normally. All the Nicaraguans wanted was a functioning country. They had already started with excellent progress by establishing literacy programs. And, in the new Nicaragua, medical care was a right not a privilege.

This revolution would be a major focus of Theresa's and my life from 1979–1990. For over a decade we went back and forth to Nicaragua like yo-yos. Theresa led her first delegation to Nicaragua with people who had helped to finance the revolution. She found herself translating for Tomás Borge, the new Minister of the Interior, and her English-speaking friends. Theresa, too, was taken by the high-spirited, electric atmosphere. Rifles were stacked at the door as disco-dancing Sandinistas continued their reunions and celebrations at the Intercontinental Hotel.

Theresa and I had anticipated making these trips together, but our seven-year-old son gave us some advice: "If you go down to Nicaragua together, Colleen and I will not have anyone to sing us to sleep." We knew he was saying more than his words conveyed. Blase Martin was concerned about our safety. We agreed with him and made a decision that we would travel individually on these missions of private diplomacy.

Children will teach you, challenge you, make you grow daily, as nothing else. Of all of the advice from all the gurus of the world and all of the ways of perfection, I would suggest one which I consider the highest: raise children. Theresa and I have laughed so many times about all the advice we gave to parents while we were in religious life. It was so simple to tell them just what to do and to spend about ten minutes of our time at it. Once our own infants come along and we realize they will be with us twenty-four hours a day, we must make a choice. Are we going to follow our selfish ways or are we going to respond to their needs? In our case, we were further challenged by the need to balance our political work and the children. When they were very young, we brought them to every meeting and every demonstration. As they got old enough to express their own preferences, we were often told they would rather not go to our meetings and demonstrations. Once Theresa asked Colleen if she would like to attend a presentation on Nicaragua and received this answer: "I know more about Somoza than anyone. I would rather stay home." And, when Colleen asked for First Communion, we invited Father Garvey to our home to celebrate mass and First Communion for her. Blase Martin was not interested. And we said that was OK.

Our children got the message of everything we did. We did not preach to them. They did not need sermons. Children simply absorb every value, every word, and every decision. Once one of Blase Martin's friends was telling my son about the hard times his family was going through. How they were out of money and had bills to pay, etc. My son said to his friend, "You had better talk to my father." I was so pleased he would say that.

Every child in the world has had either too much parenting or not enough. The younger they are, the more attention they need. Theresa and I actually served with the Indian Guides and Indian Maidens of the YMCA. We were both horrible at arts and crafts-y things, but we did them when necessary. I even think my attempt to build a tiny racing toy for my son Blase must have embarrassed him. Some of the fathers had spent weeks making the sleekest, fastest car models. The model that my son and I entered in the race was hard to distinguish from a block of wood with wheels. I believe we came in last. With somewhat more expertise, I served as a coach for AYSO soccer and Little League baseball. The Culver-Palms YMCA became a key center for the formation of our children. The staff was outstanding. Theresa and I met with the "Y" leadership to beg for a high school program as our kids were reaching that age. With Theresa's help and direction, the high school program took off with a vengeance.

Theresa and I did not always agree, however, on what was the proper balance of time between our political work and the children. Personally, I thought it worked out beautifully. We were there for them. We were not absentee parents. We did alternate on trips to Central America. Theresa still thought I should be at home more. She feared that I would become like many other people in the peace movement who often do a great deal for others while neglecting their home and family life.

Chapter 16

Office of the Americas and Nicaraguan Delegations

Theresa and I left our home in Reseda in search of some better air. My biking to work each day led me to develop bronchitis. The doctor told me, "You can't bike out here." We moved. The air was better in Mar Vista. My father was right. We were capitalists; we sold our Reseda house for twice what we had paid for it.

Our new home was becoming more and more of a headquarters. People came by day and night, visitors from Central America, friends, immigrants, and filmmakers. John Chapman told us of his new film on Nicaragua. He wanted to show it at our little house on Beethoven Street in Mar Vista. Martin Sheen came to our home to watch Chapman's film. They had worked together on *Apocalypse Now*. Martin has remained a dear and loyal friend through these turbulent years.

Theresa was more and more disturbed by the lack of privacy in our home. She began to speak of the need to have an office outside of our home so we could do our political business in a more organized fashion. We gathered friends together to discuss the possibility of forming an office, an Office of the Americas. As we formed plans to open up our office, Martin Sheen was working on a movie about El Salvador and wanted to distribute some of the money from the project. Martin was asked to play the role of priest in the TV film, *Roses in December*, which was about the lives of four religious women who were raped and murdered in El Salvador. He asked us to distribute $25,000 dollars among five groups working on the Central American solidarity. We sheepishly asked if one of those groups could be our new organization. He agreed. His $5,000 was our start-up fund. The Office of the Americas became a reality.

Theresa managed the office. She had already been instrumental in the formation of the Committee in Solidarity of the People in El Salvador (CISPES), a US group in support of the Salvadorian Revolution. After CISPES was conceived, Theresa instructed the staff in how to manage an organization. The organization became a nationwide voice on behalf of the Salvadoran people. Theresa also helped to build Medical Aid to El Salvador into a multi-million dollar source of aid for the Salvadoran people.

In the midst of all this, she was teaching at Santa Monica College, and became chairperson of the English as a Second Language Department.

Theresa spoke to Rev. Carlyle Gill at St. Augustine by the Sea Church in Santa Monica and asked her if there might be some space to set up our Office of the Americas. The woman priest was enthusiastic and delighted. She said that Theresa's call was providential in view of their Vestry meeting on the previous evening. The Church had determined to do something in solidarity with Central America. Friends came to design our new offices. Walls were installed, and we hustled desks and files. An office was in the making. We put in phones, and they began to ring. The community was ready for the Office of the Americas. We obviously filled a gap. Our scope was all of the Americas. Our initial focus, however, would be principally on Nicaragua. We determined that CISPES, with its single focus, could do well on the matter of El Salvador.

This period was so unlike the '60s, when every group thought it had some kind of a formula for the revolution. In the '80s, we were not fighting among ourselves; we were cooperating, working together in harmony and in mutual support. So often people would ask us, "Why don't you just form one giant organization for the whole country, a United Way for solidarity?" We judged ourselves to be better off as base communities, and we formed from bases all over the country. Rather than shutting down one giant organization, the government would have to shut down hundreds of solidarity groups. Yes, we were waging non-violent guerrilla warfare. Each group had its autonomy. If one group went down, the others could continue. This was guerrilla-of-peace action.

There is no way to describe the pain of listening to Ronald Reagan; an uninformed mannequin carrying out policy for the Vice President's CIA. Foreign policy was textbook fascism. It included ethnic cleansing, the massacre of civilians, the building of a clandestine mercenary army to which he claimed to belong, torture, summary execution, and all with an "Aw shucks" shake of the head. It was not the pain of the existence of a Ronald Reagan. Such people are quite commonplace. The pain was in the fact that the people of the United States bought it. The lack of discernment was overwhelming. Reagan declared a State of Emergency in the United States because of the Sandinista Revolution. He literally expressed the fear that the Nicaraguans were apt to invade the United States!

During my next delegation to Nicaragua I observed ominous developments. I could literally see the US financed mercenaries (Contras) as we scanned the border with Honduras. While the Sandinista government directed its attention to literacy, health care, and land reform, a clandestine US policy had been structured to overthrow the Nicaraguan government by force. By 1981 the Nicaraguan health care campaigns had reduced infant mortality by 40% in relation to pre-revolutionary figures.

US troops were using Honduras as a staging area for the Contra War. US troops were rotating as they also trained for control of the Salvadoran and Guatemalan Armies in their efforts to eliminate the *Frente Farabundo Martí para la Liberación Nacional* (FMLN) and the *Unidad Revolucionaria Nacional Guatemalteca*, or URNG, (Guatemalan National Revolutionary Unity). Over 75,000 US troops were in Honduras at a time. Honduras was called the air-craft carrier because of its position in the midst of the three insurgencies, not to mention its own internal conflict. Our friends in Guatemala reported that Somoza's former guardsmen were being recruited by the CIA in Guatemala and Honduras. With child prostitution and rape, the only lasting contribution made by the troops in Honduras was AIDS.

The Reagan Doctrine was cheered by death squads in Guatemala, Honduras, and El Salvador. Simply put, human rights were no longer a consideration in US policy. The slaughters became monumental in El Salvador as heads separated from bodies littered the streets daily. Guatemala followed with a scorched earth policy and the elimination of some five hundred indigenous villages. Sadistic Contra atrocities were documented internationally. Reagan smiled.

I participated in the Dialogue of the Americas in Mexico City in October, 1982. This was an international response to the US attack on the sovereignty of the Central American and Caribbean nations. During the dialogue, I received an invitation to come to the Nicaraguan Embassy in Mexico City to discuss the current situation. Daniel Ortega's wife, Rosario Murillo, greeted us there and asked the newly-forming Office of the Americas to please bring delegations to Nicaragua on a regular basis. There were no conditions placed on the request. Certainly, they would like to see high-profile people who could capture media attention in the US, but they welcomed both the known and the unknown.

I returned to Los Angeles and feverishly put together a thirty-two-person delegation. This group of celebrities and scholars departed for Nicaragua just a month later. Such delegations would follow on a near-monthly basis from 1982–1990. Philanthropist Kit Tremaine was with us and remained a friend and benefactor through these years. Producer Bert Schnider, Actor David Clennon, Director Haskell Wexler, who would produce the most accurate dramatic film about the Contra War (*Latino*), my sister, Sister Mary Anne Bonpane, Director of Stanford Home in Sacramento, California—a most engaging mix of travelers.

We met the Sandinista leadership, the junta, the cabinet, the poets, the dancers. The Nicaraguan Association of Cultural Workers, or ASTC, and

89

its Secretary General, Rosario Murillo, were our hosts. The Nicaraguans were not about to have us simply meet the leadership; they wanted us to see the entire country. We went to the areas of conflict and stopped at a point where the Contras had blown away the bridge over the Río Negro. The military commander told us we could drive the buses safely and carefully through the river. He also told us we might be under military discipline at any moment should there be an attack. Poet-author Margaret Randall traveled with us as we proceeded toward the Honduran border. We were told it was urgent to be out of the area before sunset. We visited a town overlooking Honduras and actually saw the Contras. We greeted the town militia, a handful of men with ancient rifles. We saw their trenches, their bomb shelters, and their children. Thousands of children were about to die in this slaughter—Reagan's War.

The only time I thought that we were certainly under fire from the Contras was on a late-night return to Managua from Esteli. Gunfire was blasting near the front of the fast-moving Toyota minibus. I was frightened, as was the rest of the delegation. Martin Sheen was with us. The bus driver stopped and explained that we were too close to a Sandinista military caravan and that the shots were simply a signal to stay a substantial distance behind them for our own good. Oliver Stone, John Randolph, Sam Neill and many other interested people from the film community joined us on these ventures. Journalists and documentary film makers were in abundance. The Christian Science Monitor took an interest in the work of the Office of the Americas. The late Andrew Kopkind of *Nation Magazine* came with me on an eventful delegation to Nicaragua. I told him of my respect for the oldest magazine in the United States. He said, "Yes, but it could be a much better magazine." Generally speaking, I was impressed with the absence of prima donnas among our celebrity delegates.

Our two small, twenty-passenger Toyota buses began to move south as the sun descended. We were back at the Río Negro. We attempted to cross the river by driving through as we had in the morning, but both buses became stuck mid-stream. The waters had risen during the day, and it was not possible to pass. As the sun went down, we could see the apprehension on the faces of our Nicaraguan hosts. Here were two white buses sitting in the middle of a river just at the time when fighting was about to begin. The solution: leave the buses, walk to shore through the river, and assemble on the southern side. Runners went to find Sandinista Army trucks to pull the buses out. We all boarded Army trucks and proceeded to our lodging for the evening. The Sandinistas were not trying to kill us. They were actually quite concerned about our safety. At the same time, they did not want to pamper us by simply staying in an urban setting.

We flew on two antique DC-3s from Managua to Bonanza, located in the jungle of northern Zelaya. We dropped onto the short dirt runway and met Commander William Ramirez, who was in charge of this area. Pickup trucks were waiting to take us to the famous *Tasba-Pri* (Promised Land), a very controversial location. The Sandinistas had relocated Miskito people away from the Río Coco, where they were being recruited by the Contras. The river was their life, and many were unwilling to make the change. They were forced to leave. The resettlement camp was very humane and well-organized. There were classes in three languages: English, Spanish, and Miskito. Wood homes were constructed in accord with the Miskito culture, and the health clinic was functional. *Tasba-Pri* was not a prison, as the Reaganites claimed it to be. We were among the few US citizens to ever see it. Even so, the Sandinistas admitted their mistake in attempting to relocate the Miskito people from the border river.

Resettlement is the closest thing to death that people can experience. Their relationship to that beautiful river was absolute. Interior Minister Tomas Borge made an apology saying, "We are revolutionaries and not anthropologists."

Chapter 17

Media Requests

I generally accepted any media request I received. Beggars cannot be choosers. Yet, dealing with media is always a risk. The commercial media is a cesspool of advertisements, banality, irrelevance, and nonsense. I continued, however, to accept their invitations. I was often desperate to talk about the wars being waged in Central America, especially the Contra War. Yet, the media continually concocted some diversion.

When Theresa and I were invited to talk with Ted Koppel on *Nightline* in 1982, we initially turned down the request. We had already made plans to meet with writers from the Sundance Institute about our screenplay *Epikeia* or "A Matter of Conscience" about our lives. We also had a meeting scheduled with Martin Sheen at our house to discuss his starring role in the film, and we simply told Nightline, "We don't have time." ABC-TV would not take no for an answer, and they made every effort to include our participation. They offered to send a limo so we could make both of our meetings and also be on time for the taping of the show. We accepted.

Theresa and I had a memorable session with Ted Koppel. Guests that evening included Cardinal John Krol of Philadelphia, Father Theodore Hesburgh of Notre Dame University, sociologist Father Andrew Greeley, Theresa, and me. The discussion was on priestly celibacy in the light of the film *The Thornbirds*. This was prior to the uncovering of the sexual abuse scandals in the church. The established clergy on the program all gave their allegiance to celibacy.

But the clerics seemed to miss the point of the discussion. The issue is not simply pro or con on celibacy. The issue is the counterproductive nature of the law of celibacy. Celibacy is fine. The law of celibacy is not fine. Theresa had the last word on *Nightline*. She told the clergy that it was a pity to waste so much time on institutional nonsense while bloody interventions were taking place in El Salvador, Nicaragua, and Guatemala, as nuclear madness and a starving world await our action. With that, Ted Koppel quipped, "We can all agree on that," and the program was over.

Working with commercial media was becoming even more disappointing. When Wally George called and asked me to appear on his talk show *Hot Seat*, I thought it was just another TV program. I got the call in the wake of Reagan's attack on Grenada in 1983. Once again, fact demolishes fiction. This Grenada War was certainly one of the most idiotic performances in the history of warfare. Media was on the job with a striking slogan, "We got there just in time." It was a phrase out of the radio serials of the 1930s. I have often wondered: Just in time for what? Rather than deal with the mental problems of our leadership, our military destroyed a mental hospital in Grenada and, killing hope, put an end to their New Jewel Movement.

On the day of the Wally George Show, I was ready to talk about the Grenada attack. Yet, standing in the wings, I heard Wally begin his diatribe against the guest that preceded me, a Chicano lawyer. The insults and racist comments did not stop. By the time I was to go on, I was angry at the way this Wally George had treated the attorney guest. There were two microphones in front of me: one directed toward the audience and one directed at Wally. As he began to play games with my name I simply looked at the young audience and said, "I hope you are not going to go off to Grenada and die as the enemy in a place where you are not wanted." Wally was immediately in a state of rage. He got up out of his chair, walked behind me and began to give me an advanced shoulder shake. It was assault and battery. For a mega-second I considered punching him out but instantly rejected the flash as an inappropriate response. I saw his unoccupied desk, thought of the money changers in the Temple, walked up to the desk and successfully upended it. I walked off the stage with Wally's security guards escorting me to my car. Wally used the tape of this episode hundreds of times. Actually, this was the birth of combat TV. Unfortunately the incident led to a brief national hookup for The Wally George Show.

"You won't believe what happened," I announced to Theresa and the children as I returned to our home on Beethoven Street. By the time I could explain the altercation, we were seeing it on the evening news. It became a national news story.

Wally called me the next day to say what a great act we had together and that we should do this kind of thing all over the country. I told him he was a charlatan and a liar and that I would not work with him under any conditions. Many people said that I should sue Wally. But if I sued everyone every time there was an issue, I would have time for nothing else. The theme of "turning the tables" is a great metaphor for the moral revolution we envision.

Chapter 18

Beginning of the International March for Peace in Central America

A Norwegian doctor made an appointment to speak to me at the Office of the Americas. What followed was my life's greatest challenge. "We are preparing a march through Central America. There will be some thirty countries involved and about 400 people. We have checked out the US solidarity movement and have reached the consensus that you are the person to lead the US contingent." I was not surprised. It was a call; something a renegade priest should understand. While I was very honored, I was also troubled at the prospect of a march beginning in Panama City and ending in Mexico City. All of the international experts said such a march was impossible. Three of the countries they planned to march through were at war. The others were in a state of turbulence. Nobel Peace Prize Winner Adolfo Perez Esquivel opposed it as impossible. I agreed to meet with all of the proposed leadership of the march in Vienna, Austria for a final decision. Guillermo Ungo, leader of the FDR (*Frente Democrático Revolucionario*) Democratic Revolutionary Front of El Salvador was in Vienna at the same time. His opinion: "I don't think you will get out of Panama." Having listened carefully to all of the naysayers, we decided to go for it. I considered myself called upon to find one hundred US citizens who would march through seven countries from Panama to Mexico demanding peace and justice in Central America.

I can hear the doves singing or mourning at each other every sunrise. These doves speak to me of continuing the struggle, go on . . . go ahead . . . don't be afraid, *adelante*! Rather than the singing of birds, our office and home phones were receiving regular death threats, generally directed at me. Our dear friend Joan Christie had a departure party for all of the Southern California marchers. As president of the Office of the Americas' board of directors, she and the board had generously approved my departure to lead the US contingent of the International March for Peace in Central America. It was a joyful and sad party, kind of like the singing of the doves. My children were there.

The night before our departure Theresa was crying, and so was I. It was an impossible project. We both knew that my life would be at risk. I

94

knew that Theresa would be in a more difficult position back home, in anticipation each day of what was to come. She has frequently borne much of the burden of my ventures. Theresa was very much immersed in the march back home and ultimately anchored the march from our office in Santa Monica. The Office of the Americas not only became the chief US contact-point for the march, but also the main clearinghouse for *all* of the participating countries. Under Theresa's direction, an endless flurry of collect calls, information to or from parents, friends, and lovers, was all handled by the staff and volunteers at the OOA. Theresa also made contacts with US Congress and garnered letters of approval from senators to be used in front of hostile questioners. All of this was only a portion of the burden that fell on Theresa's shoulders.

Despite both of our concerns, I simply had to do it. Over one hundred US citizens had agreed to go with us. We were by far the largest contingent in the March. Everyone had accepted the danger and the conditions. We had screened each and every applicant, simply looking for goodwill and an understanding of the dangers they would confront. This was one of the few times in my life when I felt that an entire project was on my shoulders. I generally do not feel indispensable. In this case, I was certain the march would not happen if I were not on the ground with it.

We hoped our presence would not be as negative as those who came before us. Columbus sailed the coast of Panama and called it Veragua. Here Balboa "discovered" the Pacific Ocean in 1513, and here Pizarro used the isthmus to transport his Peruvian plunder to Spain. By 1572, Francis Drake was attacking the mule trains of treasure as they crossed the narrow link from Pacific to the Atlantic. William Parker and Henry Morgan followed the example of Drake and burned Panama City to the ground in 1671. Everyone wanted the isthmus. What the Spanish lost and what the British plundered was formed into a tiny nation by the sculptor Theodore Roosevelt. Since its creation in 1903, Panama has survived the presence of fourteen US military bases and a Canal Zone. The country does not claim to be part of Central America. Nor is it thought of as part of South America, although it was formerly part of Colombia.

And now it was our turn. While Panamanians did not seem afraid of us, a carefully contrived press of dubious origin made our march appear to be a combination of the conquistadores and the barbarians.

The International March for Peace in Central America had begun. Early in December of 1985; internationalists began to assemble in Panama City at a humble suburban retreat, Centro Gomez y Gomez. We had a roof to protect us from the heavy tropical storms, but, as is common in the tropics, there were no walls. The Danes came, The Swedes, the Norwegians, the Germans, the Finns, the Australians, the

Dutch, the Japanese. There was Iceland, and Canada, France, Mexico, Argentina, Guatemala, England, New Zealand, Scotland, Ecuador, Belgium, Costa Rica, El Salvador, Nicaragua, Honduras, Panama, and the largest delegation of all, the United States of America with over one hundred members. There was something Pentecostal about the spirit, the languages, the singing, and the sports as representatives of these nations gathered, communicated, and celebrated the beginning of a historic march. This had never been done before.

The International March for Peace in Central America approaching the Honduran border from El Espino in Nicaragua, January, 1986.

With so many people and nations represented, it was crucial to balance democracy with the need for leadership. Our approach was to design an egalitarian command structure. The leadership of the march, the directorate, was comprised of seven individuals who all shared a leadership role. The directorate's role was to deliberate on issues and projects for the entire march. The directorate included myself; Torrill Eide, an activist and schoolteacher from Norway; Attorney Peter Holding from Australia; Daniel Moore, who led the Mexican delegation; Ron Ridenour, a Los Angeles native living in Denmark who coordinated the Danish delegation; and two other directorate members whose names I cannot recall. There were also representatives from each of the national groups who communicated with the directorate and an assembly of the national groups. Meetings were called by nation or by plenary session. As the march progressed, plenary sessions became the rule. Torrill Eide and I were selected to be the diplomats of the seven-member directorate and co-coordinators of the march as a whole. Torrill was brilliant, balanced, and fearless. While the six of us were almost always in sync, the seventh was so far out in left field that we called for a vote requesting his removal. We lost. In general, I believe we spent too much time in deliberations, but that was certainly better than regressing into a military model. Ultimately, we had jelled into one entity.

As a member of the directorate of the march, I was preoccupied about how we were going to keep ourselves together for the six weeks ahead. Our logistical problems were endless. For months we had planned on how we might maintain 300 to 450 people in the tropics (the numbers varied because people came and went from the ranks). The hygienic Norwegians wanted to bring portable toilets but this proved impractical. We had not answered all of our own questions. But we were determined to begin. While the marchers had little knowledge of Central America, they did have a great desire for world peace. These were not passively obedient people. There was a pronounced individualism, almost adventurism, an eagerness to try anything in the name of peace.

We gathered outside of the National Lottery Building in Panama City for the official beginning of the march in the late afternoon of December 10, 1985. I had never felt so essential and so vulnerable. Why this game of chance? Was our hope of creating peace and justice in Central America the same as the false hopes of poor people who intend to win the lottery?

Graham Greene was the most prominent figure at our departure-day ceremony on that sultry evening. He did not like to speak in public so he gave his words to a reader as he stood anonymously in the small crowd of well-wishers. After this reader read the welcoming statement by novelist Graham Greene, Panama's senior spokesman and former president, Jorge Illueca, gave the opening address. Illueca reminded the audience that today was the 37th anniversary of the Universal Declaration of Human Rights and that, as a nation involved in the Contadora Process, Panama sought a solution to the Central American conflict without war. Illueca spoke of the heroic sacrifices of the marchers: "This is a struggle not of soldiers with arms but of messengers of peace. As the dove which brought good news to Noah, you marchers are bringing an olive branch to the convulsed isthmus of Central America in order to promote worldwide peace." The statesman ended his presentation strongly supporting the non-aligned movement.

We were welcome in Panama in spite of the red-baiting of the Panamanian press and paid ads placing slogans foreign to our march under our logo; in other words sabotage. Aggressive, rhetorical, dogmatic, pseudo-revolutionary phrases were listed below our peace dove. Such posters were on every lamppost in Panama City. And who might do such a thing? The same elements that burned old glory at our peace marches in the US. The CIA had been hard at work to discredit our march. The same entity that was in command and control of all areas of the Central American war was not about to tolerate an international bid for peace. At a very well-attended press conference, I asked a reporter from *Newsweek* to remind the CIA of the peril such propaganda could cause us.

Panamanians, however, did not seem afraid of us. A few of them joined our ranks. Our first actual march was in commemoration of the raising of the Panamanian flag over the Canal Zone in 1964, when twenty-four Panamanian high school students were killed by US forces. This act led to the breaking of relations between Panama and the United States by President Chiari. We retraced the steps of the students. We were an undisciplined unit. Hence we decided to dedicate a good bit of the following day to discipline and preparation for our march on Fort Howard.

We gathered at the tomb of General Omar Torrijos, which is located in Balboa within the Canal Zone. It was time for speeches by us and the Panamanians. The hero's father was there, and his sister. Our homage was genuine, but some of our marchers had to take cover from the tropical sun. The critical need for hats and canteens was demonstrated at this event. Monitors, who were represented by each nation and whose job was to make sure everything was in order, were trained, and we became a more serious marching group.

We stood at the Miraflores Locks of the Panama Canal and sang peace songs to the passengers of various ships, including the famous Love Boat as these vessels sank low enough to pass on into the waters of the Pacific.

We had expected Jesse Jackson to join us in Panama City. He phoned that afternoon to let us know that he could not participate in the march. While I was disappointed with this news, his words struck me with unprecedented power. This was his message, which I recall almost verbatim from my memory:

> The Rainbow Coalition supports the International March for Peace in Central America. It is as Gandhi's March to the Sea and King's March to Washington, to Montgomery, and to Selma. People who are willing to put their lives on the line are bringing light to Central America by this March."

> This is a time of genocide in Central America. This is a time of military oppression. The US government should meet with President Ortega. It would be mutually beneficial. This is not the same as Somoza's period

of tyranny. We must respect the sovereignty of Nicaragua and end our sanctions. We must create relations which will make us all proud. We must support the Contadora process, not by ignoring the Contra invasion of Nicaragua, by acknowledging it and stopping it.

Many are dying on bloody battlefields; others are choked off by the International Monetary Fund and bear the burden of years of economic domination.

I am happy that Reagan and Gorbachev met in Geneva, but they made no accord on human rights. This is not a matter of peace between East and West. This is a matter of peace with justice in Central America.

I want to express my support for the gallant men and women marching in Central America. Political colonizers have been conquered; Economic colonizers have not been conquered. We must remove the debt. People want peace as opposed to quietness.

My prayers are with you, and know that peace is the presence of justice, health care, housing, and job training. The golden rule is the measure of foreign policy, and there is no way we can have peace without justice. We must light candles in the night and in the day. We must look for honest people.

This march will have an impact on the United States. We cannot turn the light out on Central America.

I will be with you soon, brother, and remember,

The Lord is our Shepherd, we shall lack nothing. Though we should walk through the valley of the shadow of death. We shall fear no evil.

The words of the 23rd Psalm had never been more meaningful to me than on that torrid day in Panama when Jesse called.

Our march at the Southern Command was disciplined and effective. Norwegian leader Torrill Eide, and I went ahead to make sure we were at the proper entrance of Fort Howard, and we made a few wrong turns before we were ready to give the signal to marchers waiting on the highway. Our tactic was to tell the military exactly what was about to happen so they would not panic or overreact.

People from twenty-five countries marched up the hill to the entrance of Fort Howard to be met by the commanding officer, a Panamanian. While the officer would not permit the passage of the march through the base, he did cooperate fully with our alternate plan. Each and every one of the three hundred marchers would request permission to enter the base, and he would subsequently deny permission individually. This was done in the spirit of the Posadas, the Christmas custom in Latin America of reenacting the search of Joseph and Mary for a place to stay. Had the officer not been a Latin American, this cultural act would have been impossible. The Panamanian commander caught the symbolism instantly and entered into it. Group after national group arrived singing and waving the flags of their countries. Fort Howard was selected because it is the center for the forces of state terror in Central America. From here bombs are delivered to El Salvador for the indiscriminate bombing of the Salvadoran people. From here, the training of Contra mercenaries takes place.

Standing behind the Panamanian commanding officer were two US Air Force officers who were not anxious to talk until someone brought up the subject of retirement in Panama. They were for it. The entire demonstration took about three hours. We left Fort Howard knowing that our position in history had been established. Our march was the first demonstration of US citizens and internationalists at the Southern Command in Panama. Our efforts would have been a success even if we had gone no further.

I made phone calls to key people in Costa Rica, the next nation up the Pan American Highway. There was trouble. Word was that it may not be possible to enter the country. Our visas had been cut back to twelve hours. The march may reach a dead end at the northern border of Panama in the state of Chiriqui. I called US Ambassador Lewis Tambs in Costa Rica, and he assured me he would seek cooperation from the Costa Rican government for an extension of our visas. He said, however, as it stood now, we would be undocumented aliens in Costa Rica after twelve hours. We certainly have many friends in the US who share that status back in the USA.

Theresa and the staff at the Office of the Americas were calling friends in Congress and at the State Department asking their support for our safe passage.

Later the same day, Ambassador Tambs assured Senator Cranston's office that a political officer of the US Embassy would be at the border to observe the International March for Peace in Central America. We were leaving Panama with warm feelings for and from the Panamanian people and the Panamanian support committees that made the march possible. Some of these people were blown away by US bombs in George Bush's Christmas Massacre of 1989.

To deal with the impasse at the Costa Rican border, Torrill Eide, Daniel Moore, and I flew from Panama City to San Jose, Costa Rica, to seek governmental permission and to remove any fears the government might have of our presence. As we departed by air, the march continued by land toward the Costa Rican border. Neither we nor the rest of the marchers expected that they would be detained for some forty-eight hours at that border.

When our delegation of three arrived at San Jose, President Monge had already denounced the march as an action of the extreme left. Terror was in the faces of the Costa Rican preparation committee when we knocked at La Casa de Amigos at 3:00 AM. They knew we had arrived at the airport at 9:00 PM and could not understand why it took us six hours to get from the airport to the city. Well, it required two hours to get through customs.

When we realized some people were looking for us, we avoided them because they looked suspicious. We did not recognize anyone. We finally acknowledged our reception group after we had studied them carefully. They cordially understood our apprehension. Unfortunately, their vehicle became dysfunctional as we headed for San Jose. All of this was responsible for our 3:00 AM arrival at La Casa de Amigos. The folks at the Casa thought we had been arrested or kidnapped.

Word from the border informed us that the march was being threatened by Costa Rica Libre. Until this moment, I did not know there was such an organization. It was described as a group of Contra mercenaries, Cuban exiles, and right-wing Costa Ricans with a fascist orientation. I called the minister of security and was greeted with a flood of negativity. The march could not go to the university because his ministry does not have jurisdiction over the university. We could not have any public meetings. We must be out of the country in twelve hours. We may not visit anything or anyone. We are in transit, and we must keep going. Those who are on the border now may not come to San Jose. If there is a confrontation of any kind, the march will be expelled by police escort directly to the Nicaraguan border. I was speaking to Benjamin Pisa. This grim minister of security insisted that groups of Costa Rica Libre were waiting to attack us. He said that sixty to eighty taxis representing the movement were preparing to block the Pan American Highway.

This was my first of various phone calls to Pisa. I wanted to maintain contact with him under any circumstance. For some reason I found him accessible. On a Sunday morning I called to ask, "May I come by your home and talk to you personally?" He agreed. Benjamin Pisa was the godfather. Our local committee informed me that Pisa was not only Minister of Security, but founder of Costa Rica Libre. Sitting in his palatial home, he said, "I don't think I can protect you." I had heard the same words almost twenty years before in Guatemala. At that time it was from the US Ambassador. The phrase is a diplomatic threat. I asked him if he would please allow our march to come to San Jose for humanitarian reasons. By now they had been held up at the border for almost forty-eight hours with little food and less water. They had no shelter. Costa Rica Libre was there to taunt them. It was ironic; the horn of one cab was playing the Nicaraguan revolutionary song, "No Pasaran" (They Shall Not Pass). In this case, the words applied to our march.

At last, Pisa agreed to let the group come into San Jose if they remained under virtual house arrest at the youth hostel where the three of us were staying across from Colonel Sanders Kentucky Fried Chicken.

Chapter 19

The Long March
through Central America

The marchers were finally released from their detainment at the Panama-Costa Rica border. Hundreds of Costa Ricans in solidarity with the march were waiting as the buses arrived at the hostel in San Jose. It was a welcoming scene of jubilation. Benjamin Pisa was outraged at this demonstration of support. From the moment the march arrived at the Costa Rican border, he repeatedly stated that if there was a demonstration of any kind, we would be expelled under police escort to the Nicaraguan border. I was pleased that Costa Rican security forces stood guard in front of the youth hostel because the pro-Contra opposition was there en masse screaming insults at the marchers as they descended from the buses. Apprehension took over, however; as the buses continued to arrive, the Costa Rican security began to fade away. In their place, the threatening members of Costa Rica Libre multiplied.

The attack began. Costa Rica Libre Contras threw grenades of CS gas at us. The canisters were imprinted "Made in USA." This is not old-fashioned tear gas, it is tear gas on steroids, much more powerful and dangerous.[2] The US is not permitted to use CS gas in international warfare, but has frequently used it domestically. The same CS gas was used as crowd-control in the Poor People's March of 1968 and to attack the Branch Davidians at Waco in 1993. The gas sickened marchers as they attempted to enter the youth hostel. I caught a whiff of it and knew it was not standard. A deadly barrage of bricks and stones followed. We were under attack for about two hours, and we were wall-to-wall people. The missiles were hitting us. Inside, tables were placed in front of windows. The youth hostel was in shambles. The Red Cross arrived to take away some of the injured. When is this going to stop? Several members of the march directorate called the embassies representing the marchers, asking for protection. I awakened a sleepy Marine at the US embassy at about two in the

---

2 CS gas stands for 2-chlorobenzalmalononitrile. It is a white solid powder usually mixed with a dispersal agent, like methylene chloride, which carries the particles through the air.

morning. He said he would "do what he could," which basically meant that we were on our own.

At approximately 2:30 AM, Benjamin Pisa appeared in the street in front of the hostel. I went out to meet him. He had arrived just as we were expecting the attackers to invade our lodging. Pisa waved off the bloody organization he had founded, Costa Rica Libre.[3] He then entered the hostel and ordered us to be out of San Jose by seven in the morning. Pisa's threat: "If you do not leave here, I am turning you over to Costa Rica Libre." The interplay between Security Minister Pisa and the extra-governmental organization, Costa Rica Libre, helped our marchers to understand the relationship between the security forces and death squads in El Salvador and Guatemala.

The marchers were exhausted. Some were emotionally upset and others were injured. I was very worried about the safety of everyone, myself included. The directorate of the march determined not to awaken the group for a 7:00 AM departure. It was now close to 3:00 AM. I decided to simply let them sleep, which they did. The following morning we were not ready at seven. We were not ready at eight. By nine, Benjamin Pisa appeared and said, "If you are not out of here by noon, I will remove all of my security people." He was ready to carry out his threat to unleash his dogs of war.

The marchers were so combative, especially the young ones, that they did not care. They were ready to confront Costa Rica Libre once again. I delivered a harangue on how our stubbornness could lead to personal harm for our Costa Rican supporters and that it was not fair to do what we wanted against the wishes of our hosts. It would have been a one-sided bloody confrontation between armed, violent fanatics and unarmed pacifists. I could not help but think of the early Christians being fed to the lions. Initially, the Costa Rican preparation committee said they would cooperate with anything we wanted. But finally and prudently, they said, "Look, we think it is best for you and for us if you are out of here by noon." In spite of this recommendation, some marchers still wanted to vote on whether or not we should leave.[4]

Prior to our summary expulsion from Costa Rica, there were two significant meetings unobserved by the Costa Rican authorities. The

---

3 The revulsion of Costa Ricans to the brutal attacks on us may have led voters away from the favored and pro-Reagan Angel Miguel Calderon and contributed to the election of Oscar Arias, who was to win the Nobel Peace Prize for his role in ending the Contra War.

4 The documentary film *Viva La Paz*, produced and directed by Kelly Holland, and winner of a Gold Medal at the Houston Film Festival, saves many of these scenes for posterity. Kelly was one of the marchers and expended heroic efforts to make this film.

first was with Jose Figueres, former president and senior statesperson of Costa Rica. He invited all the marchers to his hilltop home and assured us that such a meeting could not be considered public because his home was private. Figueres was a significant figure. He abolished the Costa Rican military in 1948, giving an example that every Central American president should follow. Figueres was ashamed of the growth of the neo-fascist Costa Rica Libre organization.

Our second unobserved meeting was with Archbishop Arieta of San Jose, Costa Rica. After attending Mass at the cathedral, I approached the archbishop in the sacristy. He recognized me instantly and said in English, "Father Bonpane, we understand your program." I asked him if he would support the march and he began a ten-minute ethereal commentary on how he could not support the march and how the Church was for peace. To my surprise, the prelate concluded his discourse saying, "Yes, you can celebrate Mass in this Archdiocese for your peace march . . . but not in my cathedral." We had planned to celebrate such a Mass in the open air, but the Ministry of Security had other plans.

Under pressure to leave, we finally agreed to depart by noon. Yet, some wanted to force the Costa Rican security forces to drag them onto the buses. I explained to them that we were not in a US policing situation and that it would be hard for the security forces to drag anyone while trying to balance an M-16 at the ready. We left San Jose under heavy security, Costa Rica Libre screaming obscenities and stoning our buses as we faded into the countryside.

Some weeks after the attack in San Jose, we were pleased to read in the Spanish press reports that the Costa Rican Association of Jurists had demanded President Monge dissolve Costa Rica Libre precisely because of its attacks on the International March for Peace in Central America. Government officials were living in terror of this organization. Costa Rica Libre was directly linked to the Contra mercenaries and, as such, opened up opportunities for unemployed murderers, rapists, and thieves.

The US media censored this historic march into oblivion. Even though journalists from major US television, radio, and print media, including CNN, PBS, CBS, UPI, AP, were in evidence during the entire march, little or nothing was aired in the US. Why? Because of the uncritical support of US foreign policy by major media. Certainly the press accepts an opinion piece here or there to demonstrate its openness. But hard-news reporting generally implies that the US side is the right side. No major media outlet was ready to say that the US is practicing terrorism in Central America. The hard fact is that the terror and death caused by US policy in Central America in the 1980s far exceeds the suffering experienced during the civil wars that split Yugoslavia in the 1990s.

Media coverage in Central America, Mexico, and South America, on the other hand, was intense. The International March for Peace in Central America was a major item in the Central American press from December 10th through January 22nd. Reports were filed from each of the seven countries on our route. Press conferences were held in Panama, Costa Rica, Nicaragua, Honduras, El Salvador, Guatemala, and Mexico. Attendance was excellent. We even received positive press in Honduras. The basic theme in the Central American media was to state the error of their nations in banning such a march.

The march was now a reality. We had actually traversed the jungles of Panama and the Mountains of Costa Rica. Even though every venture of this kind for me begins with a certain depression and questioning, "Why am I doing this? Wouldn't it be easier to stay home?" We were now an organic whole. Violent resistance had molded us into an organic unit. Making decisions together and making mistakes together, I and the other marchers hoped to become even more united. But this was not a realistic hope. If only five people were walking together and planning to have a picnic, they might have disagreements about how to do it. I could not expect that over three hundred people could make decisions while traversing seven countries without severe disagreements. We practiced the democracy of listening to everyone, hearing them out, and attempting to come to collective decisions, in most cases with consensus.

There was little complaining about the hardships of the journey. Within a few days, people became accustomed to sleeping wherever they could, be it in the open or in union facilities or schools. I had never done much camping even as a child. It was a good feeling to know that we pampered gringos could live under the Central American sky for an extended period of time. Most of the time sleeping was on the ground. I was always so exhausted I had no trouble sleeping, and sleeping on the ground seemed to actually help my creaky back. Insects were a great problem. There were many bites. I had a strange bump on my forehead—some sort of parasite.

Water is a problem in Central America. It is not so much the quantity but rather the frequently dubious quality. There were the usual gastrointestinal diseases. Food at best was simple and frequently sparse. I suffered only from the loss of some good-riddance weight. Our discussions and differences, however, were fortunately on matters of tactics and strategy rather than on the Spartan living conditions.

We were not in a posture of military discipline, and it probably would have been easier if we had been. Military discipline is what we were trying to avoid. Only in extreme situations was our directorate expected to "give orders" without time for discussion.

The spirit of the march was one of achievement and optimism. Even though we often asked ourselves, "If things are so difficult in peaceful Costa Rica, what will be our reception in El Salvador, Honduras, and Guatemala?" Such apprehensions did not last long.

Yet, a sudden current of concern jolted our march as we neared the northern border of Costa Rica under heavily armed escort. Because we were prisoners, the Costa Ricans could have turned us over to the ARDE Contras (Eden Pastora's group) since there was no direct contact with the Sandinista Nicaraguan government at the Costa Rican border station. After previous firefights between the two customs gates, the Nicaraguans had moved their station some five kilometers back into their own territory, leaving a swath of no-person's-land which was highly contaminated with mercenary killers. It was not paranoia to speculate that the Contras would be waiting in this sinister location.

But the Nicaraguans were not about to leave us stranded in such a vulnerable spot. They personally came through the no-person's-land to meet us near the Costa Rican customs gate. This was a risk for the Sandinistas, but they were accustomed to taking risks for their friends. I was extremely relieved and honored by their reception. Our Costa Rican committee had informed Managua of our expulsion from Costa Rica, so the premature arrival was not a surprise to the Nicaraguans. Father Ernesto Cardenal, the Minister of Culture, had been waiting for us much of the day. I was happy to see him and to have some time to talk about developments in Nicaragua.

We passed through this war-scorched area without incident. It was a devastated and dismal region. When we arrived at the Nicaraguan customs gate, we were admitted as a group, with no complications or paper shuffling. The entire community was waiting for us a few kilometers up the road. We were recipients of gifts, including a well-preserved deer head and FSLN neckerchiefs. I exchanged greetings with town elders, Children and Mothers of Heroes and Martyrs. This latter organization is established in every community of Nicaragua as living witnesses to the terror inflicted on Nicaragua by the Contras.

Much of our time in Nicaragua was spent in areas with a Contra presence. There was a strategic value to our presence. The Contras were less apt to attack while observed by such a large group of international witnesses. We were spontaneously received in village after village. People who had been living with terror welcomed non-threatening guests. In Palacaguina, we began singing, "*Cristo ya Nació in Palacaguina*" ("Christ was now Born in Palacaguina"). The townspeople continued as a choir.

President Daniel Ortega and most of his cabinet met with the entire march in a *Cara al Pueblo* (Face the People: a direct dialogue between government and the community) session just outside of Managua. He was awe-struck by how many countries we represented. He remarked "You are citizens of the world. You are brothers and sisters of the citizens of Central America." He responded directly to the questions of the local community and the marchers late into the night. There were both silly and serious questions. We asked about the ecology of Nicaragua, the United Nations, and the United States' role in Nicaragua. Some marchers asked questions to sense out the humanity of the government. They wanted to know that Nicaragua was not being run in Soviet style. Was there adequate health care and education? President Ortega answered them all. He spoke to us about the new health care structures that had been built, the development of literacy programs, and the increased quality of education. All this was verified by UN data which was in sync with Nicaragua's assessment of its health care and education programs.

Throughout Nicaragua, we received nothing but good will and welcome. It was a nation at peace. Unfortunately, its peaceful and nonviolent people were being attacked from the outside, and they responded as peaceful and non-violent people by defending their families and their country.

Nicaraguan students welcomed us at the coffee co-op known as El Chaguiton, comprised of both Nicaraguan and US volunteers.[5] The Contra threat here was such that we could go no more than one kilometer from camp during the day and no more than fifty meters at night (that was the distance to the outhouses). Contra devastation was everywhere. These imposed limits were taken seriously by all but the Spanish delegation. They wandered off into the mountains and were not expected to return. Inexplicably, they came back unharmed.

Word was coming from many sources that we were unwelcome in Honduras. This was a pall hanging over our march within this island of goodwill called Nicaragua. Honduras is the only country to the north with a Nicaraguan border. El Salvador has no border with Nicaragua (a fact that Washington should have understood, but somehow did not). I began to fear that Nicaragua would be the northern terminus of our odyssey.

We made our way up the Pan-American Highway to the border town of El Espino in the Nicaraguan province of Madriz. We were greeted with sheer hostility by the Cobras, an elite group of Honduran troops who wore gas masks and had M-16s at the ready, to prevent our nonviolent

---

5 For further information on Nicaraguan co-ops see Laura Enriquez, *Agrarian Reform and Class Consciousness in Nicaragua*. Gainesville, Fl.: University Press of Florida (1997) and *Harvesting Change: Labor and Agrarian Reform in Nicaragua, 1979–1990*. Chapel Hill: University of North Carolina Press (1991).

attempt to cross the border. The town had been completely destroyed. There was not a living soul in El Espino. We made our stand here for seven days in an attempt to enter Honduras by land. Ironically, behind the company of Cobras was a sign, *"Bienvenido a Honduras"* (Welcome to Honduras).

We stood at the Nicaragua-Honduras border. We sang, we chanted, we talked to the troops, but they would not respond to us. Using a tactic similar to the Fort Howard demonstration in Panama, we began individually going to the very line of the border. Each person would state their name and country and point to their visa for Honduras. The Honduran soldiers were impassive. Their gas masks and bayonets on their rifles threatening.

Our overnight encampment was some several kilometers back from this border crossing. As in the case of the Costa Rican border, it was necessary for Nicaragua to move its gate back from the actual Honduran border to avoid firefights with the Hondurans. The area where we spent our days was a no-person's-land of Contra activity. We were staying in an abandoned school near El Espino, a ghost town. One morning, as we returned from our border confrontation with the Honduran military, many of the marchers sat on the highway to rest. I was not among them. They were stung simultaneously by an intolerable itch. In a cynical trick, the Honduran military had crossed into Nicaragua at night and covered the highway with Pica Pica, a powder from a poison plant. The *Los Angeles Times* covered this act of sabotage on the front page.

I received a gesture from a man dressed in white on the Honduran side. I crossed into Honduras and asked if our group could enter. He said, "No, you will never enter Honduras." He asked me if I was a priest, and I answered in the affirmative. He said that priests should be in their churches and should not be involved in political activities. He asked me if I had seen arms in Nicaragua. I told him that I was not a military man and was not able to identify what kind of arms they had. He told me that Nicaragua had only shown us what they wanted us to see. He also said that Nicaragua had to disappear. He then asked to see my passport and read it through page by page. He said, "You have been in Nicaragua too many times. You must know more than you are saying. I do not believe that you do not know more about Nicaragua. You say you have seen schools. You say you have seen churches. I want to know what else you have seen." His tone was ever more threatening. He repeated, "You will not pass." I asked if we could simply be given freedom of transit to El Salvador or to Guatemala. He said, "No, Honduras is a country of peace. We do not need a Peace March in Honduras. We are peaceful people."

I told this man, who would not identify himself but who was obviously in charge, that I had recently visited with Edgardo Paz Barnica, the foreign minister of Honduras. I was referring to a quick trip made by me and two other marchers from Managua to Tegucigalpa to visit with the Honduran Peace March preparation committee. Dr. Juan Almandarez, a former rector of the University of Honduras met us at the airport. He took us to a union hall to meet members of the university community and union members. Women were demonstrating in the plaza of the Cathedral, demanding that our march be admitted to Honduras. In spite of the fact that it was Christmas Eve, we were welcome at the home of the foreign minister, Paz Barnica. He assured us that we could enter the country legally as long as we had visas. We all had visas. But when I told the man in the white suit that Paz Barnica was enthusiastic about our visit to Honduras, he was not impressed. He viewed government officials with contempt. This immaculate vision in white had so much authority that dust from the road feared clinging to him. The only power greater than the Honduran military was the US military in Honduras.

The approval of our march by the Foreign Minister was obviously futile. The lines of governmental authority were anything but clear in Honduras. Without question, the Honduran military had the last word. We began to understand that what we could not accomplish by land, we might achieve by air. A strategy developed of filtering our people into such countries in small groups and by air.

It was time to plan our arrival in the three countries where we were clearly unwelcome, Honduras, El Salvador, and Guatemala. After seven exhausting days on the Honduran border, with little food or water, we were ready to retreat to Managua to plan the next moves.

We rented one room at the Intercontinental Hotel to serve as a communications center. From there, we began to distribute marchers throughout the three countries. The plan was simple enough. A few would go by air to Tegucigalpa in Honduras, report back by phone and give us approval or disapproval regarding the sending of subsequent groups. The Office of the Americas back in Los Angeles had the difficult task of arranging flights and getting tickets for everybody to Tegucigalpa. I visited embassies and made several phone calls. I went to the Honduran embassy in Managua. The plan worked, and our Honduras team was able to communicate with Miskito Indigenous, who were press-ganged into serving as Contras. While sending marchers into Honduras, we simultaneously began to send small groups into El Salvador, once again awaiting their report upon arrival, and then sending more groups.

In Honduras, the bitter opposition of the Honduran people to the occupation of the US military was clear. People on the street were quick to express their antipathy for the denationalization of their country. Honduran misery was not alleviated by hundreds of millions of US dollars expended for military purposes. To this day, literacy has not improved, infant mortality has not decreased, the job situation is not better than it was. Honduras remains a conquered, occupied country with a high level of resentment. It is very difficult to find any military coup in Latin America without the imprint of the US on it. The 2009 overthrow of democratically elected President Manuel Zelaya was no exception to the rule.

Arriving in El Salvador, the marchers were inspired by the response of the Salvadoran preparation committees. There was a welcoming march of over one thousand Salvadorans, who declared themselves members of the International March for Peace in Central America. The Salvadorans used the same slogans and symbols as our march. This was the boldest gesture I had observed to date. They began marching from San Salvador to San Francisco Gotera, where they were physically stopped and ordered to return to the capital. There were interrogations by the military, and there were violent threats. Salvadoran Brigido Sanchez was arrested and imprisoned. The military commander put his arms around Brigido and stated sarcastically, "We will take care of you, Brigido."

The entire group of Salvadorans and internationals began a three-day vigil in the basement of the Cathedral of San Salvador. After this respite, the Salvadorans began to march west toward Santa Ana. This effort was also stopped by the Salvadoran military, and the group was once again ushered back to the capital.

The segment of the march that arrived in El Salvador reported an attack from a US warship. The FMLN forces were attacking the Salvadoran military battalion Cuscatlan in the area of Usulutan. The ship coming to the rescue of the Salvadoran military was described as similar to the destroyer Spruance, a type containing missiles that are nuclear-warhead capable. The US Department of Defense denied the presence of such a ship as well as the alleged attack.

Some of the Salvadoran segment of the march remained to find out exactly what happened to Brigido Sanchez, who had been detained by the military at the outset of the marchers' presence. He symbolized for them the many Salvadorans held without charges. They remained in touch with his case until documenting his release over a year later.

The Salvadorans were determined to march with or without us. We repeatedly asked them if we were jeopardizing their safety by marching with them. The consensus of their replies was that they were always in danger and that our presence would not hinder their safety. In each

111

country the greatest wisdom came from the local citizens, and the safety of our marchers was assured by listening to them.

I reflected back on the opinions of the experts we had consulted prior to the march. Nobel Prize-winning Perez Esquivel of Argentina was convinced the concept of a peace march in Central America was entirely too dangerous and would not succeed. Some said we would never get out of Panama. Others said we could in no way get beyond Nicaragua. Here we were, already present in Honduras and El Salvador. I was anticipating the greatest challenge of all. Guatemala: the ultimate police-state. To even mention peace in Guatemala was a subversive act.

Chapter 20

The Celebration

We attempted to charter a plane from Managua to Guatemala City. Charters, however, come under the jurisdiction of the Guatemalan military so that was not a good idea. As in Honduras and El Salvador, we flew group after group into Guatemala as tourists. Guatemala was preparing for the inauguration of President Vinicio Cerezo Arevalo. The march was to be unveiled as a unit on inauguration day, January 14, 1986. It worked. This was the right time for our presence. Guatemala tried to give the world an image of democracy. Our march carried an array of banners and international participants were joined by members of Mutual Support Group (GAM or Grupo de Apoyo Mutuo), the families of the disappeared. People merged into our ranks as the March passed through the capital city.

In the high country of Huehuetenango, the jubilant International March for Peace was joined by indigenous people as if the marchers were long awaited and expected. The Mayor of Quetzaltenango greeted the marchers in a strong statement of solidarity.

Almost two hundred marchers were now together in Guatemala. We did not think this would be possible in a nation with one of the world's worst human rights records. One of our segments was permitted to visit a "model village." These camps were structured in the same way as the strategic hamlets of Vietnam. People are thrown together from various linguistic backgrounds and are living in utter misery. The schools are non-functional, and terror is in the faces of many. Hundreds of thousands of indigenous men have been forced into Civil Patrols. Movement from place to place is by permission only.

I was concerned that after successfully traversing Guatemala, marchers might think they would be home-free in Mexico. While the entire group was still in Guatemala waiting to cross into Mexico, the Mexican preparation committees began militant revolutionary chants. I asked them to stop and at least give our people a chance to get on the Mexican side before they became too enthusiastic. The Guatemalan security apparatus could have clamped down at any moment.

As we poured across the border at Cuauhtémoc into the state of Chiapas, we were overwhelmingly embraced. Minority parties, such as the Trotskyists, Communist Party of Mexico, and the Partido de la Revolución Democrática (PRD), while supportive of our march, also tried to take advantage of us by surrounding us with their symbols and banners. We met with these parties and asked them to respect our autonomy as a march representing no partisan interest. We were worried they would deflect the goals of the Central American Peace March. We were there to support non-intervention, self-determination, human rights, and the Contadora peace process. Two representatives of one of the minority parties objected, asking, "Don't we have a right to use our banners as we wish?" My response was, "This is not a matter of rights, it is a matter of tactics among *compañeros*." Our conversation led to a full agreement and demonstrated for us the maturity of the Mexican political parties. They also accepted our intention not to focus on Mexico's many domestic problems. Mexico was not aiding the Contras. Our attention was on Washington, and we considered Mexico to be the key to the success of the Contadora peace process.

We proceeded to San Cristobal de las Casas to be received by the great Bishop Samuel Ruiz Garcia. He had taken the responsibility for some hundred thousand Guatemalan refugees in Chiapas. The Mexican government refused to give us permission to visit refugee camps. Such a refusal was ineffective. The refugees were everywhere. The march around this frigid, high-altitude colonial city was followed by a festive ecumenical celebration at the Cathedral.

The celebration helped the anti-religious Europeans have a deeper understanding of Liberation Theology. They had not previously seen Buddhist Monks receive Holy Communion. They had not heard marimbas in the sanctuary. They had not heard the commentary of people interpreting scriptures for a here and now. They had not heard a bishop break into tears during the first sentence of his sermon, saying, "The people of Latin America are oppressed and I'm sorry to say many of the oppressors call themselves Christians."

In Tuxtla-Gutierrez, the capital of Chiapas, hundreds of locals marched with us. They presented our directorate with *sarapes*. There were speeches of solidarity, peace, and justice from marchers and Mexican citizens. We were in friendly territory. Even the notorious Mexican Federal Police, now serving as escorts to the march, were not intrusive.

In Tehuantepec we were hosted by Bishop Arturo Lona Reyes. Habitually dressed in Levis and a T-shirt, with a tiny wooden cross around his neck, Lona lives for the rights of the oppressed indigenous people. A unique leader and spiritual brother of Bishop Samuel Ruiz

Garcia, the threats and attacks on Lona had been so pervasive that he generally had to sleep in a different location every night.

The march arrived in Puebla, the city that defeated the forces of France on May 5, 1862 (Cinco de Mayo). My last visit to Puebla was in 1979, when the Pope arrived for the meeting of Latin American Bishops. It was here in Puebla that Pope John Paul II got an earful on Liberation Theology. Archbishop Oscar Arnulfo Romero was at that meeting of Latin American Bishops, as was Father Ernesto Cardenal. The Puebla Conference ended with a sound condemnation of unrestrained capitalism and no condemnation of Liberation Theology. Theresa and our children, Colleen and Blase Martin, were also at that historic gathering. While I had missed them throughout the march, it was here in Puebla that I was growing homesick. During these moments, I often thought of those in the military who are away from home. I was voluntarily gone for seven weeks. But military people are often away from their families against their will for very lengthy periods.

It was now January of 1986. As thousands of local citizens came out to walk with us in Puebla, I began to sense a celebratory mood in our odyssey.

After delays, opposition, attacks, injuries, insects, hunger, thirst, anxiety, disagreements of all types, and sleepless nights, we arrived in Mexico City exactly according to plan. We were definitely in a distinctly new political situation. The Mexican political parties, including the all-powerful Institutional Revolutionary Party (PRI or *Partido Revolucionario Institucional*) had endorsed our march.

We were unprepared for what was to greet us in Mexico City. Some fifty thousand people were gathered as we approached the Juarez monument. They were there in support of the International March for Peace in Central America. It was the largest gathering that country had seen in five years. They marched with us to Chapultepec Park and to the Monument of Niños Heroes. Members of the Legislature of Mexico marched with us.

Archbishop Mendez Arceo, former Archbishop of Cuernavaca and now revolutionary bishop to the world, presided over the formal conclusion of the march in Mexico City. I had met him several times at many areas of conflict in Central America over the two past decades. *Would to God* that the Mexican Bishops Samuel Ruiz, Arturo Lona and Sergio Mendez Arceo were the rule in their land. They are, in fact, rare exceptions.

The Mexican press was positive about the impact of the march. I was overwhelmed that our goal had been achieved. The climax of the march was a high-spirited, joyful, and unifying experience. We celebrated the final hours of January 22, 1986, with a huge fiesta. Participants from the thirty nations gave their cultural best for the Mexican people. We slept on the floor of the Sports Palace that night, very happy to be inside during Mexico City's frigid weather. The energy of the marchers was astounding. I, however, was exhausted and amazed that after a day of marching, singing, and celebrating, some of the younger stalwarts began a soccer game at 1:00 AM.

I went directly to Washington, D. C. with a delegation from the march. On the 24th of January, we held a well-attended press conference. We demonstrated near the Vietnam Memorial and conducted a vigil at the State Department. The rest of the day was spent lobbying Congressional offices to end the Central American Wars.

Our objective in such a march is to change the methods of change by asking the world to reject militarism. The march was one such instrument as a tool of change. Fidelity to the past requires such mutations. Those who repeat the ignorance, the racism, the brutality of the past, are unfaithful to the past. Those who are willing to seek these new instruments of change are faithful to the past because they have learned from the past. Now that we have lived through this most violent of centuries, it is time to identify instruments of change that are effective, strong and nonviolent.

I was profoundly grateful that the march was completed without the loss of life. The non-violent examples of Dr. Martin Luther King and Mahatma Gandhi have been used successfully in various national campaigns. Our objective was to apply these methods at the international level. We certainly had anticipated that lives could be lost on such a venture. We talked of that eventuality, and all of the marchers were aware of the perils. I was certainly aware of it. Theresa and I had discussed the dangers of this march. I am grateful that Theresa supported my involvement, as I knew it was very difficult for her.

I was inspired by the general atmosphere of courage and willingness of marchers to do almost anything for their objective. I found it necessary to restrain people who had bizarre or adventurous ideas that they intended to carry out in a spontaneous fashion. Time and time again, I witnessed people about to do things that could have harmed themselves and their companions. The greatest safety valves for the march were the local preparation committees. We were able to avoid extremely damaging actions because we listened to them. If marchers were not concerned about their own lives, we had to convince them to be concerned about the lives of those who remained behind after we left.

Chapter 21

Reflections on the International March for Peace

Reflecting on the International March for Peace in Central America, I cannot help but recall the Book of Exodus. After fleeing the oppression of Egypt, Moses was confronted by people who missed Egyptian food. Like us, they complained. They set out, not knowing where they were going. In similar fashion, our day-to-day insecurity led to anxiety. We made no attempt to claim this as the best march in Central America. It was the only march in Central America. It was a hope for nonviolent change. Success does not depend on how far we walked, but rather on the fruits of our walk. I wanted to avoid a "can you top this" atmosphere.

Our principal unity had to be on the objectives of the march, rather than on how, or where, we marched. There were constant differences of opinion. Some of the young people wanted to log in more kilometers a day. Often, it was not possible to walk even five kilometers a day because of the armed conflicts and rigid opposition to the march in Costa Rica, Honduras, El Salvador, and Guatemala. Many times it was necessary to repeat the axiom of Jesus, "Sufficient for the day is the trouble thereof." Calm and confidence were essential to combat anxiety and disaster.

I felt that every step of the march was on my shoulders. I knew that if I lost personal control at any moment, it would be disastrous for the unity of the march. I found it necessary to debate other members of the directorate publicly. I had to ask people not to be so in love with their idea of the march that they would refuse alternative plans. I believe that what an individual wants to do is not necessarily the best thing for the group. Many great actions of history have required waiting. Milton said, "They also serve who only stand and wait." Gandhi, Martin Luther King, and Nelson Mandela knew when to wait. It is much harder to endure conflict than to attack.

One member of the directorate—who I quickly understood to be totally out of sync with the peace movement—came up with a bizarre idea to get us to El Salvador. His proposal: take motorized canoes from Potosi, Nicaragua across the Gulf of Fonseca and land at the Salvadoran town of La Union. The Gulf is a convergence of El Salvador, Honduras, and Nicaragua. US warships frequently patrolled this area.

I personally opposed this proposal. It would have been an intrusion into one of the most strategic areas of the Central American conflict. In spite of my apprehension and the fact that the proposed action was planned for media purposes, a substantial number of marchers, especially the Danes, proceeded north on the way to Potosi. I kept thinking of the Gulf of Tonkin. Lyndon Johnson had used the Gulf of Tonkin as a contrivance just to get troops to Vietnam. We did not need to become part of a contrivance for the US to send even more troops to this conflict.

Fortunately, the Nicaraguan government was alerted and the dissident group received a plea from the Sandinistas to cease and desist. The government spokesperson told them that the Salvadorans would not permit the launches to land at La Union, and that any such action would be taken as a provocation by Nicaragua. Nicaragua simply did not need more accusations of aggression as it bled from Reagan's war. The Danes reluctantly returned to the body of the march undaunted by having nearly created an international incident which could have been used against Nicaragua. Such adventurism always required urgent attention.

This same member of the directorate also called me a liar. When I called ahead to Costa Rica to tell them we were assembled and ready to proceed to their peaceful land, the spokesperson at the Quaker House in San Jose said, "Please listen, you have a member of the march who was arrested in Costa Rica some years ago. He is not welcome. The authorities here will pick him up and the march will be discredited. Please tell him to proceed to Nicaragua by air and rejoin the march there. He must not come to Costa Rica." I thought that message would be easily related by the individual named by the Costa Ricans. His response, however, was rage. He screamed that there was no such phone call from Costa Rica and that I was doing this to keep him out of the leadership of the march. In his view, my intentions were subversive and paternalistic. He then got hopelessly drunk. This thorn in the side remained, agitated, provoked, annoyed, and disruptive, for the duration of the march. What ultimately shocked me and taught me about the power of demagoguery was that some marchers looked to him as a legitimate leader.

I was disturbed by the lack of discernment on the part of various marchers. I was upset by the willingness of some marchers to follow near-psychotic, divisive, and anarchistic elements who seemed eager to break the unity of the experience. At worst, I thought of certain individuals as suicidal. Fortunately, each US citizen on the march had agreed in writing that he or she would leave the march if the leadership judged their presence to be counterproductive. Unfortunately, many of the other nations that participated had not put any such clause into their applications. Without a doubt, the US delegation was the most carefully screened and the most disciplined. During our seven-day vigil on the Honduran border, some of the participants from other nations were conspiring to simply march in defiance into the arms of the battle-ready Honduran Cobra Special Forces. In their view, such defiance was a sign of fortitude. They believed that the armed Honduran forces would not open fire. I did not share their enthusiasm. We were in a war zone.

Despite such tensions and conflict between the marchers, the contemplative heart of the march was the Buddhist monks. Their constant chants, drums, and prayers served as a unifying element. For several days in Managua, they chanted from sun-up to sun-down. They prayed through several days at the destroyed Cathedral of Managua, not eating or drinking.

One of my happiest recollections of the march was the chance to spend several hours with Rigoberta Menchu.[6] Here is my translation of her words, which I taped as we sat together that blessed day. I write her words here in poetic form to represent the rhythm of her speech. A linguistic scholar told me that this great woman, who would soon receive the Nobel Peace Prize, actually speaks in verse. When I met her, she had only recently learned Spanish.

The new president will make demands,
But his demands will not be permitted.
The military is going to select the Minister of Defense,
Not the president.
Power has been militarized.
Our men are mobilized into Civil Patrols.

A special *cedula*[7] awaits
Members of the fundamentalist churches.
People of Nahuala have become fundamentalists.
People who used to be Catholics.
Why have they changed religions?
Because they are allowed to go further from the village
To look for firewood if they have a fundamentalist *cedula*.

---

6 Please read her book, *I . . . Rigoberta Menchu: An Indian Woman of Guatemala*, Verso Press, London, 1984.

7 Internal Passport

People are forcibly acculturated.
They build highways.
They grow wheat instead of corn.
We are now living in total misery.
The new government will change names
But not reality.

We lack salt.
Salt is sold in pinches.
It costs three or four *Quetzales* per pound.
No one buys a pound,
So it is sold in pinches rather than pounds.
We are losing our culture.
There is no other way to preserve our lives
But to lose our culture.
Our people are prisoners in Chiapas.
We lack water.
Those in Campeche have it better.

Do you know that two thousand people died in Alta Verapaz
Rather than to give in to the army?
The army was going to put them into open prisons.
They refused.
This was not the only massacre.

They use certain churches to oppress us,
The Mormons.

A woman told me recently that she could no longer
Make *huipiles*.[8]
But now that we cannot make *huipiles*,
We must make history instead.
After we make our own history,
We will make *huipiles* again.

Perhaps we are guilty of triumphalism.
We thought victory was right around the corner,
But this is not the case.
We must remember the slogans of

---

8 Hand-woven blouses

Grupo Apoyo Mutuo.
To die honoring the names of our beloved.
They took them away living.
We demand to see them living.

The risk is very great,
Grupo Apoyo Mutuo[9] is an obstacle to the new government,
And the new government might strike out at them.

I know my parents are dead, and I am very proud of them.
But in my dreams I see my brothers and sisters.
I do not think they are dead.
Many times I dream they are alive.
They were captured by the army,
Taken away by night.
I really don't know if they are dead or alive.

And now I live in airports,
An international diplomat for the indigenous people of Guatemala.
I do not have a family, a house, a roof.
I do not have a country,
But hundreds of families are supporting me.

I have hope we can arrive.
We can have greater joy.
Drugs take people away from the realities of life,
But I have a vision of great change in the world.
People must make history.
I am disturbed by the level of ignorance in the United States.
I am disturbed by the degree of unconsciousness in the United States.
Your culture wants people to say, "Oh, I didn't know that."

Rigoberta is the personification of the indigenous militant nobility that is sweeping through the Americas. Her words remain as an accurate account of what was happening in Guatemala at that time.

I often wondered about being in a position of authority. As a white male over fifty and a US citizen, for many my status represented everything that is wrong with the world. The US group—especially—marched

---

9 In English, "Mutual Help Group." This is a women's group in Guatemala that demands accountability of those who have disappeared and have been illegally detained by Guatemalan security forces.

with the weight of US imperialism on our backs. Yet, I found that the more I was engaged with the marchers and the local people, the more this burden was overlooked.

I was also ambivalent about my role as a director while living in such immediate contact with all of the marchers. Military tradition separates officers from enlisted people in order to retain authority. But we were organized in anti-military fashion. Our egalitarian setting made it difficult, however, to be in a position of authority. In times of crisis, I wanted to take a "quasi-military" approach. These were moments when I needed to make a strong firm decision without discussion. We were creating a new model. Such difficulties must be expected.

In trying to avoid the traps of "super-democracy," I often used the analogy of an airliner. In the super-democratic model, two passengers might arrive at the cabin in the midst of a flight and demand to take the controls because, "they had just as much a right as the pilots to fly the plane." Or suppose the usurpers should make such a claim on behalf of gender or racial balance, never taking into account that they were not pilots. If we erred on the march in regard to authority, it was by attempting too much democracy rather than too little. I often did feel that I was more capable of tackling problems that arose on the march simply because I had previously spent so much time in Central America.

The Danes and the Spaniards were aggressive, defiant, fearless, adventuresome, and ready at the proper moment to give a completely united front. Most of the Europeans were anti-religious. At the beginning of the venture they had no concept of Liberation Theology. They did, however, come to respect the spiritual power of the Japanese Buddhist Monks. For instance, the dauntless Danes marching defiantly up to the Honduran Cobras, who were ready to kill them. All the while, they sang in Danish the "Ode to Joy" from Beethoven's Ninth Symphony. The image of these tough, hard-drinking people will remain forever in my memory.

Some of the more pious, obedient, and thoughtful marchers simply could not take the strain and left the march. The Canadians, who were particularly religious, often got fed up with the attitude of the more flamboyant types, such as the Danes and Spaniards who could sing all night, joke at everything, and pay no attention to the needs of others who might have to sleep. Perhaps they could be categorized as thoughtless and selfish. Ironically, in spite of their constant complaining and all-night revelry, these thoughtless and selfish people were making history. They were able to persevere through the march simply by being themselves, while the more pious and obedient types were compelled to leave the march. It was as if the constant complainers were actually energizing their ambition to continue. By constantly reaffirming who they were and by being themselves, the Danes and Spaniards were able to go on. Even today I wonder: What would we have done if the Danes and Spaniards had stopped complaining?

The women complained less than the men did. How great women can look even without makeup, laundry facilities, water, and fancy clothing. Their femininity seemed enhanced along with their courage. I remembered the hymn, "How beautiful the feet of those who preach the gospel of peace," and reflected, not only the feet, but the whole person. They seemed to glow with an authentic spirituality that was not pietistic, that was not self-righteous, and not sectarian. It was whole. Some of them had endured such harsh conditions before. For instance, the British women had served at the Greenham Common antinuclear demonstrations.

Occasionally one of the women would understandably become hysterical. The male members responded with their own version of hysteria: they became more macho and louder in an attempt to cover up the very real fear in carrying out the march. The constant exhaustion and threatening atmosphere began to take a toll on everyone.

At times the marchers looked to me like children, angry at their father. Apparently, I was the father figure. I frequently heard, "We're going to live our own life; this is our project, and we're going to do it our way." It was necessary to point out time and again that the most dangerous acts were not necessarily the most effective, and that sometimes the most dangerous acts were the most selfish. Even though I was often met with resistance by the young marchers, I considered my role as "father figure" necessary.

For instance, one young marcher was desperately ill; he became partially deaf and remained behind in Esteli, Nicaragua to rest and get some medicine at the local hospital. This was not sufficient. I came down from the Honduran border, went to his sickbed, got him up and put him into a cab bound for the Military Hospital in Managua. In obvious pain, he shouted, "I don't want to go to the military hospital. I'm a pacifist." I countered, "You are going to the military hospital." In Managua, the efficient Nicaraguan doctor at the military hospital carefully diagnosed a mastoid infection, gave shots, medicine, and a series of future appointments. There was no charge. Medical care was free in Nicaragua for *everyone*, including foreign visitors. The young man improved rapidly.

Ultimately, the International March for Peace in Central America was just the beginning. Our march had no historical precedent. Several nations came together as a family to observe areas of conflict and to petition for a peaceful settlement. Afterwards, many of the marchers stayed in Central America or returned later to do volunteer work. This was an incipient international solidarity movement that has now evolved globally.

Jorge Illueca's prophecy that our march would significantly influence Central American peace negotiations became a reality. Illueca was the senior Panamanian statesman and pillar of the Contadora peace process who spoke on the first day of our march in Panama. On that day, he said: "The march of these messengers of peace will light a flame of hope in the region and will contribute to creating a climate to stimulate and revitalize the Contadora negotiations." On February 10, 1986, his prophecy was fulfilled. All eight foreign ministers present at Caraballeda, including Mexico, Panama, Venezuela, Colombia, Peru, Brazil, Uruguay, and Argentina, representing 85% of the people of Latin America, presented themselves to Secretary of State George Schultz in Washington, D.C., with the following demands:

> A permanent solution to the Central American conflict must be Latin American. It must not be considered part of the East-West conflict.

> Self-determination, non-intervention, and respect for territorial integrity. Observance of human rights.

> Suspension of international military maneuvers.

> Formation of a Central American Parliament.

> Reestablishment of conversations between the United States and Nicaragua.

> No political, logistical, or military support for any group intending to subvert or destabilize the constitutional order.

It was as if the Foreign Ministers could have taken these slogans directly from the banners of the International March for Peace in Central America. We believe that our constant support for Contadora as the avenue to a peaceful settlement prepared the way for the bold proposals of the meeting at Caraballeda in Venezuela on January 11 and 12 of 1986.

It was my hope that the relationship between malicious US military adventures in Central America and the dismal domestic conditions in the United States would now be more obvious to US citizens.

In the wake of the march, the Costa Rican Association of Jurists also demanded of President Monge that Costa Rica Libre be dissolved because of its attack on the International March for Peace in Central

America. The revulsion of the citizens of that country at the conduct of Costa Rica Libre's attacks on our march was so great that it appeared to tip the scales away from the pro-war candidate and lead to the election of the more progressive Oscar Arias.

The presence of peace marchers with the indigenous people of Guatemala as well as with the peasants of El Salvador and Nicaragua had a strategic value in protecting these people from attack. Peter Holding, an attorney from Australia and a member of the march identified the forced recruitment of Miskito Indians in Honduras for service in the Contras. He judged the Honduran judiciary to be non-functional and declared Honduras to be a de facto military dictatorship.

The people of Central America now understand that they can call on the international peace community to accompany them in times of struggle. I am extremely grateful to the people of the United States and the rest of the world who contributed their time, their efforts, and their money to support this march. We believe we made an impact for peace in Central America. Central America certainly made an impact on us. We will let history make the final evaluation.

Chapter 22

Returning Home

Returning from such an experience is usually the joyful part. I do not regret any of the countless trips, delegations, or caravans. They were all meaningful. Coming back whole, however, elicits much gratitude. For some reason it reminds me of the feeling I had after long summer days working for the Southern California Gas Company when I was fifteen. When I jumped off that truck after a long day in the ditches, I felt a great sense of achievement. "Weeping we go to sow the seed, but we shall come rejoicing bringing in the sheaves."

Theresa and I always made an effort to be a normal family, to visit relatives, understanding that neither family nor friends were much interested in our adventures. After returning from war zones to the US, there was always a sense of "culture shock." It was as if the US was a vast unconscious machine. Often on a return home from afar, someone at a family gathering would say, "Tell us about your trip." But they were usually not really interested. This was fine, as I was not anxious to expound on my adventures either. I did not comment on my activities unless asked a direct question. We were living a different life than many of our family members. We were simply in different ballparks.

Colleen was fifteen. Blase Martin was thirteen. These formative years were our constant preoccupation. The children knew and absorbed what we were doing, but they could rarely participate directly.

After the International March, I had to determine whether such long-term absences from family and office would be my future course of action. There were many reasons for a negative answer. Theresa was not happy with such long ventures away from home. She was concerned with the family and the development of our children. The death threats came in not only on our office phones, but just prior to my departure for the march, the threatening calls were reaching our private home phone as well. I could see the logic of not spending long periods out of the country unless absolutely necessary. Many of the problems in Latin America have their origin in the United States. Much of the work of the Office of the Americas could best be handled from within the United States. If it were necessary to spend more time away, I felt certain this could be done. On the other hand, many people in military service spend months and years away from their loved ones. Therefore, shouldn't we, the peacemakers, be as dedicated to our service as the enlisted soldiers? Fortunately for my family and me, the majority of my work does not require leaving the United States.

We never pressured our children to join the peace movement. So we were surprised when our daughter Colleen told us she was eager to go to Nicaragua. Theresa was orchestrating a new project and challenge that I would never have imagined: "Let's bring teenagers to Nicaragua." While Theresa was planning this project, we never encouraged Colleen to join. Yet, Colleen told us she wanted to go.

I could not have managed this kind of a project. Theresa did it. The Contra war was in full force. We would need written permission from each family, as well as documents for the immigration authorities in all countries concerned. The teenagers had to pay their own way on these delegations, as did the adults. As executive director, Theresa had to keep a tight control on the budget. We refused to borrow money or to go into debt. That bank balance always miraculously hovered near zero.

The first teenage delegation was a life-changing experience for the people who went. Young people will rise to the occasion if adults have the courage to take this kind of risk. While in Nicaragua with these delegations, the teenagers were introduced to Sandinista soldiers who were no older than they were. They socialized together, swam together, and parted as the teenage soldiers returned to the mountains to fight against US-financed mercenaries. Over the years that have followed, these "teenagers" who are now adults still thank Theresa for her courage in bringing them to the site of a war crime committed by the United States. The International Court of Justice unanimously condemned The Contra War and demanded restitution by the offender. Colleen was so touched by the Nicaraguan people that after her return to the States, she asked if she could go back to Nicaragua for several more weeks of the summer. She went back. "They have nothing, but they are so happy," was her comment.

Chapter 23

El Salvador

After returning home from the Central American Peace March, Theresa and I decided to turn over our delegation work to organizations that were imitating what we were doing. We never attempted to compete with any-one. And we were not "looking for work." There was always more to do than we could handle. Why should the Office of the Americas continue to send delegations when other organizations were doing them well? My decision was to travel only when I felt my contributions and presence were absolutely necessary.

One such trip was to El Salvador in 1988. These were US union lead-ers in solidarity with the Salvadoran labor movement. I traveled with Don White, the major leader of the Committee in Solidarity with the People of El Salvador (CISPES). We were both clear about the negative aspects of the US unions in foreign relations. The American Institute of Free Labor Development (AIFLD), a coalition of corporate capital and the AFL-CIO, received heavy input and involvement from the US government and CIA, both of which were intent on destroying militant Latin American unions. In a miscommunication between the death squads and the CIA in El Salvador, two representatives of AIFLD were murdered at the San Salvador Sheraton Hotel. Since then, AIFLD and the CIA lived in a state of unholy matrimony. The Jesuits at the University of Central America (La UCA) were taking a risk by inviting the US unionists to have this conference on their campus in El Salvador. An umbrella movement for Salvadoran labor was in formation, The National Union of Salvadoran Workers (UNTS). This was considered to be some kind of subversive act by the Salvadoran government.

The US-directed death and destruction in El Salvador was out of control at this time. And in spite of this bloody environment, the Jesuits not only opened their campus to us but their superb faculty participated in the events of this labor conference. Military helicopters buzzed the auditorium where we met. While they did not fire, they did make it hard to follow the proceedings. The rector of the university, Father Ignacio Ellacuria, is etched in my mind. He was a scholar, an activist and a courageous prophet speaking truth to power. While he was not necessarily supportive of the National Liberation Front of Farabundo Marti (FMLN), he was outraged that a people's movement was being brutally attacked. It was clear to him that the US was in command and control of this conflict. I was conscious of the danger that Ellacuria was in as I took notes on his talk about the relationship of the United States to this blood bath.

We boarded buses at the university and drove directly to rebel areas held by the FMLN. Our bus went to Tenancingo, a town that had been declared a peace area and was placed under the jurisdiction of the Archdiocese of San Salvador. We drove past the Ilopango Airport and on to the last military checkpoint. At the blocked highway, I flashed letters from Senator Cranston asking that we be given every consideration. What a clear indication of being in a denationalized colony! Letters from a US Senator legitimized our passage into rebel territory. I don't think letters from any Salvadoran authority would have had the same impact in the United States. As we made our way up the dirt road to Tenancingo, white flags were everywhere. FMLN rebels and Salvadoran military were in close proximity.

Many of the civilians had left Tenancingo. While technically under the jurisdiction of the archdiocese of San Salvador, the town was actually under FMLN control. I walked into a busy clinic and found a religious sister hard at work caring for the sick and wounded. I asked the sister if there were FMLN guerrillas in the area. She suggested I go out the side door. There, playing with a child, was a young rebel armed with an M-16 rifle. He spoke with us in a friendly manner. "Where did you get that rifle?" I inquired. "We get everything from the barracks of the Salvadoran Army, or we buy weapons from officers who are inclined to sell them," he responded.

More rebel troops casually came up to speak with our delegation. We were standing openly in the plaza at the center of town. They were asking for food and money. I heard and saw the approach of Huey helicopters at very low altitude. Quite frightened, I asked, "Shall we take cover?" I was struck by the complete confidence of the FMLN guerrilla who said, "No, that won't be necessary," as he and the rest of us stood about thirty feet below the passing chopper. I was unbelieving and could almost feel bullets piercing flesh. The rebels were correct. They knew we would not be fired upon. Trying to understand this event, I could surmise that the military knew we were a delegation of the US and did not want to add to the list of murdered US labor representatives.

On the way back to San Salvador, we were stopped at the military checkpoint. Our driver was verbally attacked and threatened by the lieutenant in charge. I approached the officer, showed him my passport and cover letters from Senator Cranston, and asked that any blame attributed to the driver for traveling out to this area be placed with us and not with him. After all, we were the ones who hired him. Why should he be punished for driving us where we ordered him to go? The lieutenant allowed us to return without further incident with the understanding that there would be no retaliation against the driver. When we arrived back at the capital, we celebrated with music, dance, and food. Despite hardship and deadly oppression, the Salvadorans were victorious in their hopeful struggle. The slogan, *"La lucha misma es la victoria,"* (the struggle itself is the victory) was central to their environment.

The meeting at the university was the last time we saw the Jesuits alive. Six of them were murdered along with their housekeeper and her daughter. Graduates of the School of the Americas at Fort Benning, Georgia, directed the slaughter. Those graduates represent the "quality" of troops we have trained at our School of the Assassins hellhole. The rapists and murderers of the four US religious women were also under the direction of this school of scoundrels. The murderer of Archbishop Romero had the same scholastic background at the School of the Americas. The officers responsible for the El Mozote massacre of over seven hundred civilians had that same high-tech schooling. These atrocities are only the tip of a bloody iceberg.

I recall the faces of so many who have been killed in El Salvador: Masa, a local solidarity leader in El Salvador who worked with CISPES, behind the desk of the much-attacked UNTS building, Febe Velasquez, leader of a major Salvadoran labor organization, who I met at the University conference where I served as translator, and then the Jesuits. Salvador's finest have been martyred. This was Vietnam in Central America. Surely one of the prime characteristics of empire is to have no learning ability. Create an absolute disaster and holocaust in Vietnam. The program fails, millions die. Repeat the program in El Salvador, repeat it in Nicaragua, and in Guatemala. Destroy Honduras in the effort. Empire does not learn; it just self-destructs.

When I checked in at the El Camino Hotel, the desk person looked at my passport and said, *"El famoso* Dr. Bonpane." It did not feel like a compliment. My free translation: "We know who you are, Dr. Bonpane." El Salvador had a way of creating a chill in its visitors. So much for traveling anonymously.

After this trip to El Salvador, my name was posted at the airport in San Salvador with all of those to be forbidden entrance to the country. I discovered this from Sister Pat Krommer, who was also refused admittance to El Salvador, and saw my name on the same list that denied her entry. Over the years I have been expelled or forbidden entrance to Costa Rica, Honduras, Guatemala, and El Salvador.

My next trip to El Salvador during the war was with CISPES to support the UNTS labor umbrella and the demand of Archbishop Romero that the US stop military aid. Mother Theresa was in El Salvador during this 1990 delegation. I was once again traveling with Don White. His courage and leadership ability was contagious. We did not meet Mother Theresa personally, but we groaned when we saw her on TV. I remember three words: "aceptar, aceptar, aceptar," ("accept, accept, accept"). She was basically telling the people of Central America to accept the torture of their people and destruction of their communities. For all I know, the words may have been superimposed on what she actually said, but we groaned nevertheless. While not working to change political structures, Mother Theresa was doing important work by helping the sick and dying in India. But the words attributed to her in El Salvador were not impressive.

With some apprehension, Don White of CISPES called a press conference in the middle of the Capital at the UNTS office. We knew that we were under government and military surveillance. We wanted to talk about the possibility of peace in El Salvador and call attention to Archbishop Romero's proposals for peace: the need for dialogue, the need for a democratic convergence, and the support for non-violent change. We basically took the memory of Archbishop Romero, killed on March 24, 1980, and used it as our focus for the news conference. Archbishop Romero is certainly the most remembered person in El Salvador, so we thought it would be effective to base our goals for peace on his observations. The media actually showed up, and they even aired the conference. I could not help but think of how many times the media neither responded to nor aired our press conferences in the United States.

I had an excellent visit with Ruben Zamora on this same visit. He was trying to establish the Democratic Convergence, a coalition of political parties that would be capable of winning an election. He was wearing a bulletproof vest as he arrived at his office. He explained to us that he could only campaign within the city of San Salvador and its suburban limits. He could not go farther into the countryside because these areas were under the direct command of the military. Ruben did not come with us on that Sunday as we headed out to a zone of conflict in San Vicente. I was once again edified by the ability of the Salvadorans to celebrate. Never mind that the military might attack at any time. Never mind the fear. Celebrate life. And, with them, we did.

Chapter 24

Demonstrations

Throughout the 1980s, our solidarity with Central America was foreign and domestic.

Aside from the constant delegations to Nicaragua, the International March for Peace in Central America, fact-finding in Colombia, and El Salvador, we were conducting peace demonstrations—which often had a component of civil disobedience—in Los Angeles. Father Luis Olivares, the Pastor of La Placita, was in full participation with us. This is the mother church of the city of Los Angeles. The full name is Nuestra Señora Reina de Los Angeles, originally an outstation of the Mission San Gabriel some two centuries ago. It is the epicenter of the great city that bears the name Los Angeles. This was also the Mecca of my spiritual quest as a teenager, and also the place where Theresa and I decided to get married. And now it was a place of refuge for the displaced of the Reagan-Bush wars. Numerous demonstrations originated from this sanctuary from 1983 to 1989.

Father Olivares and Cardinal Mahoney had a tense relationship. The homeless were welcome to sleep in his church every evening. Olivares did not consider any human beings to be illegal, so he also had many run-ins with the immigration service. We would meet at La Placita on Wednesdays at 7:00 AM. The gatherings were spiritual without the obfuscations of unintelligible dogmas, but with a clear moral compass. After the 7:00 AM. meeting, a march would follow to the Federal Building at 300 North Los Angeles Street. Celebrities and prominent citizens were with us. Actors Edward Asner, Martin Sheen, David Clennon, Kris Kristofferson, producer/cinematographer Haskel Wexler, musician/singer Jackson Browne, Santa Monica City Attorney Robert Meyers, and so many more. We formulated a liturgy commemorating the dead in Central America. We read their names and responded to each, *"Presente!"* As in the case of Vietnam, Iraq, and Afghanistan, the Central American Wars were pure and simple state terrorism on the part of our country. These were evil acts perpetrated by our government. A pledge of resistance was formulated. A crucifix would be carried by the first wave of marchers; it was constructed of mock M-16 rifles. The Christ figure was Central America.

In view of the large-scale horrors being committed in Central America, the number of US resisters was relatively small. What Father Dan Berrigan stated in preparation for the Catonsville Action in 1968 was still true. "Our resistance is not proportional to the evil being done in our name."

Support from the local churches was disappointing. Father Luis Olivares was certainly an exception to the rule. He was an example—similar to Archbishop Romero—of someone who previously identified with the lifestyle of the wealthy and later experienced a conversion. Romero was initially considered a stereotypical conservative bishop in El Salvador. As the best of his clergy were being murdered by ever-present death squads, he realized it was a result of their identification with the poor. His conversion led him to become the voice of the voiceless. The Archbishop was shot and killed on March 24, 1980 while celebrating Mass.

The murder of the Jesuits at the University of Central America in El Salvador in 1989 resulted in a large number of religious personnel participating in our demonstrations. Archbishop Roger Mahoney even joined us at the Federal Building. When the time came for the civil disobedience component of that demonstration, I thought the prelate was going to be arrested with us. The final police warning was given. We were blocking the entrance to the Federal Building. When the Federal Police moved in to arrest us, the archbishop had stepped aside just in time.

Since many of these demonstrations included civil disobedience, those who risked arrest were carefully segregated from those who wanted to demonstrate legally. We did not want anyone arrested who was not planning on it. We were arrested many times. I did not consider this the best thing to do, but often non-violent civil disobedience was the only strong statement we could make, our only available weapon. The Democratic Congress was basically ignoring us. The President suffered from Alzheimer's, the Supreme Court was off in space.

Seventy or more of us would be arrested at any one time. We sat in holding tanks, frequently our handcuffs were left on as a punitive measure. Try urinating with handcuffs on. The willingness to be arrested is a step forward for middle- and upper-middle-class people, to say nothing of those in the upper classes. I think it is really most difficult for people who are poor, because they are constantly the object of attack by law enforcement. The arrests, aside from calling attention to the holocaust in Central America, helped us to be in touch with the treatment of the poor in our society. Our prisons have become concentration camps for people of color and the poor. Twenty-five percent of the world's prisoners are in the United States. We have only 4% of the world's people.

One day, I was in a holding tank at the Ramparts Division Station. There were six of us in a tiny glassed-in cell with no water and no toilet. During the entire day we could monitor the behavior of the LAPD at this notorious station. Chief Gates was still in charge. Everything was sadistically funny to the police on duty as they made up rules and regulations as sick jokes. One detainee asks to go to the bathroom. "That is up to the arresting officer," was the response. The arresting officer could have been fifty miles away by now. We received a long and unwanted sermon about the horrors of communism from a Vietnam veteran LAPD officer. We saw a Spanish-speaking arrestee brought in and chained to a bench. "We won't have anyone who speaks Spanish until next week," quipped an officer.

Police science is necessary. But I am unimpressed when someone asks if I am pro-police or anti-police. I am pro police who are professional law enforcement officers. I am anti police who are racists, abusive, and trigger happy. The "them and us" attitude is destructive. For instance, my son was on his first day of driving with a license, so his performance may have been a little less than smooth. As he drove in West Los Angeles with his African American friend, an unmarked police car stops them, a pistol is jammed into his face, "What are you on? What are you on?" was the question. This is not a professional police officer; this is simply a bully in blue.

One day in a cell at the Central Los Angeles jail after being arrested at the La Placita demonstration, the Captain came in to see me. "I am Captain Kozak. I used to monitor your classes at California State University Northridge." That's right, the LAPD had the gall to have secret agents in my classroom! Here is a case where we did sue. Some fifteen of us who had been under surveillance by the LAPD filed a lawsuit through the ACLU. We won a judgment against them. They admitted their crime and were required to pay damages. It was not enough to have the FBI, CIA, DIA, and many other agencies keeping files on me. I have obtained thousands of pages of such material by way of the Freedom of Information Act. But the LAPD?

During this same arrest, there were two or three other lawyers being held with me. As we languished there, the guards opened the cell door and threw in a teenager saying, "Please excuse us for throwing in this piece of shit!" It turns out this young man was from Mexico, and the officers had beat him up. The lawyers who were also in the holding cell decided to take up the case. It turns out that the young man was undocumented. In this case, the lawyers determined it was best for the kid to be able to return to his home in Mexico without any further time in jail. It would have been different if the boy had been from any country farther to the south. The attorneys would have sought political asylum.

I was arrested with Martin Sheen and several others for pouring fake blood on the sign outside the Federal Building. The blood symbolized the real human blood that had been shed by the Contra War in Nicaragua. The baby-faced prosecutor told the judge that we had damaged federal property. The ancient judge questioned just how much damage we had caused. The federal cop witness replied that the blood had already been washed off the marble sign. "Then they did not damage federal property," said the jurist, "they were littering." He let us go on our own recognizance.

I was really nervous about being detained on this occasion because I had not planned to be arrested that day. I threw the blood from the vial after others did. And I have always recommended to others that they not choose civil disobedience in a spontaneous fashion. Spontaneity is not a virtue in such situations. My nervousness was partially related to thinking of all the things that I should have been doing that day had I not been locked up.

On occasion, the judge would declare me the ringleader of these civil disobedience demonstrations. It was difficult to answer a judge who would make such an allegation. We were trying to develop a model where there would be no supreme leader. Not a Martin Luther King, nor a Mahatma Gandhi. We had a collective leadership that was truly admirable. Such actions were developed by consensus in planning meetings. We listened to each other and were generally in sync. Thus, I have to confess I enjoyed the title given to me by the indomitable Don White, one of the pillars of solidarity. He called me the "Pope of the Movement." I enjoyed this title because of the feigned ecclesiastical tone and because I knew that no one would take it literally.

Law enforcement often showed us a great deal of contempt during these actions. There were, however, always some, even in law enforcement, who understood exactly why we were there. "I have never seen such dedication in the faces of arrestees," said one observer in the federal lockup.

The religious component of the peace movement has generally been the most authentically radical (getting to the roots of the problem). The Catholic Worker movement and Dorothy Day initiated a militant non-violence that has transcended anything offered by the sectarian "left." I am really tired of sectarian ideologues placing dismissive tags on others and remaining passive practitioners of non-action. Of course the same tiredness also applies to inactive liberals and unconscious conservatives. Actually, I don't think this planet is going to be saved by any rigid religious or political ideology.

Theresa thought that our son Blase might be excessively worried about my frequent arrests. "Do you think Dad will get arrested today?" he said. What Theresa discovered was a more practical concern; Blase Martin wanted to use my car. If it were parked downtown while I was being held, he would not have transportation.

These arrests were frequent, and for me, always very distasteful. But such inconvenience was nothing compared to what the Central American people had endured. Sometimes we were held in large underground rooms, men and women together. Generally, the police would not remove our handcuffs. Yet, we were usually cited and released and out of the tank by nightfall.

These frequent arrests for civil disobedience did not make my ability to find teaching jobs easier. Throughout my twenty-eight years of directing the Office of the Americas, I did accept several teaching positions. There was always questioning of my "political" activities by the administration. But surprisingly, during this period I was at least tolerated by academia.

My distaste for demonstrations and civil disobedience has grown with the years. I am very jealous of my time. I do not like to be in a literally captive situation where hours and days can be spent waiting for some bureaucratic resolution of one's status. I often considered staying out of these long confrontations with law enforcement. Each time we would ask ourselves collectively if there was something better we could do. Yet, since the media and the government were typically supportive of the rape of Central America, I often concluded that civil disobedience was necessary. We never approached the level of dedication we see in hundreds of political prisoners like Father Roy Bourgeois, Father Louie Vitale, Sister Megan Rice, Dan and Phil Berrigan, Kathy Kelly, Father John Dear, and an endless number of others who have spent years of their lives in prison as prophetic witnesses to peace.

Demonstration at the Los Angeles Federal Building after the massacre of the Jesuit Priests, their housekeeper and her daughter in El Salvador, September, 1989.

Our helicopter lands in a war zone on the East Coast of Nicaragua together with the Veterans Peace Action Team leaders, Colonel Phil Roettinger and Brian Willson. We are greeted by Sumo Indigenous Sandinsta troops, 1989.

Anti-intervention demonstration at the US Embassy in Managua, Nicaragua with Martin Sheen and Daniel Ellsberg, 1984.

Office of the Americas delegation to Tasba-Pri, Miskito Indian relocation camp near the Honduran Border. November, 1982.

John Randolph and Oliver Stone on an Office of the Americas delegation, 1985.

Sandinista military celebrates arrival of Theresa's delegation, July, 1987.

Bill Becker offers water to a Sandinista soldier during the peace march of 1986.

Dinner in Managua with Minister of Culture, Father Ernesto Cardenal and California attorney Carmen Ramirez, 1983.

With Colonel Philip Roettinger, Brian Willson and the Veterans Peace Action Team in Nicaragua, 1989.

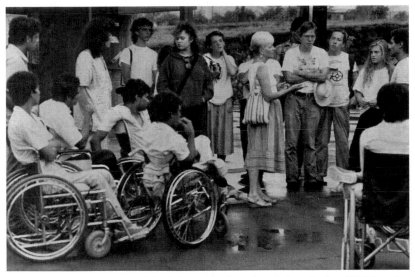

Theresa, Founding Director of the Office of the Americas, brings the first US delegation of teenagers to Nicaragua. They are visiting wounded Sandinista soldiers, July, 1987.

Theresa leads a delegation to visit the Contra War, 1983.

With Ron Kovic as speakers at Anti-Iraq War demonstration in Los Angeles, 2002.

With Kris Kristofferson and Brian Willson at the Peace Accords in Sapoa, Nicaragua at the Costa Rican border, 1989.

Chapter 25

Liberation Theology

Traveling in war zones can lead to hours or days of delay. On the evening of September 17, 1987 our delegation was in such repose on the outskirts of Managua. In response to numerous questions about Liberation Theology I gave the following presentation:

Liberation Theology is a response to many things associated with organized religion. Liberation Theology is an attempt to discover an authentic spirituality removed from the trappings of empire. The Roman Empire that crucified Jesus became the model for the Church established in his name. Most of us have learned religion in an imperial manner, from the top down. Our religious views have been impacted by capitalism. Salvation is private enterprise. It's God and myself; my personal savior and my personal profit. Churches have focused on personal sin. Guilt is wholesaled and forgiveness retailed.

Liberation Theology was developed in places like Guatemala where we worked as priests and understood religion as something more than church and sacraments. Having tens of thousands of parishioners we could have spent day and night administering the rituals of the church. I had my awakening in the community of Aguacatan in Huehuetenango. Suppose five hundred indigenous people want to go to confession. Let's not do this individually. Let's celebrate forgiveness and reconciliation for all in a ten-minute ceremony. I did not want to continue baptizing malnourished children. Was God going to throw these suffering innocents into hell? I would prefer to vaccinate the children and let them walk in and ask for baptism as adults if they chose to do so. You will notice this component in the Campesino Mass which you will attend this evening. We can celebrate what we are about to do or what we have done. We cannot expect the celebration to do the work. Consider a social event—the party is to celebrate what we are doing or what we have done—a graduation, the beginning of a new position, a marriage. Everyone knows, however, that the party will not do the work. Why do I mention this? Because there is a theme in imperial theology which implies that the sacraments will do the work (*ex opere operato*). It seems to me that the basis for this is a desire for the "faithful" to remain in a posture of non-action. Is that not what empire wants? The sacraments will not feed the poor, only political organization will do that. Then we have something to celebrate.

The themes of Liberation Theology are democratic. The church was never meant to be a top-down society. The Pope is not a line officer in the military who gives irrevocable orders. The key unit is the base community. Picture a group of people like us gathered to consider a problem, to pray or meditate over it and make, (1) an observation, (2) a judgment, and (3) a praxis (a reflective act we have arrived at by consensus).

Many people became part of this Central American Revolution because of their faith. They accepted the call of doing God's work on earth, as it is in heaven. We don't have to put heaven in order but we do have to put the earth in order and make it into a beautiful garden like the beauty that surrounds us here at Ticomo. The spotlight is away from the dogmas which have divided the world for centuries. Liberation Theology does not care to argue about the virginity of Mary, the divinity of Christ, the nature of the Trinity. These sectarian issues have led to separations, hatred and inquisitions. And the same is true of political sectarianism.

We are actually very much in sync with people like St. Thomas Aquinas who remind us that theological thinking is analogous thinking. If we refer to God as Father, that is an analogy. Liberation Theology would have us focus on the use of our time here and now. What is fitting conduct for us and why?

Some social scientists say there is no such thing as the common good. But Liberation Theology is common good oriented. Together, people can create collective genius. Together we can pursue an authentic spirituality without being sectarian. We are not interested in getting another member for our church. We don't want to imply that the Roman Catholic Church is *the* church. Do any of us think that Jesus would define his way as Roman Catholicism? We do not wish to say that we have the truth and all others are in error. Such is the theology of inquisition, the theology of fundamentalism. Theology of Liberation is the antithesis of fundamentalism. We do not claim to have all truth. We do not claim that those in 'dogmatic error' must be punished.

It is important to understand that the culture we have just left in the United States is a culture of nationalistic fundamentalism. The Iran-Contra scandal is based on the same paradigm as the inquisition of old. Please recall that the inquisition was extremely active in this hemisphere. You are a Jew. You are not free to be a Jew because error has no rights and you are in error. You must be punished: you may repent or be killed. And the same applies if you are a Protestant or an atheist. Notice what happens when you go back to the US The argument for killing Nicaraguans will be based on the accusation that they are communists. Communist means, "OK to kill," just as Jew, Protestant and atheist did in the days of the inquisition. Remember how we justified the killing of three million communists in Vietnam? Yes, that includes the babies, the mothers, the invalids, all of them! We can only break the fundamentalist, inquisitional pattern by searching for what is human and humane. Now do you see why I call our home culture nationalistic fundamentalism?

Atheistic humanists and theistic humanists can get along very well. I certainly found this to be true in Guatemala. At first the position of our movement was classically anticommunist. Around 1966 we put our anticommunism (OK to kill) aside. The dope trade, the mafia, every dictatorship and the US had used anticommunism to promote their might-makes-right policies. We let go of our anti-communism and began working with people who were humanists, both theistic and atheistic. Some were Marxists, some were not. It was clear, however, that anticommunism was not the road to democracy.

We wanted to know how to get democracy across where it had never been practiced. The right to be, the right to study, the right to see what 'freedoms' should be taken away: the freedom to be illiterate, the freedom to die of hunger, the freedom to be a prostitute, the freedom to get polio. Once we can agree on the common good, all of these things can be done.

In seeking common good consensus we don't go for a 51% majority. On basic common good issues we can go for the will of the vast majority. For example, we might ask how many approve of the smog in Los Angeles. Just a few hands would go up out of the nine million people living in the area. Once the will of the people is established, we can proceed to get rid of the smog. How many want effective rapid transit? All hands would go up. How many want low cost housing? This is the effort being made here in Nicaragua. People want to build an economy based on need.

Yes, that's socialistic. The profit motive is not accepted as the ultimate motor force in society. This theme is part of Liberation Theology. Biblical literature of the Old and the New Testament targets the rich in society as the problem. They are not targeted because they are bad rich. They are targeted because they are rich. It is a societal problem. Because of their riches, others are poor. Distributive justice, the matter of the distribution of goods and services is a fundamental moral problem.

Liberation Theology would have us look at the collective devils of hunger, ignorance and disease. The attack on these evils can be done with joy, enthusiasm and a sense of making history. It includes getting our minds off of our navels. We can be victimized by traditional religion. Is not the message of many sermons, "First I must become perfect, and then I can do something for someone else. Because I am imperfect, I am not able to do anything yet. When I stop smoking, I will start doing something for someone." What does this mean? It means I will never do anything. Perfectionism is not a formula for action, it is a formula for non-action. Non-action on the part of the people (peasants) is the mode of imperial theology. You don't know enough yet. You're not good enough yet. You are not an authority on that subject. Everything is waiting. Everything is tomorrow. They are homeless, yes, but they have no one to blame but themselves!

Liberation, on the contrary, requires engagement and risk. It requires an intolerance of social injustice. Liberation Theology does not ignore personal failings, it simply believes that personal failings are best 'cured' by engagement in life. The world is changed by people who join together and do what they judge should be done. If there is any road to perfection, it is that of doing what needs to be done: careful parenting, for example. I cannot imagine a higher level of asceticism. As we become a conscious part of a collective effort, we do not lose our identity, we find it.

The Pope came to this country [Nicaragua] and created one of the great moments of church history in this century. In the early church there was a history of speaking up to the Pope. St. Paul is addressing St. Peter, the Pope, when he says, "When Cephas came to Antioch, however, I opposed him to his face, since he was manifestly in the wrong." (Galatians 2:11) Such democratic dialogue was evident until the time of the Emperor Constantine when the empire that killed Jesus became the model for the church. The pre-Constantine church was an illegal, clandestine organization. As such, it was very clean and very revolutionary. It was in hiding. It was communal. They had nothing of their own; they shared everything in common, to each according to their needs and from each according to their abilities. Religious orders retained this form of micro-communism and they have done well by it. What was once a system for all members of the community (the church) became the exclusive system of the clergy and full-time religious personnel. The pursuit of profit is not a good model for the economic system of the future. We are not speaking of the systems of the Soviet Union or Cuba. No one is interested in static imitation. The thinking must be dynamic, with new concepts and new ideas. It must not be rhetorical or dogmatic. This requires an atmosphere of experimentation, of listening, especially listening to the poor. We can identify with the wisdom of the poor. Think of it. The rich and powerful are wrong most of the time. They are holding on to something very tight, and that makes them paranoid and full of falsehoods. The rich and the powerful are not in a position to make decisions for prisoners, or for homeless and hungry people. They are out of it.

And so the Pope arrived here in Nicaragua. The people were terribly upset. Fifteen teenagers had just been slaughtered by con-tra terrorists and their mothers insisted that the Chief Shepherd make reference to this. They were asking for a blessing, a consola-tion, an acknowledgement. The Pope interrupted them by saying, "*Silencio!*" [silence]. They knew of no reason why they should shut up for the Pope. They don't shut up for the Pope. They don't shut up for Ronald Reagan. They don't shut up for anyone. Ronald Reagan knows nothing about Nicaragua except to authorize its destruction. The Pope knows little or nothing about Nicaragua except what he received from Cardinal Casariego of Guatemala, a man of comic opera stature.

The women of Nicaragua reacted to the Pope the same way a forty-year-old daughter might react to a sixty-year-old father. They showed love, honor and respect. But they do not accept his jurisdiction on how to run their country, on whether to be a social-ist or not, a Sandinista or not. These issues are not in his realm of competence. The objective is to practice democracy and to incor-porate democracy into spirituality. A central theme of Liberation Theology is you cannot be an imperialist and have an authentic spiritual life. It is out of the question to practice 'might makes right,' and to also have spiritual vitality.

There is but one race, the human race. There is one very small globe on which we live. It is in grave danger of being totally unpopulated. Together we can save the planet by working for international law and order. Nation states cannot make decisions which require global consensus. US laws cannot stop the pollution of the oceans, the pollution of the air. We don't have the jurisdiction. All nations must work in harmony, giving up a portion of their "sovereignty" to make global decisions possible.

Liberation Theology is an integration of religious and political thinking. It brings an end to those old categories which segregate the spiritual from the political, the natural from the supernatural. This reminds me again of my respected mentor, Eric Fromm, who when I asked why, after writing books like *The Art of Loving*, people refer to him as an atheist. He said it was because they do not understand the reverence in ancient rabbinical teaching. When he learned about not taking the name of the Lord in vain, he was not learning about what we call swearing. He learned about not trying to conceptualize about God, about not saying the name of God. What we hear from the fundamentalists is simply irreverence. God will do this. He won't do that. People play around with God to make him into their image and likeness. Reverence will not do that. Liberation Theology is so reverent that it is not even sectarian. What would Jesus say about atheists? I think he would say that some people believe in moral behavior even though they don't believe in God. They don't believe in rewards and punishments. Such people are to be admired and respected.

This movement is a challenge to existing churches because it does not create something new. Sometimes bishops will claim that people have formed a new church, a popular church. They are thinking about examples such as that of Martin Luther some five hundred years ago. There was so much corruption in Rome that he established a new structure and promoted a Reformation by stepping away from Vatican power and control. The approach today is different. It is only indirectly confrontational. Without getting into arguments with the Pope or other authority figures, a message is transmitted, "If you don't want to bring good news to the poor, the gospel, why don't *you* leave the church. You are not indispensable."

There seems to be more rapport between Liberation Theology and socialist thought than there is between Liberation Theology and capitalist thought. Some Latin American prelates have made statements about not being able to coexist with atheistic capitalism. There is not one ounce of theism in the capitalist system. It is just grab the money and run. But we have experienced years of equating socialism falsely with godlessness and capitalism with God. Liberation Theology has nothing to do with the union of church and state. It is the integration of political and spiritual values. I am the same person spiritually as I am politically. There are ugly political concepts and beautiful political concepts. Ideas such as, "stay out of politics," are only fitting for a monarchy. No one should stay out of politics. Everyone has to be in politics all of the time, but must never promote an organized religion as part of the state. When a state becomes a theocracy, it becomes a disaster. It becomes a formula for perpetual war. There will always be those categorized as unsaved. Ethnic and religious outcasts will be categorized as second-class citizens useful only for cheap labor. There must be no cheap labor, just people who must have a living wage.

Liberation Theology is not simply a manipulation of Christian thought by Marxists. The spiritual message came first. Marx came later. It is most unfortunate that our culture is so protected from Marxist thought. Certainly no one in the United States is permitted to study Marx from kindergarten through 12th grade. Only demonization is applied. The same vacuum generally applies to the first four years of college as well. A rare graduate student might actually study some of the wisdom of Marx. Michael Harrington dedicates his book, *The Twilight of Capitalism*, with, "To the future of an almost forgotten genius: the foe of every dogma, champion of human freedom and democratic socialist, Karl Marx."

This new theology is really a very old theology. It's what Moses was trying to get across to the people when he told them it was not right to be in slavery. The true God liberates us. Idols enslave us. Our idols today are nuclear missiles and an imperial foreign policy. Such things are perceived as "The Will of God."

But we are among people today in Nicaragua who are sisters and brothers to us. What they suffer is what our family suffers. We don't intend to tolerate this. In the US, our development of this theology is more secular because that is the nature of our culture. Thousands of solidarity communities have sprung up which are base communities in fact. Spirituality does not have to stand out like an appendage. It must be part of the fabric of our character. Just last month we initiated our Days of Decision at the Van Nuys Military Air Base. Thirty-four of us got arrested that day. We were held inside of a hangar. Within that hangar was military equipment for use against the people of Central America. We knew we were in the right place. Our message is simple. It is the same message that was generated during the war in Indochina. Three million people were destroyed because they were "communists." It was a holocaust. Our message was, "Stop the war or we will stop the country." Nixon was ready to use nuclear bombs against the people of Southeast Asia. He had made his decision. It was the only way. We were losing the war. But he knew he could not get away with it. Nixon witnessed the largest mutiny in the history of the US Soldiers were killing their officers. He could see from the window of the White House one million patriots saying, "Stop the War." Indeed, the great movements in our country have come from the streets. Mass mobilizations gave us the eight-hour day, the forty-hour week and the right to organize.

There is great wisdom in the people at the base and there is great ignorance at the top. Wealth is going into fewer and fewer hands currently, giving our country the worst distribution of wealth in the world. Our leaders are incompetent to make decisions pertaining to health, poverty and housing. They think simply in terms of military production and it is literally killing us. Our cause is to turn it around. We only want servants in government. People who look like servants, act like servants, perform like servants or get out of government. We don't care what they want. We must demand that they do what the great people of our country want them to do.

The Mass tonight [*Misa Campesina*] will be about celebrating our freedom to do and to make history, to do and create the future, to bring justice to the planet. Tomorrow we will visit the war.

Those were my thoughts shared with a delegation of foreigners from the United States on a beautiful star filled and tropical evening just outside of Managua.

Chapter 26

Last Delegation to
Nicaragua and Reflections

We had literally brought thousands of people to visit the war. I was moved by the sincerity and concern of the numerous delegates over the years who paid their own way to visit the wars of Central America. It was hard to find a church or social organization in the United States where some member had not just returned from Central America. These people had legitimate apprehensions and fears. They left me with the thought: our people are so much better than the leadership which is imposed on them. Our people are better than the thugs in power. As in the case of Vietnam, our government was constantly lying. It was not easy, however, for Reagan-Bush to continue their ceaseless babble with any vestige of credibility. My hope is to have a government free of this corrupt leadership and worthy of the fine people who risked their lives on these Central American delegations.

I took an Office of the Americas delegation to the pivotal election of 1990. The word was out to all Nicaraguans: Ms. Chamorro will win or the war will continue. UNO (Unión Nacional Opositora/National Opposition Union) will win. The UNO coalition was comprised of fourteen political parties united in their opposition to the Sandinistas. Thousands of Nicaraguans reluctantly voted for Ms. Chamorro in order to stop the US-directed bloodbath. It must have been 2:00 AM when we realized that the Sandinistas had lost the election. There were no celebrations in the streets. The Nicaraguans—the victims of this new leadership—were trying to console us over the Sandinistas' defeat.

This was one of the most painful moments in the history of the Office of the Americas. I have been grieving ever since. But the Nicaraguans repeated the last words of the early twentieth century US labor organizer, Joe Hill, of the International Workers of the World (IWW), "Don't mourn, organize!" Reagan and Bush destroyed Nicaragua with a criminal policy known as Iran-Contra. And now fanatics like Jesse Helms wanted to be sure every last drop of blood is drained out of the Nicaraguan movement for liberation. Never mind that the International Court of Justice ordered the United States to pay seventeen billion dollars in restitution! These savage attackers of small nations don't seem to understand: the seeds of liberation have been sown and the harvest will come. The harvest has only been delayed.

The methodology of armed struggle is not the way of civil society. There is a difference between guerrilla war and imperial war. George Washington used guerrilla tactics; the British fought in an imperial fashion. Regardless of tactics, guerrilla warfare is still militarism. It is still killing. Guerrilla warfare certainly may be justified as a final resort for those who understand the right to self-defense. But this does not make it fault free. Innocent people get killed in guerrilla warfare. People like the Salvadoran poet Roque Dalton are executed by power-hungry paranoids of the "left" who think they have a right to make judgments over life and death. Children get killed in the crossfire. Peasants who want no part of the struggle are drawn into it unwillingly. Villages are destroyed, recruits are pressed into service by physical and psychological pressure.

If you ask me if I favor the armed struggle, my answer is no, I do not. If you ask me if I understand the armed struggle, the answer is yes. While I abhor armed struggle, I also understand the right to self defense. The guerrilla war model is certainly not a good guide for civil society. The FSLN of Nicaragua and the FMLN of El Salvador have encountered that reality. Any faults of these rebel organizations, however, are minor in comparison with the gross might-makes-right oppression of US-directed "low intensity conflict." The people of Nicaragua had lost mothers, fathers, brothers, sisters, wives and husbands in what was actually high intensity conflict with the United States. The Pentagon called it Low Intensity Conflict (LIC) because of the low number of acknowledged US military as compared to the internationally hired guns.

The behavior of the United States in Nicaragua from 1855-1990 demonstrated that a painful line in the Sandinista Hymn was simply gospel truth, "Yankees, the enemies of humanity." Nor could we say that this line of the hymn was exclusive to Nicaragua. Williams Blum's book, *Killing Hope*[10] expresses the worldwide nature of this denunciation.

Nicaraguans needed the war to stop. The only way to stop it was to vote for the opposition coalition UNO. There were enough Nicaraguans who wanted peace at any cost, and so this is how Mrs. Violeta Chamorro was elected. Jimmy Carter was in Managua conferring with President Daniel Ortega about the transition. No one knew better than Ortega that this was a critical moment in the history of Nicaragua. A revolutionary government was in peaceful transition to an elected opposition government. The reason for this transition was the brutal and illegal force imposed by the United States. There was no joy in Managua with this great "victory."

10 Common Courage Press, 1995

The atmosphere was grim, sad and restrained. Nicaraguans realized they had lost a battle. They had not lost the revolution. Daniel Ortega spoke of governing from below.

When the Sandinistas came to power, Nicaragua saw its landed elite run to Miami, become US citizens and then return to Nicaragua to claim land owned by "US citizens." They do not have a legal leg to stand on. So they stood with Jesse Helms who could not care less about international law.

The revolution was stomped on, tortured, lied about, attacked, and suffocated. CIA Chief William Casey begat Oliver North and other monsters to create a secret contra government. Money was begged from the Sultan of Brunei, and weapons were being piled into the Iran of Ayatollah Khomeini. Flunkies were hired in the US to pose as "intellectuals" in support of the Contra cause. These were Reagan's "yes" people: supposed "experts" working in Washington who favored the Contras. Flunkies are people who go where the power goes; they are often incapable of critical thought. I had a debate at the John Kennedy School of Government at Harvard University with one of them. I was lodged in John F. Kennedy's room. The debate was well-attended. My opponent was an ardent supporter of the Contra war. Mercenaries in the field, mercenaries at Harvard, mercenaries in the Congress. Ultimately, I was not happy about this debate. I think I sounded hostile.

All of this led to the death of some forty-thousand Nicaraguans together with amputees from border to border. What about the "class warfare" thing? Class warfare is not something that is created by mean-spirited poor people. It is the reality that exists when people who don't work "earn" hundreds of times as much as people who do back breaking labor.

And how do we keep our sanity? By engagement. It seems to me that once we are engaged in a struggle, there is no room for cynicism. There is only room for work, for risk and reflection.

I returned home from Nicaragua's elections of 1990 feeling personally and collectively wounded. My major focus and that of the newly forming Office of the Americas from 1979 to 1990 was on Nicaragua's revolution. I thought of the thousands who returned to the US after serving in Spain during its civil war of the 1930s. We, however, were not military combatants. In my opinion, the role of our non-violent international solidarity movement has a greater future than any attempt of internationals to participate in armed conflicts. We were not engaged in fantasy. We imbibed the victory of 1979, the literacy program, health care for all, the numerous varieties of cooperatives, the schools, the admission of government abuses (a rarity in most places), the humanity in the jails and prisons, the rehabilitation of Somoza's teenaged torturers, the music, the contra terror, the Mothers of the Martyrs and the CIA sabotage.

When speaking in the Southern California region Ernesto Cardenal was a guest at our home. After serving as a world-class Minister of Culture, this former Trappist Monk found it necessary to leave the Sandinista Party. We have the hope that all of the splinters will come together again with a deeper spirit of participatory democracy. We cannot ignore the failings of individuals who make a revolution. This kind of review can apply to Washington, Jefferson or Ortega. It is painful to see the current splintering of the Sandinistas—may it only be temporary. *Comandantes* may serve well in the armed struggle. But civil society is something else. Ernesto's contributions will endure regardless of the party's future. His Gospel in Solentiname demonstrates the power of people to apply the lessons of biblical literature for themselves. Ernesto Cardenal insists that culture is for everyone, not simply for a "cultured class." He was profoundly offended when the editor of Barricada was removed for attempting to evolve the Sandinista Party newspaper into an organ of critical thought for all Nicaraguans.

During our several delegations to Nicaragua we were hosted by Rosario Murillo, wife of Daniel Ortega and Secretary General of the Asociación Sandinista de Trabajadores de la Cultura (ASTC or Sandinista Association of Cultural Workers). We had a familial relationship with the leadership of the Sandinistas. We worked not only as fellow colleagues, but as friends and family. The Foreign Minister, Father Miguel d'Escoto, was a seminary colleague and dear friend. Father Ernesto Cardenal was a compañero of years, Vice President Sergio Ramirez was a guest of the Office of the Americas in Los Angeles, as were a host of Sandinista Ambassadors to the United States.

Liberation Theology was the leitmotiv of Nicaraguan revolutionary music and literature. There was the musical genius Carlos Mejia Godoy and his brother Luis, the Soul Vibrations from the Atlantic Coast, Father Molina and the *Misa Campesina Nicaraguense.* Jesus said, "By their fruits, you shall know them." The fruits of these talented, humane people were to be seen everywhere. There was the Ecumenical Center Valdivieso and the great work of the Reverend James Goff and his family. Protestants were not aliens in the Sandinista revolution.

No one could fool Sister Mary Hartman in her human rights office. After decades of work in Nicaragua, she was aware of former students who were Somosistas and now avidly working for the contras. The Maryknoll Sisters were in the most dangerous of locations. Sister Nancy Donovan was captured by the contras and somehow lived through it. Many of her parishioners did not.

But were the Office of Americas' delegates simply a cheering section for the Sandinistas? Were we incapable of critical thought? Many in the US press said we were. I recall an argument with Christopher Dickey of the *Washington Post* at the Intercontinental Hotel in Managua in the early 1980s. It was about my claim that both sides were not the same. It was about the fact that Nicaragua was far more correct than the US. It was not about perfection on the part of the Sandinistas. It was about their ethical position as compared with that of the US. It was about the US journalistic definition of "balance."

I cheered the many things we had hoped to see in our own country and internationally: medical care as a right, education as a right, and housing as a right. We delighted in the formation of the Nicaraguan Constitution, the plethora of political parties, the opposition newspaper *La Prensa*, something which the United States never tolerated during its Civil War or its World Wars. This long battle was a conflict between truth and power. We believe the Nicaraguan revolution went beyond the Cuban revolution. And this seemed to be the opinion of Fidel Castro when he visited Managua. "I have not come here to teach you, but to learn," was the theme of President Castro's presentation in Managua. We loved the place of Liberation Theology in the Nicaraguan revolution.

No, the "cheering" sections were the US journalists. They were bound to imply basic goodwill toward Nicaragua on the part of the United States. For every atrocity committed by the US paid contras, it seems that susceptible journalists had to demonstrate an equivalent evil by the Sandinistas. This was not honest; it was a contrivance. Yes, Dickey can say how bad the contras were, but then he must also say that Nicaragua insulted the Pope. Nicaragua did not insult the Pope; the Pope insulted Nicaragua. This required, necessary false notion of balance often destroys the ability of highly paid US journalists to make key value judgments in such conflicts. The United States was wrong in Nicaragua as it was wrong in Vietnam, Iraq, Afghanistan and elsewhere. Nicaragua was fighting in a defensive manner against atrocities from the US.

The piety of such journalists amazes me. They show more subservience to the Pope than did Michelangelo, who was paid by the Pope, but who was not afraid to criticize papal misuse of authority. Recently another *Washington Post* reporter was concerned about Father Jean Bertrand Aristide insulting the papal delegate to Haiti. How touching. The Vatican was the only polity in the world to diplomatically recognize the government of the dictatorship that overthrew President Aristide. Thousands of lives were lost in the aftermath. We should ask such reporters if they have made their Easter Duty.

158

Chapter 27

Delegation to Iraq

I was eager to go to Iraq. This was December 1990. An impossible peace mission was arranged. Almost everything we planned was unachieved. There was to be a chartered plane in Amman, Jordan, to meet us. There was no such plane. We were to meet with Saddam Hussein in Baghdad. We did not. We were to meet with Foreign Minister Aziz. We did not.

It was so difficult to leave Theresa behind to do the worrying. Foreseeing the impossibilities of this venture, I was despondent by the time I arrived at JFK Airport to meet the other delegates. Nothing was working so far. Will they let us in? Maybe they will not let us out. My self-critical inner voice began to chide, "What a dumb-ass idea. Why don't you go back home where you can walk and meditate on Santa Monica Beach? Why don't you stay out of areas you don't understand? You are not a Middle East specialist." Oh, God—what a bunch of doubts.

I met the rest of the delegates at the Royal Jordanian Airlines departure salon. I considered myself fortunate to be a part of this delegation coordinated by Global Exchange. We were now a delegation of ten, including Barbara Lubin, founder of Middle East Children's Alliance (MECA), who would meet us in Amman, Jordan; Kevin Danaher, co-founder of Global Exchange and the person responsible for arranging the trip; and other US academics and activists, including Barbara Wiedner, the head of "Grandmother's for Peace." There were many changes in the delegation as it was forming. As in all such ventures, we were not certain of what we would accomplish. But we wanted to be in person in this crisis. Perhaps we would be able to bring home some crucial negotiating points that the US government and media have ignored. Would Iraq agree to go before the World Court at The Hague with this conflict? Would the US? And what about linkage? Syria had achieved a military takeover of Beirut as a result of its role on the Bush team. The Saudis have received billions in aid with more on the way. Once the US lets the UN compare and contrast the West Bank with Kuwait, a political consensus will demand an end to Israeli occupation of Palestinian lands.

Why were we in Iraq? Ominous signs from Kennebunkport, George Bush's summer home. Iraq was making moves on Kuwait, a location claimed as its own from time immemorial. Ambassador Glaspie was saying "Nevermind," and Washington was looking for another "heroic" venture. The US's dear friend had become uncooperative—no not Manuel Noriega this time, but CIA buddy Saddam Hussein. The US sided with him during his war with Iran. We knew about his poison gas, we knew about his dictatorship, and we wanted him to win.

It really was not about oil. It was about the terror in the military-industrial-congressional-prison complex. The Berlin Wall was coming down. It was about a "peace scare," which could mean a decline in the endless welfare to the most incompetent sector of corporate capital and at once the most powerful. This was Mr. Bush's lobby. This was his life. Votes were actually pending to cut military personnel. A peace dividend was in formation. The permanent war economy was being threatened. An eternal channel to the hard-earned tax money of the middle class could possibly be choked off. The search for enemies must continue avidly.

As we left JFK on board Royal Jordanian Airlines, I thought of the impending war as Christmas carols wafted through the cabin. And there was even the music of the Maryknoll Hymn, "Oh Christmas Tree." At no time have I left the spirit of Maryknoll. I am simply no longer funded by Maryknoll.

It was good to see people of so many ethnic backgrounds in Jordan. Since Jordan is a transit and refugee point for people from India, Egypt, Kuwait and Iraq, the nation's total population is larger than usual. While Jordan has a population of three million, the nation's refugee population is almost equal to their native population. How any sane human beings could attempt to make a polity out of ethnicity or religion is a mystery to me. I do not think there is a future for any state based on religion or ethnicity. I would like to see the following establishment clause in every constitution and Bill of Rights: "There shall be no law regarding an establishment of religion."

We approached Amsterdam at 10:30 AM on December 30, 1990. I slept all the way across the Atlantic. I thought about my children. How can warmongers look at children? Children are the greatest argument for peace. A few simple negotiations should do it.

We are met by Mr. Ghazi, the First Secretary of the Iraqi Embassy in Amman. There is no charter plane available to Baghdad. Mr. Ghazi apologizes and tells us we are on our own. We then decide to stay at the Alia Gateway Hotel. The leitmotiv that is being played at the Alia Hotel was, "As Time Goes By." It plays again and again as we are waiting for our exit visas. I kept thinking about the movie *Casablanca*. Not only is the news bad about getting to Baghdad, it is also bad about getting out of Amman on a return trip to the US How to get from Amman, Jordan to Baghdad on December 29, 1990? Do as they do in the US, just stand by.

We explained to Iraq Airlines that we were part of a peace mission. They seemed to understand exactly what we were doing since Global Exchange had arranged for our visit in advance. The Iraqi airline officials asked us to come into their offices and talk. They were friendly, but this did not exempt us from a long wait. People from India and Africa were pouring out of Iraq. Jordan was acting as a transit point and doing a good job of it. And why were we going to war? Bush's approval rating was beginning to slip. Despite the president's "brave" attack on the poor of Panama giving him an approval rating of 80% in January of 1990, things were not looking good for him. Having no program and no imagination, Bush had only the last refuge of scoundrels, patriotism. Let there be another great war! This one would make Panama look like peaches and cream. This one would get him re-elected. At last, a glimmer of hope for the military dinosaurs. Start the marshal music and prepare the body bags. We would be saved from the sound logic of cutting the military budget. Bush wanted a war. It was his only skill, his only hope.

All of us finally boarded Iraq Airlines non-stop to Baghdad. We had a last-minute crisis regarding payment. Iraq Airlines would accept only American Express. "Don't leave home without it!" Office of the Americas had the only such plastic card, so the $2,500 for ten round-trip tickets to Baghdad was paid in this form.

The anxiety factor is high. And so is self-doubt about the validity of such a delegation. Despite all the delegations I had been on throughout Latin America, Iraq was different. We were expecting the bombing to begin any day now. Was this trip necessary? Would our actions have the desired impact, to create a peace dialogue? Despite these fears, I knew it was important to do something. This might have been an imperfect journey, but it was an important journey. After our conversation with the Iraqi airline officials, we were wait-listed for departure with a purely open return. When? No reservations, no tickets, we are off to Baghdad. This must have been the beginning of ticket-less travel.

My travel book was *The Wounded Healer* by the popular theologian, Henry Nouwen. I read on page 19:

> No mystic can prevent himself from becoming a social critic, since in self-reflection he will discover the roots of a sick society. Similarly, no revolutionary can avoid facing his own human condition, since in the midst of his struggle for a new world he will find that he is also fighting his own reactionary fears and false ambitions.

I reflected on my own reactionary fears and how we are socialized to conform to authority. I thought about my own aims to break through the pressure to conform and how we must step outside of our middle-class culture and subsequent conformity to US public policy.

We arrive in Baghdad without incident and are met by Iraqi authorities. Fortunately, we have two Arabic-speaking delegates with us. We are billeted on an island in the Tigris River, which in normal times is used as a honeymoon location. During our time in Iraq, it is functioning as a "Peace Camp." In the meantime, Baghdad was about to be blasted by US bombs and missiles.

At the "Peace Camp" I meet Mother Theresa's representative, an Irish Roman Catholic priest, who was trying to arrange for her visit. I also meet some really weird French fascists who wanted to fight in the ranks of Saddam Hussein. The group that touched my heart, however, was the Gulf Peace Team. Forty of these international peace pilgrims under the direction of Jean Drese of Belgium and including Kathy Kelly of the US were camped on the border between Iraq and Saudi Arabia. They were all ages and from different religions and ethnic backgrounds. Their camp was a plea for peace. The Baghdad authorities respected them in spite of their open rejection of both sides in the conflict. Like them, the Iraqi government did not want war.

We went to the world's oldest university, Al Mustansria, and spoke with students and faculty. This was during Christmas time. There are many Christians in Iraq of Assyrian background. They informed us that this coming Saturday had been declared a day of prayer and fasting. Churches in Holland and the US followed the leadership of these Iraqi Christians to pray and fast.

We were well-received by the faculty and the administration. In these conversations, we focused on the need for peace in the area and stressed that a peaceful solution was possible. They knew that we, like them, were not happy with the US leadership and the impending bombing in Iraq. The students were talkative yet reserved regarding political issues. Agents of the government were visible everywhere on campus. In spite of being a police state, Iraq was the most modern of the Arab States. Women are part and parcel of the society. They have positions of authority in the universities and the government. While we did not meet any of these women within the government, I came across Iraqi women in prominent positions at the university. Women represent 40% of the faculty and are a majority among the students of the arts whereas men are a majority among the students of engineering.

The students we spoke to had just sent a letter of protest to President Bush. They wanted Bush to know that the key problem in the Arab world was the Palestinian question: "Mr. Bush, if you attack us, we will fight back. We want the world to listen to the Palestinians who fight with stones against their oppressors."

It was New Year's Eve. Merry Christmas is literally written in lights on the Baghdad skyscrapers. I went with the other delegates to a restaurant in the heart of the city on Abu Nawas Shariah. One of the delegates, a scholar of the Middle East, explained that this street was named after a tenth century romantic gay poet and alcoholic. The restaurant served and prepared food in the ancient tradition: fresh river fish is taken out of a tank, thrown on hot coals and served with bread. I thought of the breakfast Jesus prepared for his disciples.

On New Year's Day, we went to Babylon. Ancient palaces and temples were in the process of being rebuilt. The entire project was probably destroyed by the US blitzkrieg a few days later. Men are singing, beating drums and cymbals. Men and women are socializing intensely, but separately. For a moment I was taken back to one of my countless delegations to Nicaragua. The poor of the earth have always been hospitable. I have not seen this kind of hospitality among the affluent. Those living the life of extreme frugality tend to be generous. A completely open and friendly group of men and women—yet still separated within the group—wanted us to share their food, drink and joy. Solidarity is an excellent substitute for war! "To him who can see, nothing is profane," says the French Jesuit Teilhard de Chardin.

Sharing this idyllic New Year's Day with the local Iraqis was a spiritual experience. I could only reflect on what would come to mind countless times in Nicaragua, "You are about to be killed by my country and yet you are offering us heartfelt hospitality." Again I thought of Nouwen:

> The basic principle is that no one can help anyone without becoming involved, without entering his or her whole person into the painful situation, without taking the risk of becoming hurt, wounded or even destroyed in the process. The beginning and end of all leadership is to give your life for others.

I began to understand that the apprehension, fear and anxiety I felt in Iraq was because I was holding on too tight to my comfort zone and ordinary surroundings. This is part of our culture: we are taught to hold onto what we have and not let go. Yet, we must let go and let God. Personally, I don't think the fear of death is as strong as the fear of irrelevance.

For security reasons, the Iraqi group leaders who helped coordinate our visit revealed our agenda on a piecemeal basis. One night we were expecting to meet a high-level negotiator who was in opposition to the upcoming war. Our trusty Toyota Minibus, which we had used throughout the visit, took us to a gated community. We entered an upper-middle-class art deco home. This was unexpected. This was the home of our host for the evening: Yasser Arafat. Barbara Lubin, who had done so much work on the behalf of Palestinian children, made this visit possible. There were some five or six uniformed Palestinians with him who spoke no English. Despite this security, the tone was informal and homey. For more than five hours we ate from his modest buffet table and talked about the advent of war. Arafat was clearly upset with the long shunning he had endured from the West, especially from Israel and the United States. Here is my summary of Arafat's comments, which were in English on that memorable evening in Baghdad:

I have mediated in intra-Arab disputes for twenty-five years, but your country will not accept me. I can talk to all sides effectively. This war is unnecessary, it is a lose-lose situation. This war will be a disaster. The environment will be destroyed not only in Kuwait, but in the whole area. It is our duty to find a solution, to speak frankly. They are not coming here for Kuwait. They are coming here to break Arab unity. Let us have an international conference for the Middle East and for the Gulf Crisis. We can work together to achieve peace for all of us. We can put all of the problems on the table. I mediated the cease-fire between North Yemen and South Yemen, now there is one Yemen. I mediated between the Saudis and the Emirates, between Sadat and Gaddafi. This is an old conflict between Kuwait and Iraq. I mediated between Kuwait and Iraq in 1972. Why not rent the island of Bubiyan to Iraq for ninety-nine years? But Washington does not want Arab unity.

Yasser's words represented the hopes and anxieties of the Palestinian people. Yasser himself has always been under threat of assassination. Yet, his dedication to his people was clear. Yasser Arafat continued saying:

Some say there is no comparison between Iraq's subjugation of Kuwait and Israel's subjugation of the West Bank. But the UN has repeatedly demanded that Israel give up its conquered territories. Both the US and previous Israeli governments, not to mention Israel's Peace Now movement, claimed to have committed themselves to withdrawal. The 1967 war does not legitimize Israel's annexation of East Jerusalem and the massive Israeli settlement program in the West Bank. Neither did the six-day war license Israel to trample Palestinian human rights and civil liberties by ignoring UN resolutions.

164

Saddam Hussein will retreat from Kuwait if there is some significant movement on Palestinian demands. Such parallels raised by Iraqi moves in Kuwait can be the occasion to leverage not only an equitable settlement for Israel's occupied territories but for a peaceful solution to the entire Gulf conflict. We hear talk about Iraq wanting to control the world's supply of oil. On the contrary, the US wants to control it. We hear the endless new mantra of the CIA: "Iraq might have a nuclear capability!" The real problem is that Bush has nuclear weapons and is ready to use them from Southern Turkey.

Our evening with Arafat ended with mutual gratitude and photos.

Back to Jordan via Iraq Airlines we saw Iraqi military fathers kissing their children goodbye in the Baghdad Airport. I doubt if any of those fathers returned to their homes alive. We were surprised to actually get on the Iraqi Airlines flight to Jordan. Bombs from our homeland were imminent.

From Amman, I connected via phone with my nephew, Edward Joe Crummey, Jr. a Los Angeles talk show host for KABC. Before I left, my sister told him I was going to Iraq. Joe Crummey had incorporated his family onto his program several times before, including a contentious conversation with his mother, my sister. This was his style. This time however, the conversation was not contentious. I spoke about the importance of negotiations at this critical moment. He did not argue the point.

Absolutely everything was wrong with our peace mission to Iraq. Nothing went as planned. There was no chartered plane in Amman, Jordan to meet us. We never met with Saddam Hussein as planned. And we never met with Foreign Minister Aziz. Yet, as we left Amman— unbelievably on schedule—we realized that things went better than we could have ever anticipated. We met many members of the Iraqi government. We met Yasser Arafat. We were well-received by the students and the local people.

There is always a crisis of re-entry when coming back to the US from a Third World country. While I was not shocked, I was still surprised by the absolute censorship posture that we received from the "free press." There was no interest in our visit nor our message. Given this silence, we determined that mass-mobilization was our only avenue of expression.

Theresa and I together with my son had demonstrated at the Los Angeles Federal Building long into the night on January 15, 1991. There were over one thousand of us protesting the upcoming war in Iraq. I thought: "Why is war so popular? Why does military action so please the populace?" I only wish I knew. Is seems to be the logic of the great football game? US number one! But in war, there is never an equal playing field.

165

The teams, in this case the US and Iraq, were very uneven, however, and there were no rules except might makes right. The demon of patriotism was being whipped by the wimps of war. Because the ideas of every age are the ideas of the ruling class. The owners of the presses control the "freedom of the presses." The owners of the media control the "freedom of the media." It is so obvious once we reflect. The poor are taught to hate their fellow poor, and might even parrot the phrase, "They don't want to work because they are lazy," against their brethren. As a result, the poor have become victims of the ruling class, whose thoughtless and a-historical mind control has imposed this nonsensical ideology on them. William Randolph Hearst was a wimp of war for the Spanish-American conflict. Yellow journalism was in its primitive stages at the time. In the 1990s it has been perfected. Presidents are not fact-checked, they just blabber. Scholars are fact-checked and called controversial. Nothing is more controversial than straight talk.

We are arrested at the Los Angeles Federal Building as the US drops 88,000 tons of bombs on Iraq in January of 1991.

Theresa, Blase Martin and I went back to the Los Angeles Federal Building with a large contingent of students and people of all ages on the next night, January 16th. Theresa spoke to the students about the draft and how they shouldn't have to fight in an unnecessary war. My son Blase Martin sang for the demonstrators, and before long about a hundred of us were arrested for blocking the doors of the building.

Our hands were cuffed behind us and we were ordered to lie on our bellies on the marble floor. Later, we were marched to holding tanks. One tank for women and one for men. After several hours of waiting, with our handcuffs never removed, we heard that the bombing of Iraq had started. I thought that I will be delighted to tell my grandchildren just what I was doing when that damnable holocaust began. When we were finally released and reunited, Theresa, Blase Martin and I agreed that being handcuffed in the Los Angeles Federal Jail was the best place for the three of us to have been when that filthy war of aggression started. That evil, unnecessary, malicious destruction of the cradle of civilization, Iraq and its people that has now continued uninterruptedly for over twenty years!

When people are asked, "Where were you on December 7 1941?" Many today will respond, "I was not yet born." But those old-timers who were alive in 1941 will generally recall clearly where they were and what they were doing when Pearl Harbor was bombed. Likewise, when I am asked, "What were you doing when President Bush began his personal war in Iraq?" I can answer, "I was in jail, my wife was in jail, and my son was in jail."

Chapter 28

L.A. Uprisings & Campaign for House of Representatives

I was asked to teach a political science course at Los Angeles Harbor College. I really thought I was unemployable. This was January 1991. There were thousands of pages on me in the "Freedom of Information Files." And Harbor College was still offering me a full-time position? Fortunately, I only had to teach three nights a week and alternate Saturdays, which left my days and most nights open for the Office of the Americas.

As I had done at California State University Los Angeles and UCLA during the days of Vietnam, I began my position at Harbor College with a student teach-in that waged a stinging attack on militarism and the Gulf War. The teach-in became front-page news in the college newspaper. The response by faculty was vastly different than my days as a professor during Vietnam. This was the friendliest relationship I ever had with a college administration. Only one faculty member, a Professor of Physical Education, seemed hostile. Even the Dean of Instruction seemed to appreciate my position. The students were also responsive to the event. I was unaccustomed to such acceptance of my political views within academia. I found the students receptive, the faculty cooperative and my politics tolerated. Was I in heaven or what?

Why the change? I realized that I had not taught in higher education since the fall of the Berlin Wall. The Cold War was over—certainly not won—but over. The United States no longer had an official story. That former official story was about an evil called communism which, as the cause of the world's problems, had to be eliminated. The ideology of anti-communism became our national mantra. New ideologies were in formation. Terrorized by the possibility of losing funds, the CIA began avidly looking for enemies. The new mantra was, "We think you might be making an atom bomb. Prove to us you are not making an atom bomb." Rather than sniping at individual nations our objective should be the abolition of nuclear weapons internationally. The United States has failed to show leadership in this entirely doable and necessary action.

In the meantime, my radio programs were being up-linked weekly to the National Public Radio satellite. I remember a letter from a despondent listener in Houston, which said in part:

"Every place around here has 'Support the Troops' on it; there are yellow ribbons and flags everywhere. The other day when going out to eat a hamburger . . . it had a small flag stuck into it!"

At 5:00 AM the following morning my response materialized. This is what I said on air:

A flag for your hamburger!

How appropriate to have a flag jammed into your hamburger.

It should be called the Iraq Special.

We are the penetrating flag and they are the hamburger.

First we cut it off and kill it, then we eat it.

Oh, wave the flag and let it serve as your opium.

Each wave is another child killed in the name of ignorance.

Each wave is a mindless gesture of absolution.

But no matter how hard you wave the guilt remains.

Let us never serve another hamburger without a flag on top.

Oh, Holy McDonalds, Oh, Burger King.

You, Mr. Bush, Burger King of the world, who will you grind up next?

Look, Mr. Burger King, there is Fidel, think what fine hamburger you can make.

French-fried napalm, your napalm from hell, and here's to your fuel air crematorium bombs.

Oh, put flags on the French fries too. Napalm the potatoes. Let every French fry be a reminder of what our kinder, gentler country does to children.

Indeed, we should make a law that every hamburger and every serving of French fries be topped with a flag so we can remember forever the holocaust of 1991 and the unnecessary wars of the '60s, '70s '80s and '90s.

These are the wars that destroyed our cities and our souls.

Wave the flag, ye merchants of death!

These are the wars that killed our youth. Wave the flag and genuflect please.

Oh, kinder, gentler Bush, Oh, holy one of Kennebunkport.

Oh, sacred Ayatollah, may we no longer burden you with elections. You are surely king of the universe.

Let us declare you son of God.

Let our CIA pollsters extend their loaded questions forever!

Do you support the Burning Bush?

And let those who do not support you, Oh, Holy One, Oh, Eminence, let those who do not worship you be excommunicated from the chosen.

Cast them forth! Let the polls go on.

Do you love the President?

Curse forever those who say no.

Do you support the President? Yes, I pay taxes so he can kill the world. Have you ever had a bad thought about the President . . . alone or with others?

Did you take pleasure in your bad thought?

Wave, oh, wave the flag!

Worship the craven image!

Did you ever think negatively of, "Cut it off and kill it," Powell?

Did you ever doubt that there was life in Brent Scowcroft?

Tell the truth! Wave the flag a thousand times.

Did you ever question Cheney's snarl?

Did you ever doubt Mr. Baker's honesty?

Wave, oh, wave the flag!

Did you ever wonder what happened to the Congress?

They are on a long winter's nap to be followed by a long spring nap to be followed by summer vacation. And in the fall, let them raise their salaries!

Oh, blessed patriot, fornicating with idols, wave your flag.
Conquer the enemy!

The enemy is everywhere.

The trauma of the massacre in Iraq renewed toxic feelings of Vietnam War days. To hear the snippy voice of Bush saying, "There is no peace movement," gave me much consolation knowing that the exact opposite of his babble was where truth could be found. The yellow ribbons and "Welcome Home" parades after the Iraq holocaust were just one more insult to the Vietnam veterans. Almost 60,000 had died on the battlefield in Vietnam, but more than that committed suicide after they returned home. It was not the absence of silly parades that depressed them. They realized they had been lied to and they had conducted a genocidal war against innocent people. As one of the vets in good physical health put it, "I died over there." And now the Gulf War vets are dying of depleted uranium used in the very weapons they fired. They were not informed of the toxicity. The Veterans Administration will not acknowledge the link between the use of depleted uranium and the veterans' illness.

One of my only consolations in the wake of the Iraq massacre was the dedicated labor of former Attorney General Ramsey Clark. Ramsey conducted tribunals in cities throughout the world to document the atrocities of the war. My testimony in Los Angeles as a personal witness in Iraq became part of the record.

One night I was teaching at Harbor College in Wilmington when all hell broke loose in the megalopolis. Returning home on the San Diego Freeway I could observe Los Angeles on fire. Los Angeles snapped as a result of the resentment created by the acquittal of the officers who attacked Rodney King in 1992. Before things got out of control, Theresa and many others from the Peace Center, where the Office of the Americas is currently located, went down to Parker Center—police headquarters—to protest the court action. Yet, the demonstration quickly raged and the proponents of non-violent peaceful protest, which included Theresa, had to leave the scene. The fires started raging, and the Police Station at Parker Center was under attack.

We tried to conduct business as usual at the Office of the Americas. We did not think our presence would help during the raging of arson, looting, shooting, and the military occupation of Los Angeles. This was a spontaneous uprising and it was terrorizing. As soon as some calm was evidenced, we joined many others from all over Los Angeles and began digging out the ashes in South Central. Food distribution was rapid and effective. I did this work with Theresa, Blase Martin, together with Alice and Dick Powell.

Our main strategy was based on the belief that if hundreds of people from all races and ethnicities and class backgrounds were present in South Central working, distributing food and digging out the ashes, there would be less possibility of police or military abuse. Let's face it, if many white faces were seen in the midst of South Central, the response of the security forces would be milder.

I experienced a very real fear during the L.A. uprising: the fear that the riots would lead to complete social disintegration and endless violence. I am certain many others felt this way as well. We brought that fear with us to South Central. The fear did not go away but we assimilated it in work. Helping to dig out the wreckage was a meaningful diversion. A husky African American man came up to a group of us whites who were digging out pure ash. He said, "We have evidence that you are digging in asbestos, just leave it be, it is too dangerous."

At the same site near Western and Century, I came across Edward James Olmos and his friends helping to clean up. I had met Edward at the Sundance Institute some years earlier. He was equally convinced of the "strategy of accompaniment." Both in South Central as in Central America we found the power of simply being present to have a healing effect on people who have been oppressed. We call this "accompaniment," which has frequently saved lives as international witnesses stand in solidarity with victims of domination.

I don't recommend such uprisings but I do wish that the authorities would get the message. The LAPD has a culture of racism and oppression of poor people. There are unwritten rules of police behavior. For example, at the end of a vehicle chase, the person on the run is often beaten, especially if black. There is also a Mafioso silence present in police culture: one shoot, all shoot; lying on the witness stand; manufactured evidence and on and on. Chief Darryl Gates was still in charge!

After the ashes had cooled in Los Angeles, I felt it was time for a new political movement. The burning of Los Angeles was one of the motivations for my congressional race. I felt the need to get on the street. I was frustrated with what was going on in L.A. and Iraq. I thought it might help if I could get into the actual operation of the government. I wanted to make it clear that we stood for peace and the abolition of war in all forms. Yes, to Theresa's dismay, I would begin my fourth political campaign. We both understood that this was one important way to make our peace work known. Even if I did not win per se, we would win by getting our message out there.

I ran in the area of Central Los Angeles that was among the hardest hit by the uprising, this included Korea Town, East Los Angeles, Hollywood, and Echo Park. Since the Green Party had just qualified on the California ballot, I was nominated as one of the first Greens to run for national office: the US House of Representatives. On the Green primary ballot, we had a unique statement: citizens could vote for "None of the Above." This meant they could actually state on the primary ballot that they did not want me to run. Some 2% voted for my not running; the rest of the Greens were affirmative. I moved on to the general election of November, 1992, running against a Democrat, a Republican, a Peace and Freedom Party candidate and a Libertarian.

My manager was Ruth Shy, a veteran organizer, the first Associate Director of the Office of the Americas and a key player in the Nestle Boycott by the Infant Feeding Action Coalition (INFACT). She directed a dynamic campaign from our headquarters in Echo Park. We raised money, printed literature, walked precincts, held house meetings, operated a full-time office and became clearly aware of how few people were registered to vote. Our campaign literature was written in English, Spanish and Korean. We did not have literature in the eighty-five other languages of this multi-lingual and multi-cultural district.

I came in third. I was not surprised. Even though we had organized many people with the impressive Green platform, we could not break through the two-party monopoly. Democrat Xavier Becerra won the election to the US House of Representatives, a Republican physician came in second, Peace and Freedom—which had been on the ballot for over twenty years—came in fourth and the Libertarian candidate came in fifth.

Post-campaign exhaustion included the realization that I had spent far too much of our limited family resources in this venture. Yet, I found it necessary to be with the people during this urban and international crisis. I was grateful to get out on the streets to talk to people about militarism and peace. I felt that we did the best we could. We were not discouraged by the outcome. I have never felt competitive. I enjoy responsibility and would accept as much of it as necessary. Time and again I have had the feeling of simply offering my services, not seeking another acquisition. And I still felt this way after the campaign. It was a wonderful campaign. We made our point about peace and the need to abolish militarism.

Some months later it was time for Los Angeles City elections. Many of the candidates wanted my endorsement and my lists of people who had contributed to my campaign. I energetically supported Jackie Goldberg for City Council and was really pleased to see her win. She is the best we have had in Los Angeles. Richard Riordan asked me for an endorsement in his mayoral race. I had previously met Richard in conjunction with my work for Nicaragua. I wrote him a lengthy letter explaining why I could not support him. I was not in sync with him politically. I remembered his red-baiting work in Latin America. I was concerned about his policies in the US and Latin America. Although the position of Mayor is "non-partisan," he was coming from a Republican angle. Yet, perhaps I was wrong on my decision to not support him. Looking at the history of Los Angeles, he was more constructively engaged in his task than previous mayors. But, there were still about thirty homicides a week in Los Angeles.

If not electable, if hardly employable, perhaps I could serve in the Clinton administration. He won his new position in this same round of elections. I sent letters and offered my services to the new team letting them know of my background in Latin America and my willingness to serve in the State Department, preferably as Undersecretary of State for Latin America. After Elliot Abrams, some reconciliation was necessary in the hemisphere. My resumes and cover letters were sent to the appropriate sources, but I did not receive a single letter of acknowledgement. Perhaps it was a matter of my security clearance. Yet, I refuse to be cynical. I have offered my services to various presidential administrations throughout the years. It is truly offensive that an assassination club like the CIA has the right to make judgments on the suitability of public servants. I must have really "impressed" them.

Torture victim Sister Diana Ortiz, speaks as awardee at Office of the Americas anniversary celebration, November, 1996.

Opposing the bombing of the former Yugoslavia in 1999.

With Theresa and Alex Sanchez, the founder of Homies Unidos, a gang rehabilitation program between El Salvador and the United States, 2002.

Office of the Americas 20th Anniversary celebration with (left to right) Angela Sanbrano, Paul Haggis, Theresa, Howard Zinn, Dolores Huerta and Lisa Smithline, 2003.

With Amy Goodman of Pacifica Radio at the Office of the Americas anniversary, 2003.

Receiving the Distinguished Peace Leadership Award from the Nuclear Age Peace Foundation, 2006.

With Theresa as speakers at Anti-Iraq War Demonstration in Los Angeles, 2006.

Broadcasting "World Focus" at Pacifica Radio, KPFK, Los Angeles, 2011.

Chapter 29

Cuba Again

While leading the Office of the Americas delegations to Cuba in 1990 and 1992, I began to wonder if we should continue to collaborate even more with other organizations doing peace work in Central America. Office of the Americas has never been a competitive organization; we always sought to work together with organizations that we respected. This creates a kind of collective genius. We are not looking for work; we always have more than we can handle.

We decided to channel our future Cuba delegates to Global Exchange, a successful travel agency for political groups located in San Francisco. Global Exchange began as a solidarity group under the leadership of Medea Benjamin doing work similar to OOA. We admired their work and agreed with their plan to get more confrontational regarding the travel ban in Cuba. Generally, the Office of the Americas would suggest that our delegates carry a letter from their local paper or some publication assigning them to write an article about Cuba. This made them "journalists" and they fit in to the tight limitations of chosen souls who are permitted by the US to visit Cuba. The vindictive and stupid travel ban combined with the ancient US embargo (nine presidents long) was just one more attempt to isolate the people of the United States from reality. That's right; it is not technically a travel ban—it's simply a prohibition on spending US money in Cuba. The punishment for this evil act of spending precious US dollars in Cuba is simply $250,000 and ten years in prison. One might recall that the sentence for rape is generally five years. So much for family values.

By working with Global Exchange, the Office of the Americas became a "Freedom to Travel" office. The "Freedom to Travel Campaign" began in the 1990s. OOA was proud to endorse, support and send delegates to this program of international civil disobedience. The "Freedom to Travel Campaign" was premised on the right to travel and was our first step in "upping the ante on US policy toward Cuba." Our goal was to call attention to US relations with Cuba. The right to travel is an internationally recognized human right. Hundreds of US citizens came forward as "Freedom to Travel Campaign" delegates in spite of threats of prosecution and harassment. We agreed with the statement from the American Public Health Association: "The embargo's interference in the Cuban people's access to food and medicine is tantamount to the use of food and medicine as a weapon in the US arsenal against Cuba." Surely in this day, with the Cold War behind us, the most powerful nation in the world can devise a policy that does not cause suffering among an entire population in order to accomplish our national political objectives. A change in our Cuba policy is long overdue.

The second step in upping the ante on US policy toward Cuba was to invest in Cuban products. Such investments were considered "trading with the enemy" by the US government, which carries that same penalty of ten years in prison and $250,000 fine. The phrase "trading with the enemy" was strange. It has historically been used after a government declared war. We became founding partners in the *Soy Cubano!* company. This was another brilliant idea by Medea Benjamin who founded the company. Anyone who bought a share in the company could then sell shares to other interested people. In doing so, the company then enters a joint venture with Cuban factories producing a soy yogurt drink and other soy food products. Investors are informed that they should have no expectation of a financial return on their investment. What they are doing is making a charitable contribution.

The third component of upping the ante on Cuba was the Pastors for Peace Caravans to Cuba. The same US threat of prison and fine was hovering over this caravan just as it was hovering over the "Freedom to Travel Campaign and the *Soy Cubano!* company. By bringing humanitarian aid to Cuba, we were breaking the US embargo. I agreed to lead the Rocky Mountain contingent of a caravan in 1993. We began in Boulder, Colorado, and pointed our trucks south. Denver, Pueblo, Santa Fe, Albuquerque, Amarillo, Wichita Falls, Abilene, San Antonio, and finally we converged with nine other routes in Laredo.

After each day of driving there was a press conference, a reception and a place to stay. The stop in Pueblo, Colorado, was a special joy for me. When the caravan entered town we were met by an old friend, Bishop Charles Buswell. Here was a leader who had influenced me greatly when I was Regional Director of the Maryknoll Fathers in Denver, 1962–1965. Charles Buswell was over eighty now and just as humane as ever. He housed me in the local rectory. I think he "forgot" to tell the local priests that I was married with two children.

Buswell had a glorious history of wanting to "forget" some of the rigidities of canon law. I reminded him of a large ecumenical gathering of Protestants, Jews and Catholics in the 1960s where he celebrated Mass and announced to all present, "Would anyone with love in their heart please come up to Holy Communion." I was delighted to hear this. A conventional Roman Catholic Bishop would have warned the crowd that no one should come to Holy Communion who was not a Catholic in good standing.

The ten routes of the caravan reached some one hundred US cities. We received a great deal of interest from local press. Personally, I was expecting KKK responses in some of those Texas towns. How wrong I was and how the US was changing. What we found were journalists genuinely interested in why we would plan such a humanitarian caravan and refuse to ask for a license from the US government. We explained that such licenses are not necessary. International law allows contributions from one nation to another when there is a crisis.

Some one hundred vehicles converged at the Christ Worship Center in Laredo, Texas. The Local Evangelical pastor of this center is a Bible thumper and a progressive. It is a mistake to presume that all evangelicals are fundamentalist reactionaries. Not so. "You are going to cross the Red Sea. You are going to Cuba. Though you walk through the valley of the shadow of death, you shall fear no evil. Tomorrow, you are going to cross, tomorrow!" It was a good sermon. The service was marked by jazzy music, theatrical musical ups and downs typical of a classic Pentecostal-style sermon, quasi-rock, electronic music and all with family participation. The pastor told a joke about one of the church members who went to hell. The suffering soul kept asking for blankets. "Why do you want blankets, you are in hell?" was the Devil's question. The captive said, "I'm from Laredo!"

And then we met the Reverend Lucius Walker, Baptist Minister from Harlem, who was highly revered in Cuba. People tend to forget that Cuba is an African-Latin country. Lucius was involved in the complicated logistics of the entire caravan in Laredo. Here was the Martin Luther King, Jr. of the 1990s. It seemed obvious that the national press did not want to give him the attention he deserved. I think the day will come when Lucius will be known as an example of international solidarity. Some years prior, Lucius was on a delegation to Nicaragua. As his group took the river route to Bluefields Nicaragua, US paid mercenaries (contras) attacked the boat, several passengers were killed and Lucius was severely wounded. This incident led to his understanding of US foreign policy and spearheaded his efforts to project the methods of Dr. Martin Luther King into the international arena. I remember Rev. Walker's words to us as the vehicles converged in Laredo:

"Our primary purpose is political. It is to break the blockade. If our primary purpose were simply humanitarian we would ask for a license. We are not asking for a license from the Federal Government."

While the trucks were being prepared for the journey to Tampico, Mexico, where they were to be loaded on a Cuban freighter, an International Summit on Cuba was taking place at the Royce Hotel in Laredo. Ellen Bernstein, who had lived in Cuba at one time and became a spokesperson for Cuban affairs in the peace movement, asked me to chair this summit meeting. The simultaneous timing of the Cuba Summit and the Caravan was not accidental. The summit was designed to occur concurrently with the caravan and to offer a protective group of high-profile people to witness any negative behavior of authorities as we crossed the border into Nuevo Laredo, Mexico.

It was July 26, 1993, the fortieth anniversary of the attack on the Moncada Barracks, the former headquarters of the Batista military in Santiago, Cuba. The date of our event was symbolic. Fidel Castro and one hundred rebels attacked the Moncada Barracks on July 26, 1953. The attack failed and over one-third of the rebels were tortured and killed. The attack on the Moncada Barracks was the first act of the Cuban revolution.

As the International Summit on Cuba began I introduced the former Attorney General of the United States, Mr. Ramsey Clark. Ramsey gave an excellent historical background on US interventions since the time of Jefferson. But Ramsey Clark's participation was not simply academic. The following day he was helping us carry cargo across the Rio Grande by foot. The Customs Department allowed us to drive the trucks across empty. The understanding was that the trucks were coming back to the US and that they would not be permitted to go to Cuba. Customs forbad any cargo to be carried on the trucks. So, beginning with an elderly woman in a wheelchair, the first item, a computer, rolled across to Nuevo Laredo, Mexico. She was not stopped. Another and still another *caravanista* began carrying the cargo across in an all-day repetitive safari to Mexico. Hundreds of tons of goods were carried by hand in 107 degree heat. On the Mexican side we were given permission to store the cargo in safekeeping.

Mexico has full relations with Cuba, and there was no problem once the goods got to Mexico. We all made as many round trips as we physically could on that torrid day in Laredo. At the end of the day, all cargo and vehicles were safely together on the Nuevo Laredo, Mexico side.

Walking back to the US after countless trips I saw the little yellow school bus, the final vehicle, approaching. Lucius Walker was at the wheel. Customs stopped him and directed him into the US impound area. Customs intended to impound the bus based on their information that this little school bus was going to Cuba. Lucius refused to enter the impound yard and stopped his bus in the middle of the street. He asked the officer, "Why can't I go back to the Christ Worship Center? I am not crossing the bridge." Customs once again ordered him into the impound area. He refused. A huge tow truck was called. With all passengers still on board, the tow truck hoisted the front end of the bus and pulled it into the impound. "We are not getting out," said Walker.

His thirteen passengers concurred. Thus began a hunger strike which the fourteen of them conducted for three weeks. They were sustained by numerous supporters who painted the top of the bus silver to deflect the killing heat. A port-a-potty was introduced. Water was delivered in abundance by a host of loving supporters. The press was on hand. Radio reports were given. Washington was informed. And at the end, the hunger strikers won. The bus was released and is now the proud possession of the Martin Luther King, Jr. Ecumenical Center in Havana.

The Cuban media, the Mexican media, the Central and South American media covered all aspects of the story. US national media, as usual, was weak. Pastors for Peace Caravans to Cuba have continued to go to Cuba by way of Canada. This was the last venture of Pastors for Peace through Mexico.

Today major US corporations today are begging our government for permission to do business with Cuba. These corporations were deprived for decades in places such as China and Vietnam. Now they want to invest in Cuba. And they will be welcomed on Cuba's terms.

Chapter 30

Chiapas

The Zapatista conflict began in Chiapas, Mexico on January 1, 1994, the very day that NAFTA went into effect. We immediately formed a Southern California delegation to witness the reality. We flew directly to Mexico City and met with the National Network of Human Rights Workers. Our objective in meeting with that group was to be in sync with the progressive Mexican community in understanding this crisis. After a very meaningful dialogue the ten of us continued south to Tuxtla-Gutierrez, the capital of Chiapas. Heading up the mountains toward San Cristobal by bus it was clear that this was a war zone. There were frequent roadblocks by the Mexican Army. All men were ordered out of the vehicle, arms up on the side of the bus followed by a full search of the women and cargo within the bus.

Tanks and ground troops were in the main plaza of the classic colonial high-altitude town of San Cristobal. There was no cease-fire in effect. Helicopters given by the US as part of the war on drugs were being used to fire on "suspected insurgents." Walking down the Avenida de Insurgentes in the midst of an insurgency was ironic. But so is Mexico. The street name triggered many historical antecedents to the current Zapatista revolt. Father Miguel Hidalgo was an insurgent in 1810. He was given a fair trial by the Spanish Inquisition and convicted of being a Lutheran, a Jew and an atheist. He remains the father of Mexican independence. The inquisition be damned.

The Zapatistas are the legacy of Emiliano Zapata. His Plan of Ayala was the basis for a just land tenure system in Mexico. It had roots in the pre-Columbian *ejido* system and evolved into Article 27 of the Mexican Constitution of 1917. Zapata, a victim of treachery, was murdered by Colonel Jesus Guajardo on April 10, 1919, on the orders of the "revolutionary" President Venustiano Carranza. The power of the urban capitalists absorbed the Mexican Revolution of 1910. The cry of Zapata for rural justice was muted.

The fraudulently elected President Salinas of Mexico had the audacity to abrogate Article 27 of the Mexican Constitution of 1917. He also renewed relations between Mexico and the Vatican for the first time since the revolution of 1910. If he thought such a gesture toward the institutional Church would neutralize the rural cry for justice, he was gravely mistaken.

And now San Cristobal de las Casas was being attacked on January 1, 1994. Bush had begun the NAFTA "fast track" hype and Clinton took it over. But extremely intelligent people who could not read and write analyzed the NAFTA doctrine and rejected it as an attack on their nation and their culture.

We went to the office of Bishop Samuel Ruiz Garcia to meet at his Fray Bartolome de las Casas Human Rights Center. The office was full of people who were cut off from their families because of the roadblock on the highway between Palenque and San Cristobal. They could not bring in food or medicine to their families in Ocosingo and other communities. Our delegation together with the Mexican citizens conferred as one entity. Some of the US members suggested that we just walk right through the Mexican military blockade. I flashed back to our International March for Peace in Central America where we were beset with such rash urgings. The Mexican members said, "Absolutely not. We do not intend to commit suicide. They might let some gringos through but they will surely kill us." After a consensus, the Mexican locals, the Mexican human rights workers and the US delegation assembled as a group in the center of San Cristobal on January 11, 1994. We crowded into trucks and sundry other vehicles and drove to the outskirts of the city and then marched as a group to the roadblock of the Federales (the Mexican National Police). After being allowed to pass we marched on to the roadblock of the Mexican Army. At this point our procession was decisively stopped. The officer in charge gave us a long-winded lecture amounting to, "I've got my orders," adding that we would have to speak to the general regarding any change. After a period of standoff, I, along with a resident of Ocosingo, went back to San Cristobal to seek permission from General Othon Calderon to open the highway for humanitarian purposes.

At military headquarters, the first colonel we spoke to said he had more important matters to attend to. The second colonel, the one with heavily bloodshot eyes, was hostile. He would not state his name and ordered the Mexican journalist accompanying us to put down his camera. As a Mexican citizen, the journalist was offended and shouted back at the colonel about his rights. I asked the journalist to please stay focused on the matter of the roadblock. The hostile colonel did not give us access to the general.

The entire delegation reassembled at the Fray Bartolome Center and collectively wrote a letter to the governmental human rights office demanding freedom of transit for the families of Chiapas. "Even if the government does not read it, the press will publish it," said one of our knowledgeable hosts. The letter was written and the press printed it in full. While we could not reach the general by appointment, after he read the letter in the press he came to our lodging personally to object to our impertinence and to demand a list of the members of our delegation. He did not follow through with this threat, however, due to fortunate circumstances that occurred later that evening. It turns out that one of the women on the delegation had a conversation with him at a bar later that night. As they had a beer together, the general was impressed by the knowledge and fluent Spanish of La Gringa. This was quite significant as our delegate ended up talking him into letting the food go into the besieged areas! So, Wednesday morning, January 12, 1994, the highway was open. Residents began carrying food and medicine by foot to their besieged families.

I left San Cristobal by cab hoping to get to the airport in Tuxtla-Gutierrez. My cab was intercepted by another vehicle on the perilous descent from the colonial city. The interceptors were two Mexican lawyers who insisted that I accompany them as they visited the military hospital, the civilian hospital and the national police headquarters. We added our count of the dead at the hospital to the figures given by the Human Rights Network of Mexico. Although a specific total will never be known, a conservative count confirmed that hundreds were dead.

In the midst of this new war in Chiapas, some Guatemalan refugees in Mexico were attempting to return to Nenton in Guatemala and other Guatemalans were in flight from their genocidal army attempting to enter Mexico. The state of Chiapas had been militarized for years. *Caciques* (local leaders) of the ruling PRI pontificated on behalf of cattle raisers and other wealthy landowners. What was to be done? Article 27 must be reinstated. Here is the text:

Centers of population which lack communal lands or which are unable to have them restored to them due to lack of title, impossibility of identification or because they have been legally transferred, shall be granted sufficient lands and waters to constitute them, in accordance with the needs of the population; but in no case shall they fail to be granted the area needed, and for this purpose the land needed shall be expropriated, at the expense of the federal government, to be taken from lands adjoining the villages in question.

Article 27 included a continuation of the ancient *ejido* system which made it possible for indigenous people to maintain their community lands and which stated that Mexico would nationalize more lands for *ejidos* if necessary. The elimination of Article 27 was state treachery.

189

As was the case with previous delegations, I experienced a re-entry crisis. Does anyone know what is happening in Mexico? Does anyone care? There is also always the self-doubt about returning at all. Should I simply go to such areas and stay put?

Ever since my experience in Guatemala, however, I have been convinced that the majority of my work should be in the United States. It is here where the decisions and public policy are made. It is here where I can communicate and attempt to influence public opinion.

The students in my evening classes at Harbor College were always responsive to my travels. They wanted to know details and I always took the opportunity at our eight-hour Saturday sessions to explain the reality of Chiapas to them. These eight-hour Saturday classes at Harbor were designed to give students extracurricular experiences apart from the usual course work. I considered this approach important as students at community colleges are often denied the same experiences that are available at a university.

While I live on the outside of most established structures, I feel a constant nagging desire to be a part of an established order, a university, a government, even the faint memory of representing the institutional church. There is some consolation in this; the prophet must stand outside the gate of the city in order to denounce the evils therein. But there is also the desire to be on the inside, to be part of the decision-making. Perhaps this is why I have "applicationitis." I receive notifications of college presidencies and send in the necessary forms. I have all the required credentials for these positions. Yes, while I am offering my services, I am also thinking of the necessity of making a living, of supporting two post-graduate students and of not becoming financially dependent on others. Colleen was finishing medical school, while Blase Martin was completing a Masters in Public Administration.

At no time have I felt that it is superior to be on the outside. It would simply be a form of pride to consider myself better than anyone else because I am one of society's rejects. Many of the people who are part of the mainstream have just as much a desire for good as I do. We on the outside do not represent a holier group. We are privileged, however, to be able to make judgments we might not be permitted to make if we were on the inside.

The desire for acceptance, for status, for position is always there, though it is never something I will fight for. Reflections on the glory of fitting, of being accepted, simply leave me with gratitude. After a spasm of thought about the glories of acceptance, of fitting in, I revert to thanking God for my lot. *Dominus pars, hereditatem meam et calicem meam, tu es qui restituit hereditatem meam mihi* (The Lord is the portion of my inheritance, you are the one who will restore my inheritance to me). Each day is a privilege, a new challenge. I really have nothing to complain about. I only have things to thank God about.

There is a problem when one is apart from the established order. It is contempt. Confronting so much injustice, I must confess to contempt. It has not been enough to say that the wars in Vietnam or Central America were simply part of the capitalist system. I am contemptuous of those who conducted such wars. I am contemptuous of the Colin Powells who were the good soldiers at the side of maniacal presidents like Reagan and Bush. Yes, I understand the brilliant words of Scott Spencer as he comments on T. Coraghessan Boyle's novel *The Tortilla Curtain*[11]: "Contempt is a dangerous emotion, luring us into believing that we understand more than we do. Contempt causes us to jeer rather than to speak, to poke rather than to touch." I much appreciate Scott Spencer's observations about contempt. They touch me. I have been contemptuous of our government's behavior, our elected officials and our business community. How can I ever get rid of the idea that this contempt is legitimate? According to some, contempt is simply a way of feeling superior to others. Well, isn't this a spiritual problem? The old bromide, hate the sin and not the sinner, may apply here. I hate hypocrisy but when I see it personified in the Congress, how do I act as if I am not contemptuous of it and them? Would it be better were I not contemptuous? Would it help to say, "They must mean well." I suppose it would be better but I might be kidding myself. But what of our model person, Jesus? Did he not express contempt openly and frequently?

---

11 In the September 3, 1995 edition of *The New York Times*

Chapter 31

A Respite

Thanks for your patience dear reader. But I really don't want to make this book into a travelogue.

Bear with me as I suggest that many of my "adventures" may be seen my previous books:

Guerrillas of Peace; Liberation Theology and the Central American Revolution, Third Edition, 2000

Guerrillas of Peace on the Air; Pacifica Radio Commentaries, Second Edition, 2002

Common Sense for the Twenty-First Century, 2004

The Central American Solidarity Movement, Oral History Program University of California at Los Angeles, 2005

Civilization is Possible, 2008

The Blase Bonpane Collection has been established by the Department of Special Collections at the UCLA Research Library (Collection 1590). This is a compilation of all my published and unpublished writings together with transcriptions of the World Focus radio and TV programs and lectures up to the present.

And there is my doctoral dissertation: *Liberation Theology and the Central American Revolution*, University of California, Irvine, Ph.D. 1984, University Microfilms International, Ann Arbor, Michigan.

A respite from being a frequent flyer took place in 1999. Cancer intervened. I had some sigmoid tests but nothing really caught it until having a colonoscopy. It was stage three colon cancer and well into the lymph nodes. Life had always been a rather tenuous thing for me. I never expected to get out of Guatemala alive and here I was still kicking. Theresa was very upset by this cancer thing. My daughter Colleen was looking upset as well and I asked her, "Who could have ever have a happier life than I?"

Family means everything when such illness strikes. I felt like a death row prisoner when I went in for surgery. "Put your things in this bag," "Here comes the anesthetic." Theresa was there with the very painful job of waiting. Colleen was in the process of taking her medical boards as she approached graduation at UCLA Medical School. She slept on the floor in my hospital room every night of my stay. She read the medical reports and called attention to any doctor's errors.

Colleen is one who claims she often does not say tender things but, my God, she simply does them.

It seems that the hardest part of illness is to see the family distraught. There were times when I hoped they would not come to see me because I was such a mess. But such visits are beneficial even when the patient is uncomfortable to see family uncomfortable.

I followed the cut and drug methods of US medicine. The chemo was called 5-FU. The name seemed pornographic but it must have done something because I am still in action over ten years after the surgery. I believe, however, that the 5-FU led to my neuropathy. It was worth the price.

Kidney cancer followed less than a year after colon cancer. My left kidney was removed the old fashioned way. And how to deal with recovery from cancer? I cannot speak for everyone but I simply tried to continue my role as director of the Office of the Americas. In the first weeks I might have worked one hour a day. Then I tried to resume my teaching schedule at Los Angeles Harbor College where I taught evenings. The first evening I brought my beloved companero Don White and asked him to be ready to take over the class if I became too weak to teach. I said a brief hello to the class and within seconds turned the lecture over to Don. I simply could not yet function as a professor. However I believe that the effort to resume normalcy is very healing. Perhaps this is only true when doing work we love. But I would recommend it for anyone willing to experiment.

Within months I was back to full service at the Office of the Americas and Harbor College. So the first decade of the third millennium brought a change in tempo, some restrictions on my travels and a realization that the outreach of the Office of the Americas could be enhanced by an ever greater concentration on media and writing.

Then there was the attack of September 11, 2001! In the wake of the attacks in New York and Washington, D.C. Theresa organized an immediate vigil for peace not war. She created the Coalition for World Peace and received a message of solidarity from "Families for Peaceful Tomorrows," the family members of the 9/11 victims who insisted that this attack not be a cause of war. This was simply another example of Theresa's genius without which there would be no Office of the Americas and the fostering of entirely new concepts in the international solidarity movement for justice and peace.

She must also receive the honors for the implementation of the International March for Peace in Central America in the midst of the Contra War, 1985-1986. Theresa also wrote handbooks for the peace movement on how to organize as she organized a plethora of organizations for specific purposes.

A few examples: Working closely with the formation of Medical Aid to El Salvador; working with Don White for the formation of CISPES (The Committee in Solidarity with the People of El Salvador) in Los Angeles; The Bolder-Jalapa Friendship City Project; Technica (Technicians for Nicaragua); the Los Angeles PeaceCenter Coalition against the Gulf War (1991); the Lori Berenson Committee; Doctors for Peace; The Living Wage Campaign; and Artists for Peace which, with the direction of Paul Haggis, continues to build new schools in Haiti.

Theresa's skills brought internationally known celebrities into the movement. Many of these notables were arrested with us in acts of civil disobedience. Theresa's vision insisted that The Office of the Americas never became a "religion" to be protected but rather a catalyst for building a peace system to replace the rotted out war system.

My interest in theology is longstanding but I must say that much of theology is a matter of abstract fads. I know not where this adage originated but I do think of it often; "The greatest error is to take that which is concrete and make it abstract."

I don't see abstractions in the word picture which Jesus paints of the Last Judgment. It is a picture of food, drink, clothes, prisons, sick people; concrete needs. Please read the 25th chapter of the gospel according to St. Matthew.

Democratic socialism is also based on the concrete felt needs expressed by the people. From small base communities to massive gatherings we can quickly derive the super majority cravings for justice, peace, a clean environment, and a thriving public sector.

Why then are there so many tea-baggers? Tea baggers are a product of a lifetime of mythology from schools, churches, and most of all the culture of advertising.

My spiritual roots are in the Roman Catholic Church. By the time I was ordained in 1958 I began to understand that I did not want to make converts to the Roman Catholic Church but rather to make converts to justice and peace. Father James Keller of Maryknoll developed a wonderful approach with his movement called The Christophers. He urged people to go into fields that would influence their society for justice and peace. This was a non-sectarian approach for the decade of the 50s and 60s. The Christopher Movement might be seen as a prelude to Liberation Theology.

My first years in the priesthood were directed toward getting students beyond their country and their continent to have a world perspective. That is why I asked the Public High Schools to allow me to speak at their assemblies on World Problems.

I was constantly haunted by the need to grow out of existing structures. To grow beyond, "God Bless America." To grow beyond "One Nation under God," to grow beyond one institutional Church.

After seven years of promotional work (1958-1965) covering the highways of the US speaking in schools and churches to promote the mission vocations and mission financial support I realized that my message was primarily based on that judgment account of Jesus from Matthew 25. I saw the Church as a great international institution, a universal (catholic) entity that could transcend the idol worship of US exceptionalism.

At the same time I was conscious of the pathetic state of the US Hierarchy which appeared to have more dedication to the state than to world peace. This tragic condition was personified by Cardinal Francis Spellman, who ordained 48 of as Maryknoll priests in 1958. He loved his role as military vicar of the United States and appeared to believe that our foreign policy was the foreign policy of Jesus.

My assignment to Guatemala in 1965 was preceded by graduate study in Latin American Affairs at Georgetown University in Washington, D.C. Georgetown was an opportunity to observe the condition of Catholic Higher Education. More attention was given to the state than to the teachings of Jesus. Some Jesuits worked in the peace movement, especially Father Richard McSorley who was personal chaplain to the Bobby Kennedy family.

And some Jesuits tried to out-hawk the hawks; "Bomb Hanoi would resound from their classes."

Lay members of the "distinguished" faculty came directly from the State Department, the CIA and various other US agencies.

But the overwhelming impact on me during this era was the Second Vatican Council; it was concluding in 1965. My response to the Council was my organization of the Weekends of Christian Living at Georgetown.

So here are some of my thoughts on religion and spirituality: "Religo" is the Latin word to "bind fast" or "tie and store," or to "fix firmly" or to "secure." Religion is a matter of binding to a set of sacred stories and a list of beliefs. Once we are bound we can be "relegated" to a particular sectarian system. It seems that what we need in this epoch is an unbinding so we are free to imbibe in a host of sacred stories. In such a quest religious hatreds cannot be sustained.

The killer of this unbinding is dogma. Dogma binds us to an exclusive club that "has the truth." Rigid dogma is frequently tied to politics and is universally divisive.

The "Nicene Creed" of the future might say: "I believe in justice, peace, joy, love, compassion, endurance and fortitude." Once unbound, people can imbibe in the entire range of sacred stories and they will find an amazing similarity, not in the dogmas but in the fruits of the Spirit as listed above. These fruits are part of the cosmos of religious history.

In recent history this transition can be observed in what is called Liberation Theology. It began with a sharp focus on the, "preferential option for the poor." As Liberation Theology evolved In Latin America and elsewhere the deflation of dogma was clear. Imperial religion was the product of the emperor Constantine. He paid the way for the Bishops to come to Nicaea and hammer out dogmas. Once done, religion was signed and sealed. "We have the truth. Error has no rights and death to the infidels!" Militarism and religion were joined in an unholy marriage that led directly to Crusades, Inquisition and Conquest.

Ending the war system can only happen with the demise of imperial religion. The unity of the human race can only take place when war is identified as the greatest sin. In the current epoch war and mainline religions seem to be quite compatible. But religion must evolve into a substantive nonsectarian spirituality.

Yes, as might be imagined, most of my spirituality is based on my formation in the Roman Catholic Church. While having a reverence for the positive spiritual elements of Catholicism, I simply have to be unbound from the dogmatic fundamentalism.

The final verse of my mantra comes to mind:

Da virtutis meritum,	Give us the strength to finish
Da salutis exitum.	Our journey with courage.
Da perene gaudium.	Give eternal joy.
Amen. Alleluia.	Amen. Alleluia.

And that ALLELUIA can resound through Judaism, Christianity, Islam, Hinduism Buddhism and all other religious efforts which have the potential to stand in awe of the Mystery. What becomes clear with consciousness is that the religious component is not the relevant component. The relevant component is in the visible fruits of the Spirit;

justice, peace, joy, love, endurance, courage, and compassion. These fruits can exist only within the medium of truth, they do not compute with false witness. The science of advertising and public relations is a pathetic effort to "joyfully" project falsehoods like war. Thus follows the cult of patriotism and manifest destiny.

Chapter 32

Let's Not Talk About Jesus

I really want to conclude this autobiography with my thoughts on Jesus.

This is not the sectarian Jesus, this is not the one that led to the endless bloodshed of Christendom. This is not the Jesus of the Council of Nicaea or of Martin Luther.

This is the Jesus who would be so comfortable with Mahatma Gandhi and a host of spiritual leaders.

This is the non-sectarian Jesus, yes, the internationalist Jew. He loved his roots but he, as we must, went beyond the confines of his culture and his continent to a cosmic perspective. That perspective continues to be obfuscated by sectarianism.

Can you hear Jesus saying, "I am a Roman Catholic," "I am a Methodist," "I am a Mormon"?

I don't think so.

There are some similarities between Israel at the time of Jesus and the Israel of today. At that time Israel was under the rule of empire. Oh yes, there were local kings but no supreme power aside from Caesar.

And Jesus was the best known person in Israel. Think of a Martin Luther King in a present comparison. The leadership delivered him up as a political criminal because they were envious. When scriptures speak of "principalities and powers" it is a reference to the homicidal nature of imperial politics.

Jesus loved his Jewish heritage. Judaism was the only religion he ever had. Let's take a look at his perspective:

We read of his sermon in his home town of Nazareth where he picked up the scroll and read from the prophet Isaiah, "The spirit of the Lord has been given to me, for he has anointed me to bring good news to the poor, to proclaim liberty to captives and to the blind new sight, to set the downtrodden free, to proclaim the Lord's year of favor." —Luke 4:18–19

At this point everyone in the synagogue was delighted and he won the approval of all.

There was, however a second part to his sermon. He continued:

There were many widows in Israel, I can assure you, in Elijah's day, when heaven remained shut for three years and six months and a great famine raged throughout the land, but Elijah was not sent to any one of these: he was sent to a widow at Zarephath, a Sidonian town. And in the prophet Elisha's time there were many lepers in Israel, but none of these was cured, except the Syrian, Naaman.

—Luke 4:25–27

When Jesus completed this second part of his sermon the whole congregation in the synagogue was filled with indignation, they rose up, dragged him out of town and tried to throw him over a cliff. Why?

Because the folks in his home town believed that the spirit of God could not reach anyone outside of their sect. Jesus made his point that God is not sectarian. And that message is just as necessary today.

It is about peace on earth, it is not about sectarianism.

Many people simply do not get it yet. And that is why we have Catholic and Protestant, Sunni and Shia, political Islam, political Judaism, political Christianity and political Buddhism, et cetera. Jesus, the universalist made it clear, the name of one's religion does not tell us anything. The fruits of your life tell us everything. The fruits sought by every spiritual pursuit are: love, joy, peace, courage, compassion, endurance and reverence. Where we find these qualities we find truth and authentic spirituality.

It is not surprising that the followers of the non-sectarian Rabbi from Nazareth concluded that they could not serve God and serve the brutal Roman Empire. They refused to serve in the Roman military and paid for that civil disobedience with their lives. Little has changed in 2,000 years. Empire reigns today. The time has come to refuse to serve the sacred cow, the gods of metal and the father of lies.

What is called for here is a moral revolution and in concluding this review of my life I would like to offer my perspective of what that I think that moral revolution looks like.

I do not anticipate any contradiction in the concept of moral revolution as it might be viewed by:

The Vedas, 5000 BC; Moses, 1300 BC; Siddhartha Gautama, 565 BC; Jesus, 33 AD; Mohammad, 570–632 AD; and a host of indigenous spiritual traditions.

When we hear the call to prayer of Islam, the Buddhist, Jewish, Christian and indigenous chants we can understand the hopes, desires and anxieties of human race as it strives to be in sync with creation, with evolution, with truth and with peace.

Then we go beyond our roots and begin to form the one, the beloved community.

That community which transcends all sectarianism, nationalism, racism. That community which is directed at the common good.

We then can grow out of our tribal origins even as we continue to reverence them.

Jesus did this. He loved his Judaism and he knew the prophets and the message.

But he went beyond his culture and his geography to a universalist message.

A Moral Revolution

January 26, 2011

"Don't mourn, organize," said Joe Hill, the labor leader who was executed on a trumped up murder charge in Utah in 1910. And that is our task as we face so much bad news. The response must not be, "Isn't it awful?" but rather, "How can we turn it around?" The Italian philosopher Antonio Gramsci (1891–1937) insisted on facing reality and rejecting any form of denial. As we look at the world honestly we are correct to have a pessimism of the intellect. And at the same time we must have an optimism of the will. This is where the moral revolution begins. We observe and acknowledge the negative elements in the world and at the same time we believe that change is possible and we dedicate ourselves to be part of that moral revolution. "Thy will be done on earth . . ."

As we look at scriptural literature we see that faith is what we are willing to do, and not a formulation of dogmas. Yes, the moral revolution requires faith. And how is it organized? It is organized from the base. Take the Office of the Americas for example. We started with a few people sitting around our dining room table and discussing how we could move our activities from our home to an office. We had all experienced the profound negativity of US foreign policy throughout the world. The warfare state had taken millions of innocent lives. We had all seen the power of base communities in Latin America and how the formation of tens of thousands of such groups had transformed Brazil, Central America, and ultimately created a moral revolution in the Americas.

How is policy made in the base community. The group observes their reality intensely. Next a judgment is made on what must change. Next, after reflection including prayer by those who pray, a praxis is selected. Praxis is reflective action.

Everyone in the base community participates in this base community determination. Then what happens? The general policy has been agreed upon and now responsibility must be given to those who are qualified to accomplish what has been decided upon. In our case, Theresa was the world class organizer who went to work in a revolutionary fashion. "We now have five people on index cards who will support us. We will call them sustainers," she says. It is this ability to begin with a tiny seed group and to foster it into organic growth which is the required skill of a revolutionary organizer.

Let us look at the qualities that follow:

Our community, in this case, the Office of the Americas, is not competing with anyone. We will not protect our turf. We will attempt to do what is not being done and we will cooperate and network with any likeminded groups.

We are not promoting an ideology. Personally I cannot distinguish between religious and political ideologies. In both cases the ideologues presume that they will work to fit the world into their mind set.

This is futile and divisive position.

Our objective is to change the foreign policy of the United States which is the foreign policy of empire. Some people are comfortable working in electoral politics and we respect them. Personally I consider lobbying for change to be the most painful kind of work. Each visit to Washington, D. C. is a visit to, "Talk to the wall." We get the message that our tripartite system now primarily represents the banks, the insurance companies and the warfare state. And how we admire the groups like Code Pink that can confront them every day.

The matter of mass mobilization requires a coming together of hundreds of base communities and that is what occurred after 9/11. It was the largest mass mobilization in the history of the world. Tens of millions of people came out internationally to oppose a war that had not yet begun.

The message of government was clear, "We don't care what you want, we are going to have an unnecessary, illegal and immoral massacre." Pessimism of the intellect, optimism of the will.

Since that time, those who get their information solely from corporate sources are saying, "There is no peace movement." The fact is that the peace movement is in every city town and rural area of this country and represents the hopes of the rest of the world as well.

Ethics and logic are an important part of the base community. In ethics we see war as a clear and present danger fostered by lies, ignorance and malice. It must be abolished if the planet is to have a future.

And what is the logic of government? Most government and all military is governed by the fallacy of the baculum, that is the club, the stick, the threat. This is simply the logic of authority. But in centuries of study the argument from the baculum is identified as a classic fallacy. The fact that one has authority over a group, say a military commander, has absolutely no bearing on the correctness of the position taken by that authority figure. "I'm in charge here," does not mean I am correct about anything. It simply means that I can fire you, I can jail you, I can kill you. Throughout history many generals have been clearly out of their minds and that holds true for the present time. The cult of patriotism was long ago identified by scholars of government as, "The last refuge of scoundrels." It is also the delight of war profiteers. Actually most of us have been governed by the fallacy of the baculum at school, in the work place and most of all in the military. The Office of the Americas is only one of millions of base communities throughout the world but I do think it is a good example of initiating a moral revolution.

Los Angeles demonstration to stop an upcoming illegal, immoral and unnecessary war in Iraq, 2002.

There are some occupational hazards in forming base communities. For example what can be called "super democracy." On this matter let me offer a parable: 300 people are flying on a large jet aircraft and one of the passengers stands up to say, "I have just as much a right to fly this plane as the pilot does and I demand my rights!" OK so far? And here is where authentic authority comes in. This is not the baculum authority

203

this is the authority of having a specific competence. This is the respect required for actual expertise. No, you are not going to fly the plane without certification of competence. No, you are not going to keep the books of this organization if you have no background in bookkeeping. No, you are not going to plan an action in a war zone if you are not thoroughly informed about the situation.

Risk. Yes, we will take risks. Nothing can be accomplished without courage. All of the "experts" told us we could not have a march from Panama to Mexico in the midst of a war; they were wrong.

And there is financial risk. We were constantly told that we should not deal with anything negative about Israel or we would lose support. We refused to comply with these "experts" as well. "Cancel my membership," was a frequent message. The nonsensical claim that opposing the brutal behavior of the Israeli government is anti-Semitism is an insult to non-Zionist Jews and just as banal as the claim that opposing the blatant brutality of the United States government is "anti-American."

The moral revolution requires an unwillingness to accept the "official story." The more powerful the polity, the more ridiculous is the official story. No, there were no weapons of mass destruction in Iraq. No, Iraq did not attack the Twin Towers. No, Afghanistan did not attack the United States. No, the Mavi Marmara did not attack Israel. Lies are the essence of official stories.

The moral revolution requires an understanding that the nation state as the terminus of sovereignty is as outdated as the city states of old. US laws cannot stop global warming. US laws cannot stop war. International law must be respected by the singular great power. We have trashed the entire international legal system by our "might makes right" policies.

The moral revolution requires a denunciation of conventional wisdom. The ways of the rich and famous do not represent a model for us. On the contrary, we accept a preferential option for the poor of the earth. The current economic system is a failure for the majority of the people on the globe.

War making is a great business opportunity and a morally bankrupt choice.

Mohandas Karamchand (Mahatma) Gandhi gave the model for contemporary moral revolution by way of *satyagraha*, mass civil disobedience; *ahimsa*, nonviolence. He insisted on truth force in contrast to the imperial lies of the British. His weapons included non-cooperation and boycott.

I am proud to say that these Gandhian methods are the contemporary tools of the peace movement internationally.

The commercial media compares the reactionary, armed and dangerous right wing messengers of hate, racism and war to the peace movement as if they were two similar aberrations. They are not.

They have nothing in common.

Perhaps this will explain why I think the conventional wisdom of money, power and war is a waste of our time and a waste of our lives. The unconventional wisdom of the ages for us to discover.

Happy the gentle, they shall have the earth for their heritage.

Happy those who hunger and thirst for what is right: they shall be satisfied.

Happy are the peacemakers: they shall be called the children of God.

Thanks Theresa.

What makes you superior to someone else? What do you have that was not given to you? And if it was a gift, how can you boast as if you had worked for it?
—1 Corinthians: 4:7

God is love, and those who abide in love abide in God and God in them.
—1 John 4:16

There is no fear in love, for perfect love drives out fear.
—1 John 4:18

And what did the prayer and prophecy of Jesus' Mother-to-be say about the Messianic Era:

You have shown might with your arm;
you have scattered the proud in their conceit;
you have deposed the mighty from their thrones
and raised the lowly to high places.
You have filled the hungry with good things,
while you have sent the rich away empty.
—Luke 1:51–53

That pretty well expresses the goals
of the moral revolution.

Carry it on!

Hasta la victoria de justicia y paz!

A Conversation with God

from *Civilation Is Possible*

Q: What religion do you belong to?

God: I don't have a religion.

Q: But we humans do.

God: Of course religion is a human attempt to define the indefinable and to bind a certain group of people together in that effort. Religion is a fact of Anthropology.

Q: Are religions a bad thing?

God: Not necessarily, but they are bad if they separate people from the unity of the human race.

Q: What about all those people who do not believe in you?

God: That's understandable, it may be because of all of the dumb things they have been told about me. They may not believe in me, but that does not mean I don't believe in them.

Q: Are you Jewish?

God: No.

Q: Are you Catholic?

God: No.

Q: Are you Protestant, Islamic, or Hindu or Buddhist

God: No, those are human configurations.

Q: Some people say that you are many.

God: Perhaps they see many facets and individualize those facets as many gods. That could be called "many."

Q: How do people serve, and honor you?

God: by serving, honoring and loving each other.

Q: What about all of the religious figures that have been deified over the centuries? Jesus for example?

God: Here is where language is defective. Jesus demonstrated the unity between himself, me and all of humankind. Jesus was asking everyone to share in this divinity. He did not separate himself from the human race or deny the divinity of the human race.

Q: What religion was Jesus?

God: He was Jewish.

Q: Was he sectarian?

God: No, he was universal in his approach and made it clear that everyone who lived the truth understood his message.

Q: You mean, even if they never heard of him?

God: Of course. Anyone devoted to the truth, justice and peace gets the message regardless of their religion or lack of religion.

Q: You seem to be saying that we cannot comprehend the word God.

God: That is correct. You can only speak of me in terms of analogy, you can never comprehend me.

Q: What about all the various religious liturgies, customs?

God: These are all of value if they are celebrating the good you are doing or planning to do. Think of liturgy as a party, a celebration. The liturgy will not build the house, but it can celebrate the fact that you are going to build the house or that you have built the house. The liturgy will not feed the poor. But it can be the celebration that you are about to change the very structures that create poverty.

Q: Should we pray?

God: Yes, of course. This is a way to elevate your mind from the nitty gritty of daily life and enter into the unity of creation.

Q: Did you say creation?

God: Yes, I did. There has never been any conflict between creation and evolution.

Science is simply an effort to understand my work. People should revere science as an effort to know and then use science for justice and peace.

Q: Are you aware that many people and nations are using religion as a cloak for malice?

God: Yes, I am, and I find it truly disgusting.

Q: Thanks very much for this conversation.

God: You are welcome.

Index

A-bomb 79–80, 168
Acosta, Oscar 49
AFL-CIO 65, 128
Aguirre, Fr. Manuel 22
Alhambra House 39–41
American Institute for Free Labor Development (AIFLD) 65, 128
Anzaldua, Andy 65–66
Anzi, Provincia di Potenza, Italy 2
Arafat, Yasser 164–165
Arceo, Mendez (former Archbishop of Cuernavaca) 115
Arevalo, Vinicio Cerezo 113
Arieta, Archbishop 105
Article 27 of the Mexican Constitution 187, 189
Atomic Warfare 79
Austin, Pierce 57
Avalos, Romulo 64
Avoid Vietnam in Latin America (AVILA) 38

Baculum 202–203
Benjamin, Medea 182–183
Berrigan Defense Committee 35, 61
Black Hand 3
Black Panthers 38, 47, 51
Blooms Run, Pennsylvania 1
Bonpane, Betty 5, 11, 15
Bonpane, Blase Augustus 1–2, 12, 20–21, 58–59, 74–75

Bonpane, Blase Martin 66–68, 85–86, 115, 126–127, 136, 165–167, 172, 190
Bonpane, Colleen 56, 62, 66–68, 85, 115, 126–127, 190, 192–193
Bonpane, Fleurette 15
Bonpane, Margie 15
Bray, Prof. Don 29, 45
Brookline, Massachusetts 11, 13, 15
Brown, Gov. Pat 21
Buddhist Monks 114, 119, 122
Buonpane, Domenica Cecelia 1
Buonpane, Elpidio 1–3
Buonpane, Mary Jane 1
Buonpane, Vincent Jr. 51
Bush, George H. W. 100, 132, 154, 155, 160–163, 166, 167, 169–171, 188, 191
Buswell, Bp. Charles 18–19, 183
Byzantine Rites 12

California Senate Bill #40 67
California State University
    Los Angeles (CSULA) 29, 32, 42, 44–45, 54, 57, 73, 168
    Northridge (CSUN) 69, 71–74, 134
Camara, Dom Helder 34
Capodanno, Vincent 13
Cardenal, Fr. Ernesto 80, 84, 107, 115, 142, 157
Carlin, Fr. Ramon 18
Casey, William 156
Castro, Fidel 158, 185

209

Católicos por la Raza 48
Central America 88
Central American Independence Day 22
Centro de Capacitación Social 22, 27
Chamorro, Violeta 26, 83, 154–155
Chamorro, Pedro Joaquin 26
Chapman Press 65
Chávez, César 55, 60, 62, 71, 77
Chiapas, Mexico 114, 120, 187–191
Chicago, Illinois 33, 36
Chicano Moratorium 56–57
Children and Mothers of Heroes and Martyrs 107
Clark, Ramsey Attorney General 39, 78, 171, 185
Cleveland Central High School 2
Cleveland Heights, Ohio 5
Cobras 108–109, 122
Cocker, Shirley 57
Coffield, Fr. John 13
Cold War 61, 79–80, 168, 183
Comber, Bp. John 14, 17
Committee in Solidarity of the People in El Salvador (CISPES) 87–88, 128, 130–131, 194
Committee of Latin American Solidarity (COLAS) 82–83
Communist 9, 24, 33–34, 36, 61, 62, 65, 74, 114, 148, 153
Contra War 78, 89–92, 104, 127, 135, 144, 156, 194
Copley News Service 26
Costa Rican Association of Jurists 105, 124
Costa Rica 24, 26, 96, 100–101, 103–107, 109, 117–118, 131, 145
Costa Rica Libre 101, 103–105, 124–125
Cravath, Jeff 8–9
Cuba 24, 32–38, 60, 72, 101, 150, 182–186
Cuban Revolution 84, 158

Cursillos de Capacitación Social 22–27
Cursillos de Cristiandad 17–18

Daly, Mayor 33
Davis, Angela 47, 55
d'Escoto, Fr. Miguel 80, 139, 157
Dewey, Dean 44–45
Dialogue of the Americas 89
Dolores Mission 13
Dornan, Robert 58–59
Dowdy, Jack 30

Edelstein, Joel 45, 50, 67
Eide, Torrill 96–97, 99–100
Ellacuria, Fr. Ignacio 128–129
El Chaguiton 108
El Espino 96, 108–109
El Malcriado 63–64
El Mozote Massacre 130
El Salvador 25, 48, 87–89, 92, 94, 96, 100, 104, 106-113,117–118, 125, 128, 133, 137, 155, 177, 194
El Taller Grafico 64

Figueres, Jose 105
Figueres, Pepe 26
Flores, Roberto 60
Fort Howard 98–100, 109
Freedom to Travel Campaign 182–183
Frente Democrático Revolucionario (FDR) 94
Frente Farabundo Martí para la Liberación Nacional (FMLN) 89, 111, 129, 155
Frente Sandinista de Liberación Nacional (FSLN) 26, 84, 107, 155
Fromm, Eric 31, 151
Fuji, Rev. 79

Galeano, Eduardo 33
Gandhi, Mahatma 65, 70, 98, 116-117, 135, 198, 204

Garcia, Bp. Samuel Ruiz 114–115, 188
Geary, Fr. 19
Georgetown University 19–20, 195
George, Wally 93
Gill, Rev. Carlyle 88
Glen Ellyn, Illinois 12–13
Global Exchange 159, 161, 182
Goin, Jack 7
Goldberg, Jackie 174
Gomez, Arthur 60
Granaderos 32
Greene, Graham 97
Green Party 173
Grenada 48, 93
Grupo de Apoyo Mutuo (GAM) 113
Guatemala 18-20, 22–30, 36, 38, 42,
    47-48, 61, 81-82, 84, 89, 91, 96, 101,
    104, 106, 107, 109, 110, 112–114, 117,
    119, 121, 125, 130, 131, 146, 148,
    150, 185-190, 192, 195
Guerrillas of Peace 23, 27, 182
Guerrilla Warfare 19, 88, 155

Harbor College 168, 172, 190, 193
Hare, Rev. 67
Haun, Larry 39
Haun, Renee 39
Helms, Jesse 154, 156
Hidalgo, Fr. Miguel 187
Hill, Joe 154, 201
Hill, Tori 68
Hiroshima, Japan 79–80
Holding, Peter 96, 125
Holy Days of Obligation 5
Homies Unidos 177
Honduras 25, 48, 88–90, 96, 117-118,
    106–113, 125, 130-131
Hot Seat 93
Huehuetenango, Guatemala 22–23, 25,
    27, 113, 146
Huerta, Dolores 64, 177
Hughes, Ron 46–47

Humanistic and Educational Needs of
    the Academic Community 45
Hussein, Saddam 159, 160, 162, 165
Huttenhoff, Phyllis 41

Illueca, Jorge 97, 124
International March for Peace in Central
    America 83, 94–96, 98, 100, 105–
    106, 111, 115, 117, 123–124, 132,
    188, 194
International Physicians for the Preven-
    tion of Nuclear War (IPPNW) 79
Iran-Contra 148, 154
Iraq 78, 132, 144, 158–167, 171, 173,
    180, 203, 204
Israel 164–165, 198, 199, 204

Jackson, Jesse 98–99
Jalon, Fr. 25
Japan 79–80
Jesuits 7, 128, 130, 133, 195
Jesus 8, 36, 42, 43, 48, 52, 59, 117,
    145, 146–147, 151, 157, 163, 187, 191,
    194–195, 198–200, 206, 207
Jorgensen, Christine 67

Kappa Sigma fraternity 8
Killeen, Theresa 38–42, 49, 50–53,
    54–57, 60, 64, 66–69, 71-72, 80, 84,
    85–88, 92, 93, 94–95, 100, 115, 116,
    126–127, 128, 131, 132, 136, 141,
    143, 144, 159, 162, 177-180, 165–167,
    172–173, 192-194, 201, 205
Kneuer, Fr. Rudy 27
Koppel, Ted 92
Korean War 11

La Mano Blanca 23–24
Lane, Bp. Raymond 11
La Nuova Italia 2
La Paz, Bolivia 62–67, 69

Latin America 6, 16, 19, 29–30, 38, 60, 65, 85, 114, 111, 124, 126, 161, 174, 196, 201
Law in the Christian tradition 5
League of Nations 39
Lewites, Herty 82
Liberation Theology 27, 34, 41, 80, 114–115, 122, 145–152, 157–158, 192, 196
Littwin, Lawrence 69
Lona Reyes, Bp. Arturo 114-115
Los Angeles Police Department (LAPD) 38, 47, 134, 173
Los Angeles Riots 172–173
Los Angeles Times 5, 47–48, 57, 60, 74, 109
Low Intensity Conflict 155
Loyola High School 6–8

Magidson, Herb 38
Magidson, Shirley 38
Managua, Nicaragua 81–82, 84, 90–91, 107–, 110, 113, 119, 123, 138, 142, 146, 153, 155, 158
Mangurian, David 26
Marcogiuseppi, Angela Rosa 3
Marcogiuseppi, Florence 2, 6
Marcogiuseppi, Michael 2–3
Marcogiuseppi, Vincent 3
Marine Corps of the Catholic Church 9
Marine Corps Platoon Leaders Class 9, 11, 65
Martin, Fr. John 16
Maryknoll 6, 17, 22, 29
Maryknoll College 9–13
Maryknoll Development House 16
Maryknoll , Men of 6
Maryknoll Missioner 6
Maryknoll, New York 9
Maryknoll Novitiate 13
Maryknoll priesthood 6
Maryknoll seminary 10

Marymount High School 8
McCormack, Fr. John 29–30
McCrane, Fr. Gerard 19
McKay, Fr. Frank 6
Melville, Art 22
Menard, Bob 41, 56
Menard, Phyllis 56
Menchu, Rigoberta 119
Mexican American Opportunity Foundation 55–56
Mexico City, Mexico 32–33, 89, 94, 115–116, 187
Middle East Children's Alliance (MECA) 159
Minority Parties 114
Moncada barracks attack 185
Monge, President 101, 105, 124
Mosher, Thomas Edward 34–35
Murillo, Rosario 89, 90, 157

Nagasaki, Japan 79–80
National Liberation Front of Farabundo Marti (FMLN) *see* Frente Farabundo Martí para la Liberación Nacional
National Union of Salvadoran Workers (UNTS) 128–131
New York Times 84, 191
Nicaragua 26, 52, 80–85, 87–90, 92, 98, 99, 101-103, 106–109, 112, 118, 123, 127, 130, 132, 135, 138, 143, 145, 148–150, 152, 154–158, 163, 174, 184, 194
Nicaraguan Association of Cultural Workers 89
Nightline 92
North, Oliver 156
North Tarrytown 13
Nuevo Laredo, Mexico 185

Office of the Americas 78, 87–90, 94–95, 100, 110, 126, 128, 136, 139–140, 143, 154, 156-157, 161, 168, 172–173,

175, 177–178, 182, 193–194, 201–203

Olivares, Fr. Luis 69, 132–133

Olmos, Edward James 172

Olvera Street 49

Ordaz, Pres. Porfirio Díaz 33

Ortega, Daniel 83, 89, 98, 107–108, 155–157

Palestinians 163-165

Panama City, Panama 94–95, 97–98, 100

Parisi, Mr. 5

Partido Revolucionario Institucional (PRI) 115

Party Congress of 1991 36

Pastors for Peace Caravans to Cuba 183, 186

Paz Barnica, Edgardo 110

Pensamiento Crítico 36

Peru 41, 124

Peter, Sister Miriam 24

Pezzullo, Lawrence 84

Physicians for Social Responsibility (PSR) 79

Pisa, Benjamin 101–104

Pollard, Al 7

Pope John Paul II 115, 149–151, 158

Powell, Alice and Dick 172

Powers, Fr. John M. 5

Price, Fr. Fredrick 11

Puebla, Mexico 115

Quantico, Virginia 9, 65

Quiche, Guatemala 23

Reagan, Ronald 47–48, 54, 64, 84, 88–91, 93, 99, 104, 118, 132, 150, 154, 156, 191

Reiley, Fr. Charles 25

Riordan, Richard 174

Rios, Tony 55

Romero, Oscar Arnulfo (archbishop of San Salvador) 115, 130–131, 133

Rother, Fr. Stanley 18

Roybal, Edward 56–57, 59

Rudin, Fr. John 12

Saint Ann's School 5

Saint Vincent's Church 8

Salazar, Ruben 57

Salinas Gortari, Carlos 187

San Antonio, Texas 10-11, 183

Sanchez, Brigido 111

Sanchez, Mariano 24

Sandinistas 79, 80–84, 90–91, 107, 118, 154–158

San Jose, Costa Rica 24, 26, 100, 104, 118

Santa Paula School District 60–62

Sartre, Jean-Paul 31

Sato, Rev. 79

Saul Alinsky 38

Saxon, Pauline 67

Saxon, Dr. Richard 79

Seminary of the Oblates of Mary Immaculate 10

Sheen, Martin 87, 90, 92, 132, 135, 138

Shy, Ruth 173

Skedule, David 32

Spruance 111

Somoza DeBayle, Anastasio 26, 80, 82, 85, 89, 98, 157

Soviet Union 79–80, 150

Soy Cubano! 183

Special Studies Program 11–12

Spencer, Scott 191

Students for a Democratic Society (SDS) 34–35

Sunset Hill 11

Swanson, John August 59

Synanon Game 71

Tambs, Lewis 100

Tasba-Pri, Nicaragua 91, 139
Teamsters Union of America 63–64, 68
Thuc, Bp. Ngo Dinh 12
Tokyo, Japan 79
Torres, Fr. Camilo 34
Tuxtla-Gutierrez 114, 187, 189

Zapatistas 187
Zelaya, Pres. Manuel 111

Ungo, Guillermo 94
Unidad Revolucionaria Nacional Guate-
  malteca (URNG) 89
Unión Nacional Opositora (UNO) 26,
  154
United Farm Workers of America (UFW)
  60, 62–67, 69, 71
United Nations 39, 108
United States Marine Corps Reserve 9,
  11, 65
University of Southern California (USC)
  8, 10, 54, 64
US Media 37, 105

Valle, Manuel 82, 84
Vatican Council II 4, 18, 19, 195
Vietnam 13, 19, 25, 33, 38, 44, 46, 56,
  57, 60, 72, 130, 148, 171, 186, 191
Vitulazio, Italy 1

Walker, Rev. Lucius 184–186
Walsh, Bp. James Anthony 11
Walsh, Fr. John P. 10
Washington Post 30, 41, 158
Weekends of Christian Living 19, 20,
  195
White, Don 128, 131, 135, 193–194
World War II 7–9, 39, 51

Young Adult Leadership Project (YALP)
  55
Youngstown, Ohio 2

Zamora, Ruben 131
Zapata, Emiliano 187

Blase Bonpane is the director of the Office of the Americas. He has served on the faculties of UCLA and California State University Northridge. His articles have been published internationally and syndicated by the *New York Times* and the *Los Angeles Times*.

Blase previously served as a Maryknoll Missioner in Guatemala during the revolutionary conflict of the 1960s. As a result of his work in peasant organization, he was expelled from that country in 1967. On his return to the United States, Blase and his family lived at the headquarters of United Farm Workers with César Chávez, where he was editor of UFW publications.

He is host of the weekly radio program *World Focus* on Pacifica Radio (KPFK, Los Angeles). Blase previously hosted the program *World Focus* on Time/Warner TV Educational and Public Access Channels. He was named "the most underrated humanist of the decade" by the *Los Angeles Weekly*. In 2006, he was awarded the Distinguished Peace Leadership Award by the Nuclear Age Peace Foundation.

His previous books include: *Civilization is Possible* (2008); *The Central American Solidarity Movement* (Oral History Program of the University of California Los Angeles, 2005); *Common Sense for the Twenty-First Century* (2004); *Guerrillas of Peace: On the Air* (2000); and *Guerrillas of Peace: Liberation Theology and the Central American Revolution* (third edition, 2000).

The Blase Bonpane Collection has been established by the Department of Special Collections of the UCLA Research Library (collection 1590). This is a compilation of his published and unpublished writings, lectures and recordings of his programs on Pacifica Radio.